Benjamin Franklin Baker

The new choral harmony

a collection of hymn tunes, chants, sentences, motets and anthems, selected and

arranged from the works of ancient and modern masters, together with many

original compositions

Benjamin Franklin Baker

The new choral harmony

a collection of hymn tunes, chants, sentences, motets and anthems, selected and arranged from the works of ancient and modern masters, together with many original compositions

ISBN/EAN: 9783741194849

Manufactured in Europe, USA, Canada, Australia, Japa

Cover: Foto ©Thomas Meinert / pixelio.de

Manufactured and distributed by brebook publishing software (www.brebook.com)

Benjamin Franklin Baker

The new choral harmony

THE NEW CHORAL HARMONY:

A COLLECTION OF

Hymn Tunes, Chants, Sentences, Motets, and Anthems.

SELECTED AND ARRANGED FROM THE

WORKS OF ANCIENT AND MODERN MASTERS,

TOGETHER

WITH MANY ORIGINAL COMPOSITIONS.

BY

B. F. BAKER.

PREFACE.

In the preparation of their work, the Editors of the CHORAL HARMONY have had three objects constantly in view: first, to present music of a high order, appropriate to the worship of all Christian denominations; secondly, to combine simplicity with true musical effect; and thirdly, to select music that will harmonize with the sentiment of the various hymns now in common use.

A large portion of the music contained in the following pages has been culled with great care from the Oratorios, Masses, Anthems, and Motetts, of the classic writers; and a good variety of justly popular Hymn Tunes already in common use, has been inserted, interspersed with original compositions expressly for this work, which, it is believed, are not less worthy of notice.

The *variety* of music is greater in this work than in any similar one known to the Editors; by which is meant the *real* variety, not the mere number of tunes, but the diversity of *style*—the *Allegro*, the emotions expressed by the music, from the jubilant *Allegro*, the deep *Maestoso* of the Choral, to the soothing *Cantabile* and the tender *Andante*.

In the department of Anthems, hymns for various occasions, and short pieces for voluntaries before and after service, "The Choral Harmony," it is believed, will be eminently useful and practical, and present features of unusual interest.

The hymn tunes for men's voices will be found useful in College Choirs, as well as in the Masonic Institution, and such other meetings, where soprano voices are not available.

In the department of Chants, the patrons of the Choral Harmony will find a variety at once pleasing and practical, and to which hymns of irregular metre may be easily adapted.

The Editors have been impressed with the thought that the comparatively advanced musical taste, as well as the greater skill in performance, demands more varied and stronger harmonies than are found in most books of this kind, and should the singer find something more than common-place chords on the *Tonic*, *Sub-dominant* and *Dominant*, it is believed the freshness and strength they afford—the more full and satisfactory musical effect will remunerate him for extra effort.

The logical structure, the observance of the higher laws of composition with reference to subject and answer, as well in the Solfaing Exercises as in the department of Hymn Tunes, is a new and characteristic feature in this work.

Those tunes to which the author's name is not given, with the exception of the old familiar tunes, are compositions or arrangements by the senior Editor, and on which a copyright is secured.

The Elementary portion of this work has received much care and consideration. It will be found a truthful deduction from the best specimens of musical composition, full and clear, with appropriate exercises illustrative of the principles and rules of musical notation in their most practical and logical order.

With these remarks the Editors place their book before the Public, trusting and believing that the more and the longer "The Choral Harmony" is used, the more its various excellencies will be felt and acknowledged.

THE PRINCIPLES OF MUSICAL NOTATION.

CHAPTER I.

1. What is Musical Notation?

ANS. It involves the signs and characters employed in representing tones in their various relations, and also the periods of silence that may occur between tones.

2. What is that attribute with reference to which tone is first considered?

ANS. The pitch.

3. In what is the pitch of tones classified?

ANS. In the scale.

4. How many tones does the scale comprise?

ANS. Eight.

5. What are their names?

ANS. One, Two, Three, Four, Five, Six, Seven, Eight.

6. What syllables are applied to the tones of the scale?

ANS. Do, Re, Mi, Fa, Sol, La, Si, Do.

7. What is the interval called existing between two consecutive tones of the scale?

ANS. A Second.

8. How many seconds are there in the scale?

ANS. Seven.

9. Are the seconds all alike?

ANS. No; five of them are large and two small.

10. What are the large seconds called?

ANS. Major seconds.

11. What are the small seconds called?

ANS. Minor seconds.

THE SCALE ILLUSTRATED.

Eight.	..........o..........	Do.
		A Minor Second.
Seven.	..........o..........	Si.
		A Major Second.
Six.	..........o..........	La.
		A Major Second.
Five.	..........o..........	Sol.
		A Minor Second.
Four.	..........o..........	Fa.
		A Major Second.
Three.	..........o..........	Mi.
		A Major Second.
Two.	..........o..........	Re.
		A Major Second.
One.	..........o..........	Do.

12. On what is the pitch of tones, or the scale represented?

ANS. On the Staff.

13. What constitutes the Staff?

ANS. Five parallel horizontal lines, together with the spaces between them.

14. What is the general name given to each line and space of the staff?

ANS. Degree.

15. How many degrees does the staff contain?

ANS. Nine, viz: five lines and four spaces.

MUSICAL NOTATION.

THE STAFF.

```
Fifth line.
Fourth line.
Third line.
Second line.
First line.
```

```
Fourth space.
Third space.
Second space.
First space.
```

16. How are the degrees extended beyond the staff?

ANS. By adding short lines above or below.

17. How are degrees thus attained, reckoned?

ANS. From the staff

```
Second line above.
First line above.
```
```
Second space above.
First space above.
```

```
First space below.
Second space below.
```
```
First line below.
Second line below.
```

18. How is the pitch of tones designated?

ANS. By the literal name of the degree on which the note is written, representing the tone.

19. What are those literal names?

ANS. A, B, C, D, E, F, and G.

20. How is the place of these literal names of the degrees determined?

ANS. By a CLEF.

21. How many Clefs are there?

ANS. Three.

22. What are their specific names?

ANS. The G Clef, thus; ——— thus; ——— the F Clef, thus; ——— and the C Clef, thus; ——— thus; ——— or thus; ———

23. What is the place of the literal names of the degrees as indicated by the G Clef?

ANS. G, is the Clef-letter, and is found on the second line, from which the letters are reckoned in alphabetic order upward and downward, by the inversion of that order, thus;

24. What is the place of the literal names as indicated by the F Clef?

ANS. F, is the Clef-letter, and is found on the fourth line, thus;

25. What is the place of the literal names as indicated by the C Clef?

ANS. C, is the Clef-letter, and is found on the first, third, or fourth lines, according as the Clef may be placed, thus;

MUSICAL NOTATION.

Thus:

Or thus:

26. What is used to represent the tones of the scale on the staff?

ANS. On consecutive degrees; the first note, (ONE,) being written on C, the first line below, under the G Clef.

27. A character written thus, $\mathcal{O}$; whose general name is NOTE.

28. If ONE, the first tone of the scale be represented on C, the first line below, on what letter and degree should TWO, the second tone, be represented?

ANS. On D, the first space below.

29. On what letter and degree should THREE be represented?

ANS. On E, the first line.

30. On what letter and degree should FOUR be represented?

ANS. On F, the first space.

31. On what letter and degree should FIVE be represented?

ANS. On G, the second line.

32. On what letter and degree should SIX be represented?

ANS. On A, the second space.

33. On what letter and degree should SEVEN be represented?

ANS. On B, the third line.

34. On what letter and degree should EIGHT be represented?

ANS. On C, the third space.

NOTE. The pitch of a tone takes its literal name from the degree of the Staff on which the note is written, representing it. For example, if a note be written on G, the pitch of the tone represented thereby, is called G, irrespectively of any other quality that may be imputed to the tone: The Clef is, therefore, essential, for however complete the representation of tone may be in other respects, in the absence of a Clef, the notes on the Staff have neither relative nor absolute pitch. The practicability of having two Clefs, is found in the fact, that the use of one Clef only, would incur the necessity of augmenting the Staff by the use of short lines to that extent as to embarrass the reader; whereas, the two Clefs afford facility for representing the pitch of all the tones called into requisition in vocal music, mainly on the Staff.

MUSICAL NOTATION.

THE SCALE REPRESENTED ON THE STAFF.

EXAMPLE 1.

Numerals,*	1	2	3	4	5	6	7	8
Letters,†	C	D	E	F	G	A	B	C
Syllables,‡	Do	Re	Mi	Fa	Sol	La	Si	Do

NOTE. The intervals between the letters of the staff, correspond in magnitude and order with those existing between the tones of the Scale; thus, for example, the interval from ONE to TWO of the Scale, is a MAJOR SECOND; and ONE being represented on C, and TWO on D, it is therefore a Major Second from C to D. Again, as the intervals are between the tones of the Scale, so they are between the letters as represented on the Staff above.

* The Numerals, or names of the tones of the Scale as such.
† The Letters, or literal names, by which the pitch of tones as such is designated.
‡ The Syllables, indicating the vocalities given to the tones of the Scale.

MUSICAL NOTATION.

EXERCISE 1.

EXERCISE 2.

35. On what degree of the staff is ONE of the scale written under the F Clef?

ANS. On the second space, thus;

EXAMPLE 2.

1	2	3	4	5	6	7	8
C	D	E	F	G	A	B	C
Do	Re	Mi	Fa	Sol	La	Si	Do

8	7	6	5	4	3	2	1
C	B	A	G	F	E	D	C
Do	Si	La	Sol	Fa	Mi	Re	Do

EXERCISE 3.

NOTE. The Scale may be represented as a whole or in part, beginning with C, either above or below the Clef G; the pupil will remember, however, that C, ONE, and Do, are the same; and D, TWO, and RE; E, THREE, and Mi, &c., wherever they may occur on the Staff, thus;

EXAMPLE 3.

1	2	3	4	5	6	7	8
C	D	E	F	G	A	B	C
Do	Re	Mi	Fa	Sol	La	Si	Do

8	7	6	5	4	3	2	1
C	B	A	G	F	E	D	C
Do	Si	La	Sol	Fa	Mi	Re	Do

EXAMPLE 4.

1	2	3	4
C	D	E	F
Do	Re	Mi	Fa

8	7	6	5
C	B	A	G
Do	Si	La	Sol

36. How is the length of tones measured?

ANS. By beating time.

NOTE. The pupil will measure the length of the tones by making TWO BEATS, (motions of the hand,) to each note in the following Exercises.

EXERCISE 4.

EXERCISE 5.

MUSICAL NOTATION

37. How may two parts be written designed to be sung simultaneously?

ANS. On one staff, as in Ex. 6, or on two staves tied together with a BRACE, as in Ex. 7.

EXERCISE 6.

EXERCISE 7.

DIVISION 2.

38. What are the characters called employed to represent the relative length of tones?

ANS. NOTES.

39. What is the name of the note representing the longest tone?

ANS. A WHOLE NOTE, written thus: 𝅝

40. What is the name of the note representing a tone half as long as that represented by a Whole Note?

ANS. A HALF NOTE, written thus, 𝅗𝅥 or thus, 𝅗𝅥

41. What two notes are equal in value to one Whole Note?

ANS. TWO HALF NOTES 𝅗𝅥 𝅗𝅥

42. What two notes are equal in value to one Half Note?

ANS. TWO QUARTER NOTES, ♩ ♩

43. What two notes are equal in value to one Quarter Note?

ANS. TWO EIGHTH NOTES, ♪ ♪.

44. What two notes are equal in value to one Eighth Note?

ANS. TWO SIXTEENTH NOTES, 𝅘𝅥𝅯 𝅘𝅥𝅯.

45. What characters are employed to represent Silence?

ANS. REST, written thus; a Whole Rest, ▬; a Half Rest, ▬; a Quarter Rest, 𝄽; an Eighth Rest, 𝄾; and a Sixteenth Rest, 𝄿.

NOTES AND RESTS.

Whole Note.	Half Note.	Quarter Note.	Eighth Note.	Sixteenth Note.
Whole Rest.	Half Rest.	Quarter Rest.	Eighth Rest.	Sixteenth Rest.

46. How is the Accent or Rhythm of Music indicated?

ANS. By perpendicular lines across the Staff, dividing it into MEASURES. Thus:

47. What are these perpendicular lines called?

ANS. BARS.

48. In what way do Measures indicate the accent?

ANS. The note occurring on the first part of the measure, is accented, whereas that on the second part is unaccented. Thus:

MUSICAL NOTATION.

EXAMPLE 5.

Ac. Unac. Ac. Unac. Ac. Unac. Ac. Unac.

49. What is that Measure called having two parts, as above?

Ans. DOUBLE MEASURE, (two part Measure.)

50. What is the sign for Double Measure?

Ans. The figure two, (2.)

51. Where is this placed to indicate the kind of Measure?

Ans. On the upper part of the Staff next to the Clef, thus:

EXAMPLE 6.

52. In what way is the time measured given to each part of Double Measure?

Ans. The time given to each part is measured by one BEAT; the first part is sung to the downward, and the second part to the upward motion of the hand.

EXERCISE 8.

53. What other denomination or kind of note may represent each part of Double Measure?

Ans. A Quarter Note, thus:

EXAMPLE 7.

Ac. Unac. Ac. Unac. Ac. Unac. Ac. Unac.

54. Is Double Measure the same when represented with Quarter Notes as when with Halves?

Ans. Double Measure is the same as such, but the representation thereof is different.

55. What is the full designation of Double Measure when represented with a Half Note or its value on each part of the Measure?

Ans. The figure two written twice, thus: the upper figure corresponds to the number of parts, and the lower one indicates the value of each part of the Measure.

56. What is the full designation of Double Measure when represented by one Quarter Note, or its equal on each part?

Ans. The figures TWO and FOUR, thus: the upper figure stands for the kind of Measure, (Double Measure,) and the lower figure for the fractional value of each part of it.

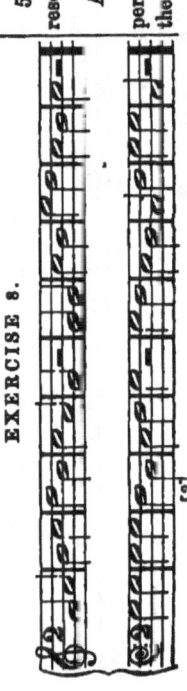

MUSICAL NOTATION.

57. What is that Measure called having three equal parts?

ANS. TRIPLE MEASURE.

58. What is the sign indicating Triple Measure?

ANS. The figure THREE on the upper part of the Staff, next to the Clef, thus:

59. With what denomination or kind of notes may Triple Measure be represented?

ANS. With Halves, Quarters, or Eighths.

60. What is the full designation of Triple Measure when represented with Halves?

ANS. The figures THREE and TWO, thus: under which the value of each part either in notes or rests, must be equal to one half note.

61. What is the full designation of Triple Measure when represented with quarter notes?

ANS. The figures THREE and FOUR, thus: under which the value of each part is equal to a quarter note.

62. What is the full designation of Triple Measure when represented with eighth notes?

MUSICAL NOTATION.

ANS. The figures THREE and EIGHT, thus: 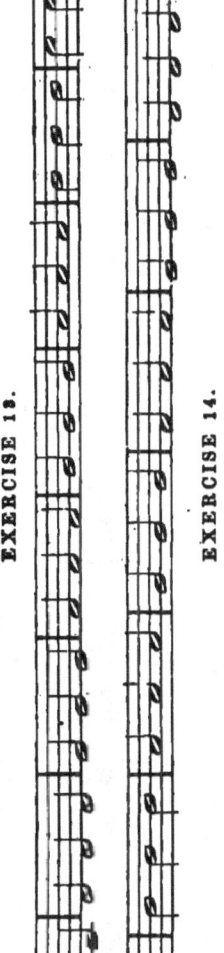 under which the value of each part is equal to one eighth note.

NOTE. The learner will entertain the idea that the UPPER figure indicates the number of PARTS, COUNTS, or BEATS, in each measure; while the LOWER figure shows the value in notes or rests of each PART or COUNT which is to be sung or passed over at one beat.

63. How is Triple Measure accented?

ANS. The first part is accented, and the second and third parts are unaccented.

EXERCISE 13.

EXERCISE 14.

EXERCISE 15.

EXERCISE 16.

MUSICAL NOTATION.

NOTE. In Triple Measure, under the figures THREE TWO, a whole note, being equal to two halves, fills two parts of the measure, and requires two counts or two beats. The dotted whole note is equal to three halves, it therefore requires three counts or three beats.

EXERCISE 17.

NOTE. In Triple Measure, under the figures THREE and FOUR, a dotted half note, thus: ♩. is equal to three quarters; it therefore fills the entire measure, and requires three beats.

EXERCISE 18.

NOTE. In Triple Measure, under the figures THREE and EIGHT, a dotted quarter, thus: ♩. is equal to three eighths; it therefore requires three counts or three beats.

64. What is FOUR part Measure called?

ANS. QUADRUPLE MEASURE.

65. What is the figure by which to indicate Quadruple Measure?

ANS. The figure FOUR placed on the upper part of the Staff next to the Clef, thus:

66. With what denomination or kind of notes may Quadruple Measure be represented?

ANS. With one HALF or with one QUARTER note on each part.

67. What is the full designation of Quadruple Measure when represented by a half note on each part?

ANS. The figures FOUR and two, written thus:

68. What is the full designation of Quadruple Measure when represented with one quarter note on each part?

ANS. The figure FOUR written twice, thus:

69. Which are the accented parts of Quadruple Measure?

ANS. The FIRST and THIRD; the first part, however, is the stronger accent.

70. How many BEATS or COUNTS are required in Quadruple?

ANS. Four: One beat or count to each part of the measure.

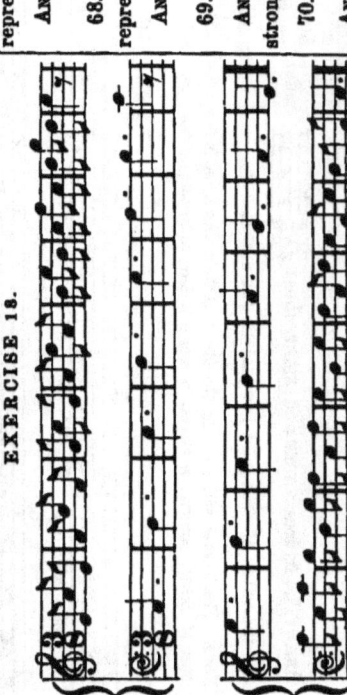

MUSICAL NOTATION.

EXERCISE 19.

EXERCISE 20.

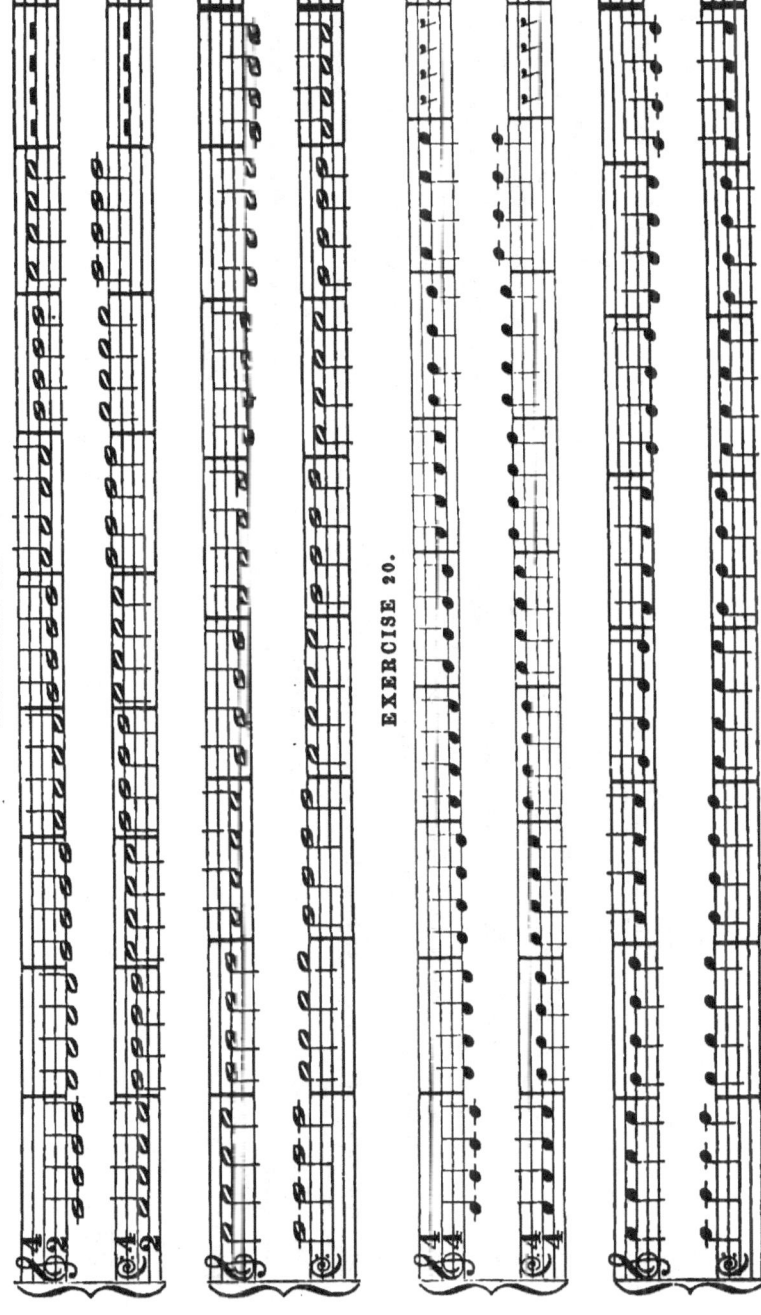

MUSICAL NOTATION.

EXERCISE 21.

71. What is that Measure called having six equal parts?

Ans. SEXTUPLE MEASURE.

72. What is the sign by which Sextuple Measure is indicated?

Ans. The figure six next to the Clef, on the upper part of the Staff.

73. With what denomination or kind of notes may Sextuple Measure be represented?

Ans. With one quarter note, or with one eighth on each part of the measure?

74. What is the full designation of Sextuple Measure when represented with a quarter note on each part?

Ans. The figures SIX and FOUR, thus: under which designation each measure contains the value of six quarters in either notes or rests.

75. What is the full designation of Sextuple Measure when represented with eighth notes?

Ans. The figures SIX and EIGHT, thus: under which designation each measure contains in notes or rests the value of six eighths.

76. Which are the accented parts of Sextuple Measure?

Ans. The FIRST and FOURTH parts, the first of which is the stronger accent.

77. How many BEATS are there required in Sextuple Measure?

Ans. Six. One beat to each part.

78. How are the motions of the hand described in beating Sextuple Measure?

Ans. Down, down, left, right, up, up.

EXERCISE 22.

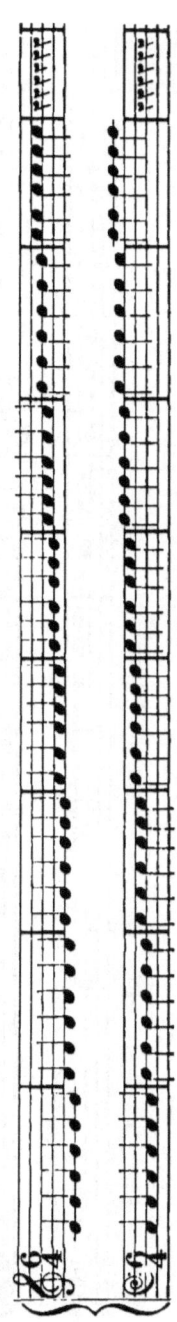

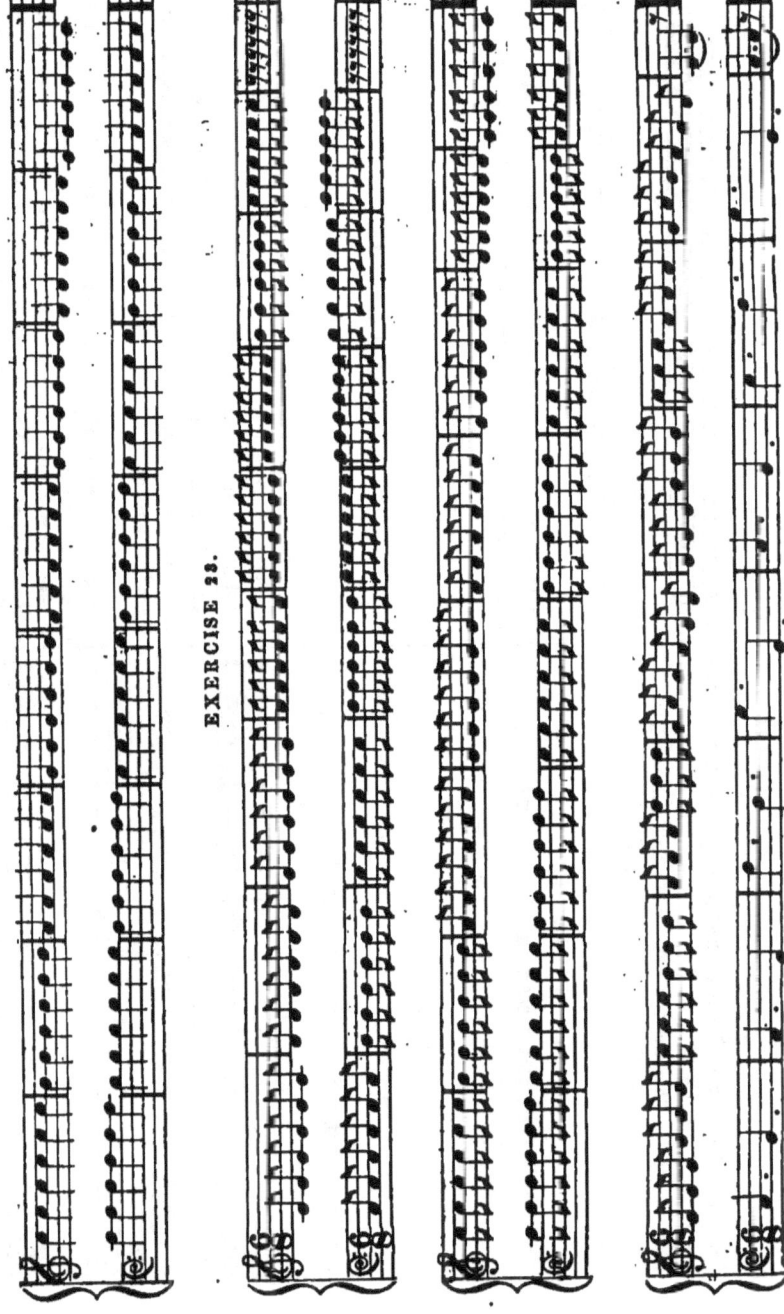

MUSICAL NOTATION.

79. How is a curved line constructed when placed over or under two notes having the same pitch?

ANS. It implies that the two notes represent but one tone.

80. What is a curved line thus used, called?

ANS. A TIE.

DIVISION 3.

OF DOTTED NOTES AND RESTS.

NOTE. A DOT adds one half to the original value of that Note or Rest after which it is placed.

EXAMPLE 8.

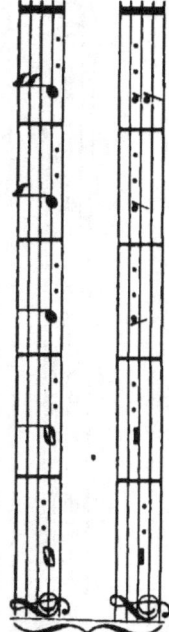

Dotted Whole.   Dotted Half.   Dotted Quarter.   Dotted Eighth.   Dotted Sixteenth.

EXAMPLE 9.

Dotted Whole Rest.   Dotted Half Rest.   Dotted Quarter Rest.   Dotted Eighth Rest.   Dotted Sixteenth Rest.

NOTE. Two dots may occur after a note or rest, the latter of which adds one half to the value of the former; thus are obtained DOUBLE DOTTED notes and rests.

CHAPTER II.

DIVISION 1.

81. How are the available tones represented between those numerals of the Scale, the difference of whose pitch forms an interval of a Major Second?

ANS. By means of a SHARP, thus: (♯) or a FLAT, thus: (♭); a Sharp elevates, and a Flat depresses the pitch of the note before which it is written.

NOTE. The Sharp placed before a note, elevates the pitch of that note to a point between two letters whose difference of pitch is a Major Second. There are no available tones represented between Three and Four, and Seven and Eight of the Scale, nor can there be represented a smaller interval than the Minor Second by the present system of notation; therefore, the Minor Second is an indivisible interval.

MUSICAL NOTATION.

THE CHROMATIC SCALE.

MUSICAL NOTATION.

82. What is the literal name of the pitch of the tone between C and D, when represented on the degree with C?

ANS. C sharp, (C♯.)

83. What is the literal name of it when represented on the degree with D?

ANS. D flat, (D♭.)

84. What is the interval from C, to C♯, D, to D♯, E, to E♭, or from D, to D♭, &c. ?

ANS. A CHROMATIC INTERVAL.

85. How many intervals may there be in a Major Second ?

ANS. Two. A Chromatic interval as from ♮, to C♯, and a Minor Second, as from C♯, to D.

86. What sign is used to restore the pitch of a letter that has been made sharp or flat?

ANS. A NATURAL, written thus, (♮) cancels the effect of a sharp or flat, and restores a note to its original pitch.

EXAMPLE 10.

NOTE. Intervals represented on one and the same degree of the Staff, are denominated CHROMATIC INTERVALS.

EXAMPLE 11.

THE CHROMATIC SCALE ASCENDING AND DESCENDING, UNDER THE F CLEF.

C, C♯, D, D♯, E, F, F♯, G, G♯, A, A♯, B, C, B, B♭, A, A♭, G, G♭, F, E, E♭, D, D♭, O.
1, ♯1, 2, ♯2, 3, 4, ♯4, 5, ♯5, 6, ♯6, 7, 8, 7, ♭7, 6, ♭6, 5, ♭5, 4, 3, ♭3, 2, ♭2, 1.
Do, Di, Re, Ri, Mi, Fa, Fi, Sol, Si, La, Li, Si, Do, Si, Se, La, Le, Sol, Se, Fa, Mi, Me, Re, Ra, Do.

NOTE. The teacher and pupils will alternate in singing the measures of the following Exercise.

EXERCISE 24.

TEACHER. PUPILS. T. P. T. P. T. P. T. P. T. P. T. P.

MUSICAL NOTATION.

87. How far does the influence of a Flat or Sharp extend?

ANS. Through the measure in which it is written, except when otherwise indicated by a Natural.

DIVISION 2.

89. What classification of voices is made with reference to four part singing?

ANS. The voices of each sex are divided into two classes with reference to their pitch; the higher class or range of female voice is called SOPRANO, or TREBLE, and the lower is called ALTO, and the higher range of the male voice is called TENOR, and the lower one BASS.

90. How are the parts ordinarily written for those four species of voices?

ANS. The custom is, to write on four staves, one part on a staff for each species of voice, respectively: the Tenor on the upper, the Alto on the next below, the Soprano next, and the Bass on the lower staff.

EXERCISE 12.

MUSICAL NOTATION.

91. How many Scales have been explained?
ANS. Two. The MAJOR and CHROMATIC Scales.

NOTE. There is still another Scale, whose structure differs from the Major Scale with respect to the kind and order of Seconds, beginning with the syllable La, on A, as the Major begins with Do, on C.

EXAMPLE 18.

THE MINOR SCALE ASCENDING. THE MINOR SCALE DESCENDING.

A, B, C, D, E, F, G#, A.   A, G#, F, E, D, C, B, A.
1, 2, 3, 4, 5, 6, 7, 8.   8, 7, 6, 5, 4, 3, 2, 1.
La, Si, Do, Re, Mi, Fa, Si, La. La, Si, Fa, Mi, Re, Do, Si, La.

92. How many tones are there in the Minor Scale?
ANS. Eight.
93. How many Seconds are there in the Minor Scale?
ANS. Seven.
94. How many Major Seconds?
ANS. Three. From 1 to 2, from 3 to 4, and from 4 to 5, are Major Seconds.
95. How many Minor Seconds?
ANS. Three. From 2 to 3, from 5 to 6, and from 7 to 8, are Minor Seconds.
96. What is the Second called occurring between 6 and 7, of Minor Scale?
ANS. An AUGMENTED SECOND.

NOTE. The pupil will entertain the idea that there are three species of Seconds; the Minor Second, between which there is no available tone, the Major Second, between which there is one available tone, and the Augmented Second, between which there are two available tones.

EXERCISE 25.

MUSICAL NOTATION.

EXERCISE 26.

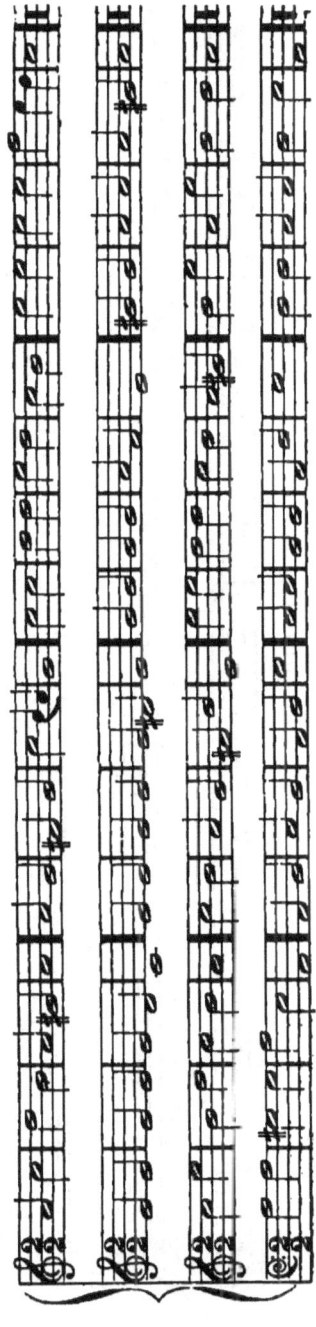

DIVISION 8.

NOTE. The figure indicating the kind of measure, is technically called the NUMERATOR, and that indicating the value of each part, is called the DENOMINATOR.

97. How are two tones of equal length represented on any one part of a measure?

ANS. By two of the same kind of notes whose value is equal to the fraction expressed by the denominator. Such two notes are called a COUPLET.

EXAMPLE 14.

98. How are three tones of equal length represented on any one part of a measure?

ANS. By three notes of the same name, whose value is diminished to the fraction expressed by the denominator, by the figure three placed over or under them; such three notes are called a TRIPLET.

EXAMPLE 15.

MUSICAL NOTATION.

99. How are four tones of equal length represented on any one part of a measure?

Ans. By four notes of the same name, whose value collectively is equal to the fraction expressed by the denominator; such four notes may be called a QUARTOLET.

EXAMPLE 16.

EXERCISE 27.

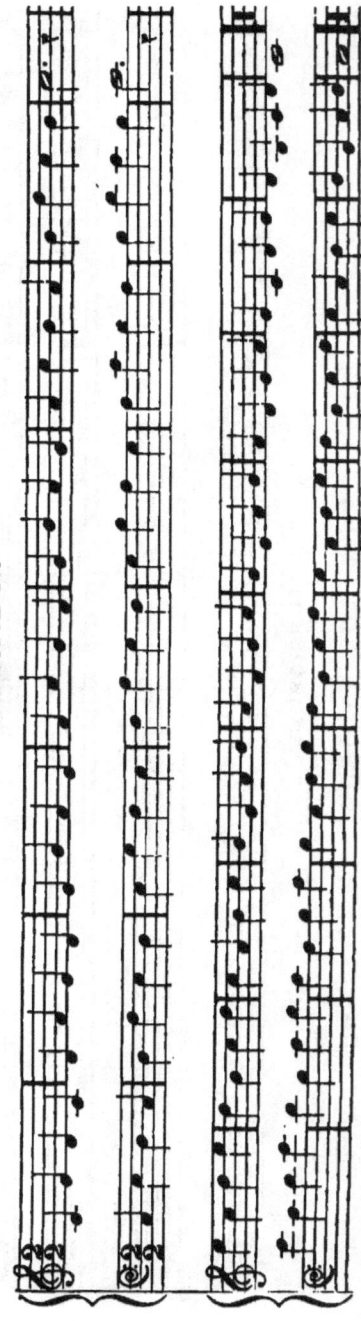

MUSICAL NOTATION.

EXERCISE 28.
EXERCISE 29.
EXERCISE 30.

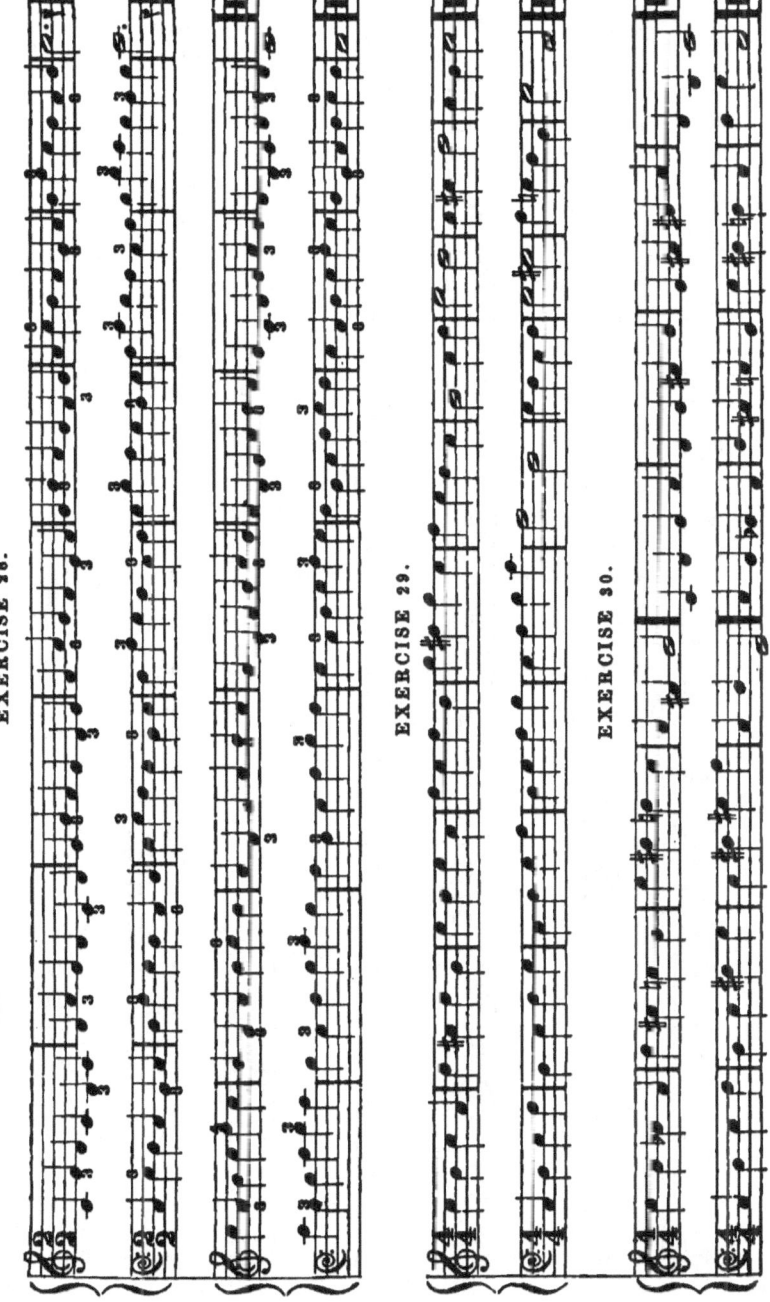

MUSICAL NOTATION.

99. How are four tones of equal length represented on any one part of a measure?

ANS. By four notes of the same name, whose value collectively is equal to the fraction expressed by the denominator; such four notes may be called a QUARTOLET.

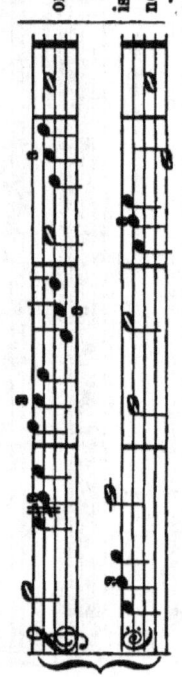

EXAMPLE 16.

EXERCISE 27.

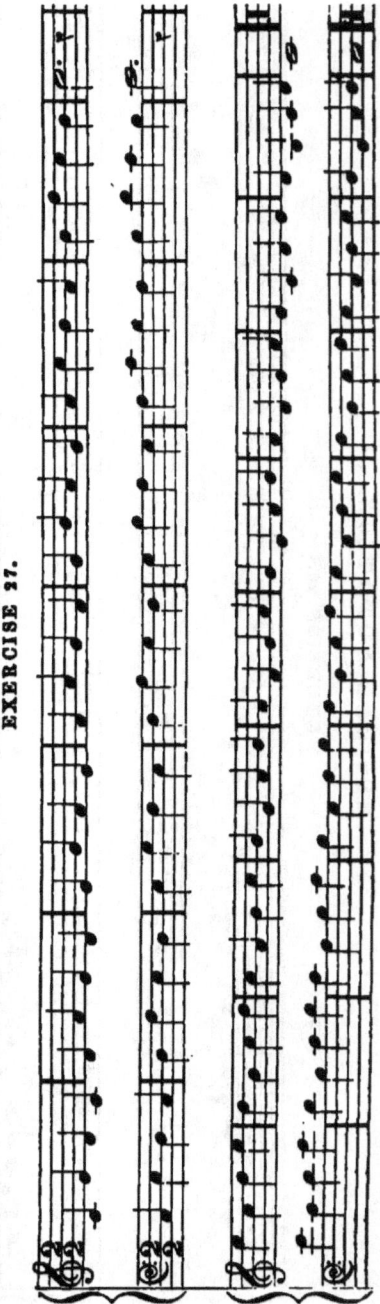

MUSICAL NOTATION.

EXERCISE 31.

EXERCISE 32.

100. What does a sign thus, > imply when placed over a note?

ANS. It implies that the tone represented by the note under the sign, should be given with strong emphasis.

101. How is music adapted or set to words?

ANS. Each word or syllable has a corresponding note, whose pitch, length, and force of tone prescribes the utterance of the word or syllable corresponding therewith, and the accent of the one agreeing with that of the other. See example.

EXAMPLE 17.

Be-hold the morn-ing sun, Be-gins his glo-rious way; His beams thro' all the na-tions run, And life and light con-vey.

MUSICAL NOTATION.

102. What does the DOUBLE BAR signify?

ANS. The Double Bar, thus: ‖ is used to divide music into phrases corresponding to the lines of poetry to which the music is adapted.

EXERCISE 33.

103. What is the name of the character placed over a note indicating prolongation of tone beyond the value of the note?

ANS. A HOLD, thus: (⌢) When written over a note, indicates prolongation of tone, and when over a rest, prolongation of silence.

NOTE. Although the Hold may be construed as indicating more or less, prolongation of time, as the leader may deem best; still, in most cases, it may be practicable to give such notes and rests twice as much time as they otherwise would demand.

EXERCISE 34.

MUSICAL NOTATION.

104. How may the accent be transferred from a strong part to a weak part of a measure?

ANS. By means of a TIE, over two notes, representing two parts of the measure; the first of which is on the weak part, and the second, on the strong part of the measure; in which case the accent is given to the first of the two notes thus tied.

EXAMPLE 18.

105. What is such inverted accent called?

ANS. SYNCOPATION. A note therefore, commencing on an unaccented part of a measure, and extending to an accented part, is called a SYNCOPATED NOTE.

EXERCISE 35.

106. Is a Tie ever used for any other purpose than to change the place of the accent?

ANS. A Tie is used to show that two or more notes are to be sung to one word or syllable. See following Exercise.

MUSICAL NOTATION

EXERCISE 36.

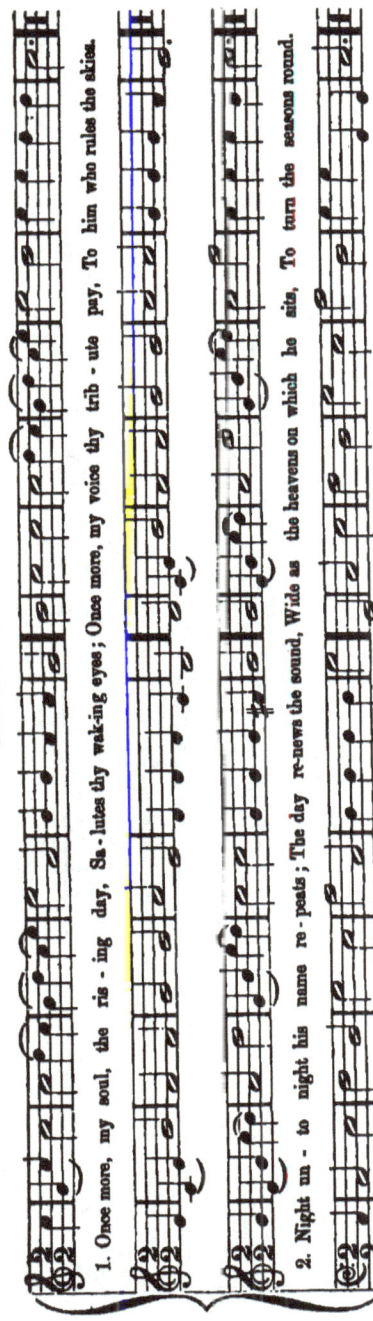

1. Once more, my soul, the ri-ing day, Sa-lutes thy wak-ing eyes; Once more, my voice thy trib-ute pay, To him who rules the skies.
2. Night un-to night his name re-peats; The day re-news the sound, Wide as the heavens on which he sits, To turn the seasons round.

DIVISION 4.

107. How are the different degrees in the force of tones represented?

ANS. By certain Italian words or their abbreviations, placed over or under a line of music or a single note. For example, the word PIANISSIMO, or *pp*,—the abbreviation of which—means Very Soft. PIANO, or *p*, means Soft. MEZZO, or *m*, means Medium Force. MEZZO PIANO, or *mp*, means Moderately Soft. MEZZO FORTE, or *mf*, means Moderately Loud. FORTE, or *f*, means Loud: FORTISSIMO, or *ff*, means Very Loud.

108. How is a gradual increase in the force of tone indicated? ANS. By the word CRESCENDO, or the abbreviation (CRES.) or the sign thus:

109. How is a gradual diminution of tone indicated?

ANS. By the word DIMINUENDO, or the abbreviation (DIM.) or by the sign thus:

110. How is a gradual increase followed by a gradual decrease of tone indicated?

ANS. By the word SWELL, or by the sign thus:

111. How is a sudden force of tone indicated?

ANS. By the word SFORZANDO, or the abbreviation *sf*, or by the sign thus: >.

MUSICAL NOTATION.

EXAMPLE 19.

pp < *p* < *mp* < *m* < *mf* < *f* < *f* > *mf* > *m* > *mp* > *p* > *pp*

A SWELL.

112. How is the repetition of a passage of music indicated?

ANS. By a succession of Dots called a REPEAT, before and after the passage designed to be sung twice. But, over a measure or phrase of music, implies a repetition thereof.

EXAMPLE 20

113. How are short and detached tones sometimes indicated?

ANS. By the word STACCATO, or the sign, thus : (׳) over a note.

EXAMPLE 21.

To be sung as if written thus ;

MUSICAL NOTATION.

EXERCISE 87.

NOTE. The letters D. C. are the abbreviation of the words DA CAPO, (from the beginning;) they refer the performer back to the beginning of the same piece of music, the end of which is indicated by the word FINE.

CHAPTER III.
DIVISION 1.

114. What may be understood by the KEY of the Scale?
ANS. The Key of the Scale is that letter on which the first note Do, of the Major Scale, or LA, of the Minor, is written.
115. In what Key thus far, has the Major Scale been written?
ANS. In the key of C, the letter on which Do is found.
116. In what key thus far, has the Minor Scale been written?
ANS. In the key of A, the letter on which is found the syllable LA.

117. May the scales be written in any other keys?
ANS. The scales may be written in the key of any letter.
118. How is the characteristic order of Seconds effected when the scale is transposed into the key of any other letter than C?
ANS. The characteristic order of Seconds is effected through the use of sharps or flats, as the case may demand.
119. How is the KEY of the Scale indicated?
ANS. The absence of flats or sharps next to the clef—the NATURAL SIGNATURE—indicates the Major Scale in the key of C, or the Minor Scale in the key A.
120. When the scale is transposed, what is the sign or signature indicating its key?
ANS. The number of sharps or flats next to the clef on the respective letters, necessary to effect the order of Seconds, beginning with the letter on which ONE, of the scale, is written.

MUSICAL NOTATION.

EXAMPLE 22.
1, Do, 2, Re, 3, Mi, 4, Fa, 5, Sol, 6, La, 7, Si, 8, Do, 7, Si, 6, La, 5, Sol, 4, Fa, 3, Mi, 2, Re, 8, Do, 7, Si, 6, La.

EXAMPLE 23.
1, Do, 2, Re, 3, Mi, 4, Fa, 5, Sol, 6, La, 7, Si, 8, Do.

EXAMPLE 24.
1, Do, 2, Re, 3, Mi, 4, Fa, 5, Sol, 6, La, 7, Si, 8, Do.

EXAMPLE 25.
1, Do, 2, Re, 3, Mi, 4, Fa, 5, Sol, 6, La, 7, Si, 8, Do.

121. What is the signature in Example 22? Ans. One sharp.
122. On what letter is the sharp placed? Ans. On F.
123. What is the Key of the scale, under the signature of one sharp? Ans. The Key of G.
124. What is the signature in Example 23? Ans. Two Sharps.
125. What is the signature in Example 24? Ans. Three sharps.
126. On what letters are the sharps placed? Ans. On F, C, and G.
127. What is the Key of the scale under the signature of three sharps. Ans. The Key of A.
128. What is the signature in Example 25? Ans. Four sharps.

MUSICAL NOTATION

EXAMPLE 26.
EXAMPLE 27.
EXAMPLE 28.
EXAMPLE 29.

MUSICAL NOTATION.

DIVISION 2.

NOTE. The pupil will observe when the scale is transposed into the key of G, that the sharp on F, is used to effect an agreement between the letters E, F#, and G—and six, seven, and eight, of the scale. The sharp, therefore, on F, next to the clef, constitutes the Signature for the scale, in the key of G, under which Signature, instead of F, F# is used, except when otherwise indicated by a Natural. When the scale is transposed into the key of F, the flat on B, is used to effect an agreement between the letters A, B♭, and C—and the numerals three, four, and five, of the scale. The flat, therefore, on B, next to the clef, constitutes the Signature for the scale in the key of F. In relation to which the same principle is active when the scale is transposed into any other key.

THE SCALES UNDER THE SIGNATURE OF ONE SHARP.

The Chromatic Scale in the Key of G.

EXAMPLE 30.

1, #1, 2, #2, 3, 4, #4, 5, #5, 6, #6, 7, 8.
Do, Di, Re, Ri, Mi, Fa, Fi, Sol, Si, La, Li, Si, Do.

8, 7, ♭7, 6, ♭6, 5, ♭5, 4, 3, ♭3, 2, ♭2, 1.
Do, Si, Se, La, Le, Sol, Se, Fa, Mi, Me, Re, Ra, Do.

EXAMPLE 31.

The Minor Scale under the Signature of one Sharp, in the Key of E.

1, 2, 3, 4, 5, 6, 7, 7, 8, 8.
La, Si, Do, Re, Mi, Fa, Si, Si, La, La.

8, 8, 7, 7, 6, 5, 4, 3, 2, 1.
La, La, Si, Si, Fa, Mi, Re, Do, Si, La.

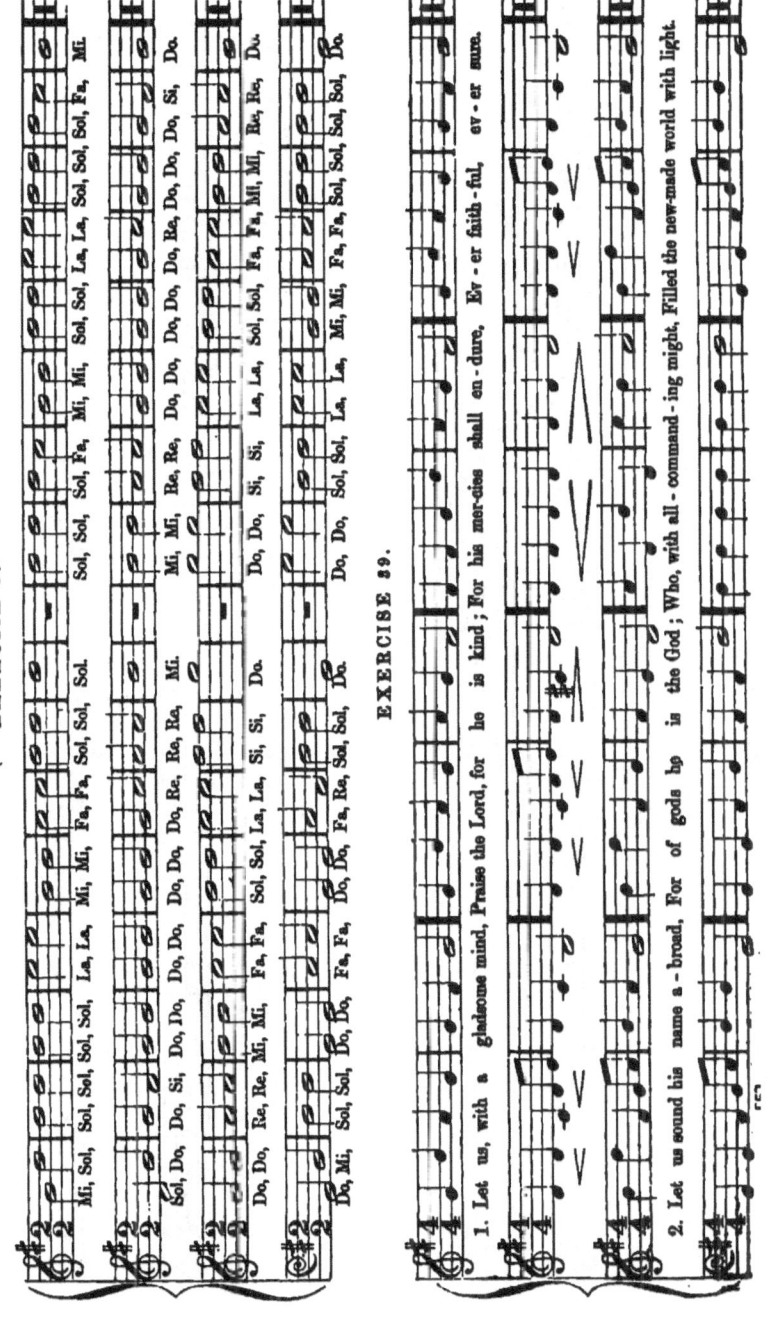

MUSICAL NOTATION.

THE SCALES UNDER THE SIGNATURE OF ONE FLAT.

EXAMPLE 32.
The Chromatic Scale in the Key of F.

EXAMPLE 33.
The Minor Scale in the Key of D.

EXERCISE 40.

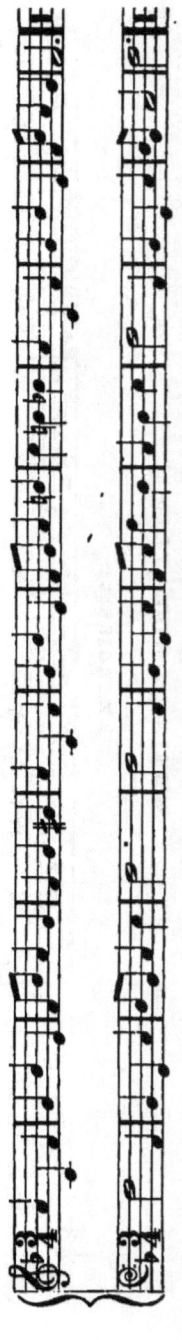

MUSICAL NOTATION.

THE SCALES UNDER THE SIGNATURE OF TWO SHARPS.

EXAMPLE 34.

The Chromatic Scale in the Key of D.

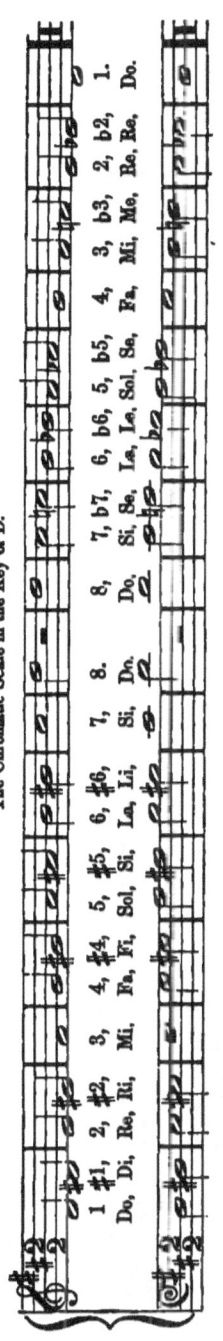

EXAMPLE 36.

The Minor Scale in the Key of B.

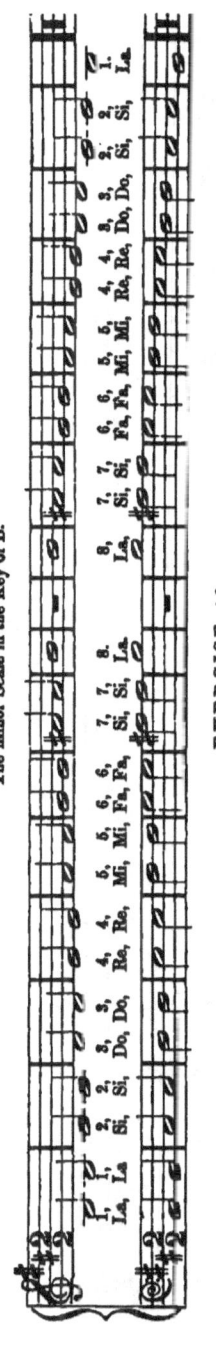

EXERCISE 40.

MUSICAL NOTATION.

THE SCALES UNDER THE SIGNATURE OF TWO FLATS.

EXAMPLE 36.

The Chromatic Scale in the Key of Bb.

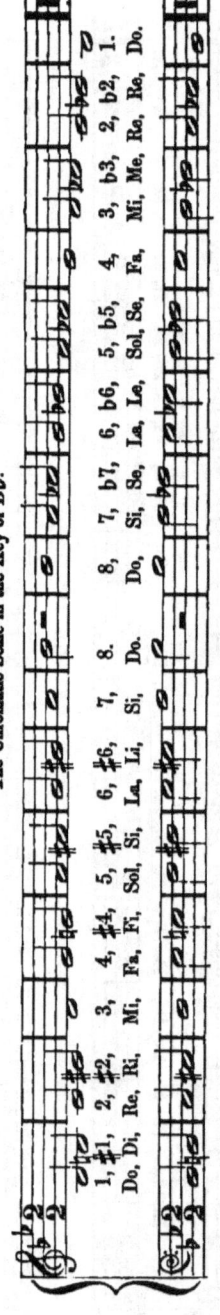

EXAMPLE 37.

The Minor Scale in the Key of G.

EXERCISE 41.

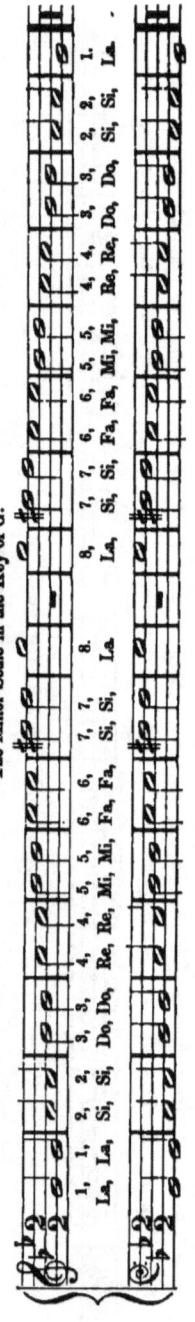

MUSICAL NOTATION.

THE SCALES UNDER THE SIGNATURE OF THREE SHARPS.

EXAMPLE 38.

The Chromatic Scale in the Key of A.

1, ♯1, 2, ♯2, 3, 4, ♯4, 5, ♯5, 6, ♯6, 7, 8, 7, ♭7, 6, ♭6, 5, ♭5, 4, 3, ♭3, 2, ♭2, 1.
Do, Di, Re, Ri, Mi, Fa, Fi, Sol, Si, La, Li, Si, Do, Si, Le, La, Se, Sol, Se, Fa, Mi, Me, Re, Ra, Do.

Note. The DOUBLE SHARP, thus: × elevates the pitch of a note that has previously been made sharp, by a sign in the signature.

EXAMPLE 39.

The Minor Scale in the Key of F♯.

1, 1, 2, 3, 3, 4, 4, 5, 5, 6, 6, 7, 7, 8, 8, 7, 7, 6, 6, 5, 5, 4, 4, 3, 3, 2, 2, 1.
La, La, Si, Do, Do, Re, Re, Mi, Mi, Fa, Fa, Si, Si, La, La, Si, Si, Fa, Fa, Mi, Mi, Re, Re, Do, Do, Si, Si, La.

EXERCISE 42.

Do, Sol, Mi, Re, La, Fa, Mi, Re, Do, Do, Sol, Mi, Re, La, Do, Si, La, Sol, Re, Do, La, Re, Si, Sol, Sol, Do, Si, La, Si, Do, Si, La, Si, La, Fa, Mi, Do.

Do, Mi, Do, Fa, Re, Sol, Sol, Do, Do, Mi, Do, Fa, Mi, Re, Re, Sol, Mi, Fa, Mi, Re, Do, Fa, Mi, Re, Ra, Do.

MUSICAL NOTATION.

THE SCALES UNDER THE SIGNATURE OF THREE FLATS.

EXAMPLE 40.

The Chromatic Scale in the Key of Eb.

1, #1, 2, #2, 3, 4, #4, 5, #5, 6, #6, 7, 8. 8, 7, b7, 6, b6, 5, b5, 4, 3, b3, 2, b2, 1.
Do, Di, Re, Ri, Mi, Fa, Fi, Sol, Si, La, Li, Si, Do. Do, Si, Se, La, Le, Sol, Se, Fa, Mi, Me, Re, Re, Do.

NOTE. A DOUBLE FLAT, thus: (bb) depresses the pitch of a note previously depressed by a flat, in the signature.

EXAMPLE 41.

The Minor Scale in the Key of C.

1, 2, 3, 4, 5, b, 6, 7, 7, 8. 8, 8, 7, 7, 6, 5, 5, 4, 4, 3, 3, 2, 2, 1.
La, La, Si, Do, Re, Mi, Mi, Fa, Fa, Si, Si, La. La, La, Si, Si, Fa, Fa, Mi, Mi, Re, Re, Do, Do, Si, Si, La.

EXERCISE 43.

Do, Si, Do, Fa, Mi, Re, Do, La, Re, Si, La, Sol, Fi, Sol, Re, Si, Do, Fa, Mi, Do, La, La, Si, Do, Fa, Mi, Re, Do.

MUSICAL NOTATION.

THE SCALES UNDER THE SIGNATURE OF FOUR SHARPS.

The Chromatic Scale in the Key of E.

EXAMPLE 42.

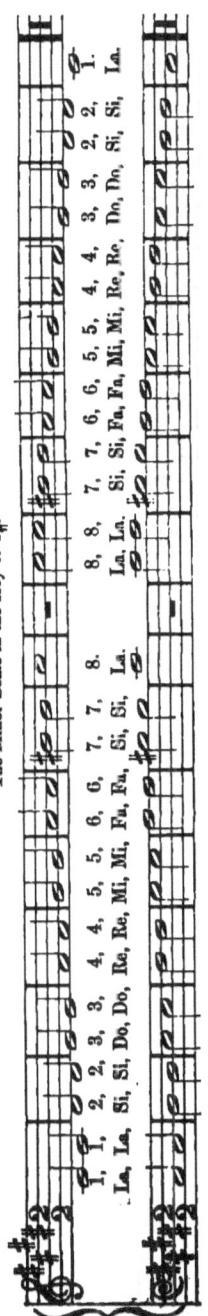

The Minor Scale in the Key of C♯.

EXAMPLE 43.

EXERCISE 44.

NOTE. A CURVED LINE over or under two or more notes, implies that they should be sung connectedly.

MUSICAL NOTATION.

THE SCALES UNDER THE SIGNATURE OF FOUR FLATS.

EXAMPLE 44.

The Chromatic Scale in the Key of A♭.

1, #1, 2, #2, 3, 4, #4, 5, #5, 6, #6, 7, 8, 7, b7, 6, b6, 5, b5, 4, 3, b3, 2, b2, 1.
Do, Di, Re, Ri, Mi, Fa, Fi, Sol, Si, La, Li, Si, Do. Do, Si, Se, La, Le, Sol, Se, Fa, Mi, Me, Re, Ra, Do.

EXAMPLE 45.

The Minor Scale in the Key of F.

1, 1, 2, 3, 3, 4, 4, 5, 5, 6, 6, 7, 7, 8. 8, 7, 7, 6, 6, 5, 5, 4, 4, 3, 3, 2, 2, 1.
La, La, Si, Do, Re, Mi, Fa, Si, Si, La. La, Si, Si, Fa, Fa, Mi, Mi, Re, Re, Do, Do, Si, Si, La.

EXERCISE 45.

Do, Si, La, Do, Si, Si, Mi, Mi, Re, Do, Fa, Fa, Fa, Mi, Do, Re, Fi, Sol, Mi, La, Sol, Fa, Sol, Do, Re, Mi, Fa, Mi, Mi, Mi, Fa, Sol, Fi, Sol, Do.

Mi, Fa, Fi, Fi, Sol, Sol, Sol, Si, Si, La, La, La, Si, Re, Do, La, Sol, Fi, Re, Sol, Do, Do, Di, Di, Re, Si, Do, Si, Se, Se, La, Sol, Sol, Si, Si, La, Re, Do, Mi, Re, Do.

NOTE. A Flat, Sharp, or Natural, when incidentally used, extends its influence through the measure in which it is written, except when otherwise indicated, and into the next succeeding measure, whose first note is on the same degree with the note in the preceding measure, before which the flat, sharp, or natural is written.

MUSICAL NOTATION

WELCOME TO MAY.

MUSICAL NOTATION.

CHAPTER IV.

Note. The pupil will commence the phrases in the above lessons softly, as indicated by the sign *Cres.*, and taking breath only at the rests.

MUSICAL NOTATION.

MUSICAL NOTATION.

MUSICAL NOTATION.

MUSICAL NOTATION.

A SLEIGHING SONG.

49

FORMATION OF TONE.

Sound is the sensation produced by the vibration of the air or some other medium with which the ear is in contact. There are three words used to describe the sensations produced on the auditory nerve, viz: SOUND, NOISE and TONE. Sound is a general term, but Noise and Tone are specific terms. Noise is that kind of sound which results from irregular, interrupted and confused vibrations, while Tone results from uniformly even, uninterrupted vibrations. Tone, in the human voice, is produced by the exercise of the vocal organ, and other parts called into requisition, in accordance with the design of nature.

A well organized throat seems to be essential to the formation of tone; but a bad voice is oftener the result of neglect, or carelessness on the part of the singer or speaker, than of organic difficulty. In a general sense, tone, or a good voice, must be taught by imitation, as are style in conversation, good manners, and the like.

In the early stages of vocal practice, the pupil should rid the voice of all pectoral, guttural, or nasal qualities, and until this be accomplished, all practice of scales and other exercises may not advance the student, but rather serve to confirm an exceptionable use of the voice.

The pupil should commence his practice by learning to inflate the chest by a single deep and silent inspiration, abstaining carefully from any sighing or sobbing sound, then allowing the breath to escape as slowly and gradually as possible; this should be repeated till the pupil can fill the lungs completely at one effort, and moreover till it come to be a matter of habit.

The learner must stand erectly, resting the weight of the body on both feet equally, and the head kept steadily in its proper position, inclining neither to the right or left; in short, let the attitude be easy and graceful.

Let the tone be formed in the back part of the mouth, behind the veil of the palate, and let it issue unaccompanied by any wheezing, gurgling, or reedy sound. The mouth should be opened sufficiently to emit the tone freely, not so wide however as to distort the feature. Avoid protruding the lips, adjusting them so as slightly to expose particularly the upper teeth. Ordinarily, huskiness and hoarseness result from an over-issue of breath; hence the less amount of breath used, the purer will be the tone.

The student should inflate the lungs and check the breath before commencing the tone. The tone must be approached with the slightest possible current of breath,—with certainty and firmness,—still avoiding abruptness. A seemingly natural and fitting position of the mouth must be secured before the tone commences; no change should take place in the shape of the mouth during the prolongation of tone, that is, supposing the tone to be on one and

FORMATION OF TONE.

the same vowel element. Neither should the general position of the mouth change when the tone is increased or diminished; for the mouth change when the tone is increased or diminished, so will also the vowel element change. Hence it is recommended that the pupil form the tone on the following vowels, viz: A, long, as in fate; E, long; O, long; and A as in far; all of which are single elements, demanding the same position of the mouth in their approach, prolongation, and termination.

The tongue should lie unmoved in its proper place, neither drawn back nor elevated. The tone should be formed without causing any apparent effort, for it is probably true that when the voice is exercised in accordance with the design of nature, it is pure,—costing the singer but little effort, and thereby rendering the tones far more grateful to the listener.

The words CHEST VOICE, HEAD VOICE, and MIXED VOICE,—which, by the way, are terms to most minds as vague and equivocal, as they are wanting in real significance in themselves,—we feel obliged to receive as technical terms, since custom has so long recognized their use. These words refer not so much to the formation, as to the characteristic quality of tones.

The Chest Voice, is that kind of tone which is clear and shrill, yet at the same time wanting in resonance. The Head Voice, is characterized by resonance, but wanting in clearness. The Mixed Voice, combines the clearness of the Chest Voice, with the resonance of the Head Voice, and this is the quality of voice which, in this work, is recommended.

In the proper exercise of the voice, the breath contained in the lungs is compressed by the contraction of the muscles of the waist, and forced upward into the Chest, thereby giving a strong impulse to the current of air passing through the trachea. This may be illustrated in part by a pipe Organ, the waist serving as a bellows, the chest as a receiver, or wind chest, the trachea as a pipe, and the head as a reflector or sounding board.

Notwithstanding the many suggestions that may properly be made to the learner in his early stages of practice, it is important, and indeed necessary, to attain excellence in the use of the voice, and form a chaste and finished style in singing, that the pupil should be under the direct instruction of a competent master, who is himself a practical singer, and whose examples are fit models for imitation.

No. 1.

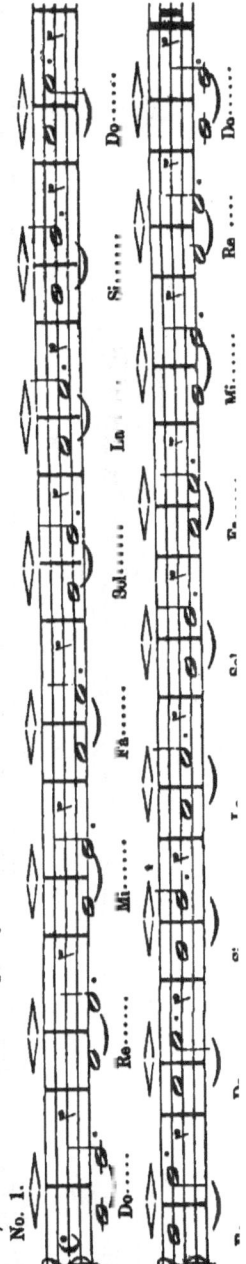

MUSICAL NOTATION.

MUSICAL NOTATION.   53

DICTIONARY OF MUSICAL TERMS.

A. An Italian preposition, meaning *to*, *in*, *with*, *according*, *to*, &c.; as *a tempo*, in time.

ACCELLERANDO. Hastening the time, moving faster and faster.

ACCIDENTAL, is a term applied to sharps, flats, and naturals, when they occur not as the signature (*see Signature*) of a piece of music, but only before some particular note or notes.

ACCOMPANIMENT (Italian, *Accompagnamento*); a term generally applied to the part performed by instruments in connection with another, or others performed by voices.

ACCOMPANIMENT AD LIBITUM, an accompaniment that may be used or omitted at pleasure, in contradistinction that cannot be omitted.

ADAGIO. Slowly; used to denote a movement faster than *largo*, but slower than *lento*; *Adagio* movements should generally be performed in a gentle, calm manner.

ADAGISSIMO. The superlative of *Adagio*, very slow, soft and subdued.

ADAGIO ASSAI. Nearly synonymous with the above.

AD LIBITUM, or AD LIB. At pleasure, according to one's choice, used with reference to the time of a movement.

AFFETUOSO. With deep feeling and emotion.

AGITATO. Indicates a hurried, disturbed manner of performance.

AL, ALL, ALLA, ALLE, ALLO; different forms of the Italian preposition *A*, combined with the definite article *il, la, lo, &c.* They mean literally *to the*, or ACCORDING TO; as *Alla Turca*, in the Turkish style, *Alla Cappella*, in the church style.

ALLEGRO. Quickly; it also generally indicates a degree of joyfulness, cheerfulness, and animation. The superlative, *Allegrissimo*, indicates that those characteristics should be heightened, while the diminutive, *Allegretto*, denotes a less rapid and joyous movement. The word *Allegro* is very often combined with other words, as *Allegro Con Brio*, and *Allegro Con Fuoco*, with vehemence and spirit; *Allegro Vivace*, very fast and with great animation; *Allegro di Molto*, exceedingly quick; *Allegro ma grazioso*, fast, but in a graceful, gliding manner; *Allegro ma non troppo*, and *Allegro ma non presto*, quite fast, but not hurried.

ALL' OTTAVA. On the octave. When written *over* notes it means that they should be played or sung an octave higher than written, and when *under* notes, that they should be performed an octave lower.

All Segno. To the sign; this directs the performer to return to the sign, ($, or §,) and repeat from that

AMBROSIAN CHANT. A peculiar kind of chant, so named from its inventor, St. Ambrose, Bishop of Milan, who lived A. D. 340-398.

ANDANTE. This term refers not only to a moderate, measured movement, but includes the mode of delivery. Alone, it indicates a gentle, calm, peaceful expression, and a movement neither so fast as *Allegro*, or as slow as *Adagio*, but one midway between them. It is very often combined with other words, as *Andante Affetuoso*, (see Effetuoso,) *Andante Divoto*, with great religious feeling, with penitential and reverential emotion; *Andante Cantabile*, is a smoothly, flowing, melodious manner.

ANDANTINO, the diminutive of *Andante*. It is yet a disputed point whether the word denotes a quicker or slower movement than *Andante*, and it is used by composers in both senses; in this book, it indicates always a quicker movement than Andante, but with the same style of delivery.

ANIMATO, or CON ANIMA, indicates a bold, vigorous manner of performance.

ANTHEM. A sacred composition, for any number of voices, the words of which are most frequently taken from the Psalms. There are several kinds of anthems, such as the *verse anthem* for solo voices, the *solo anthem* for one voice only, and the *full anthem* for voices and instruments together; this term is derived from the Greek word Anthemos, which meant a kind of common dance, to which they at the same time sung.

ANTIPHONAL. Music performed responsively, one part being sung by a solo or semi-chorus, and answered in the same manner.

A PIACERE. See *ad libitum*.

APPASSIONATO, or CON PASSIONE. In a highly impassioned manner, indicative of much more fervid emotion than *Affetuoso*.

APPOGIATURA. Commonly applied to an ornamental fore-note which forms no part of the harmony, and is usually written in a small form, thus:

ARDITO. With spirit and energy.

ARIOSO. In a light, airy, gay manner.

ASSAI. An Italian adverb, meaning very in a high degree. It occurs connected with and qualifying very many musical terms, as *piano assai*, very soft; *presto assai*, very quick.

ADAGIO ASSAI. Very slow and subdued.

A TEMPO. In time, used when the regular beat has been interrupted by an *ad lib.* or *ritard*, (see *ritard*,) to indicate that the regular movement should be resumed.

A TEMPO GIUSTO. In very strict and steady time.

A TEMPO ORDINARIO. Synonymous with *Moderato*, which see.

A DUE, for two voices; A TRE, for three voices; A QUATTRO, for four voices, &c.

ATTACCA. A term used at the end of a movement, to show that the next movement should be immediately commenced, without stopping at all between the two.

BALLAD. A little lyric story, or a few simple reflections, expressed in a few verses, each of which is sung to the same tune.

BARITONO, or BARYTONE. That kind of voice which lays midway between Bass and Tenor.

BASSO, or BASS. The name of the lowest part in harmony.

BENE PLACITO. Indicates that the performer is at liberty to embellish and ornament the text at pleasure.

BREVE. Means a note, formerly used, but now almost obsolete. It literally means *short*, and was used in contradistinction to another note called *Longa*. The *Breve* is twice as long as the note now called a whole note, and is written as follows:

ALLA BREVE measure is that measure whose parts consist of *breves*; it is now wholly disused. The expression ALLA BREVE is also *sometimes* used, and denotes a pretty rapid movement, nearly synonymous with *à Cappella*.

BRIO. Spirit, vivacity, animation.

DICTIONARY OF MUSICAL TERMS.

BUFFO. An Italian adjective, meaning comic, sportive, facetious, &c.

CADENZA, or CADENCE. Sometimes means an ornamental passage occasionally introduced by performers at the end of a piece of music; again it is used as synonymous with the word *trill*, particularly by the French; but the more proper and technical meaning, in every harmonic progression where after a dominant seventh, or also the harmony of the subdominant follows the tonic harmony. In the first case it is called the *authentic*, and in the second the *plagal cadence*.

CALANDO. Gradually becoming softer and slower.

CANTABILE. Designates a moderate movement, and a simple, unaffected style of performance.

CANTATA. A kind of composition invented by Barbara Strozzi, a Venetian lady, in the seventeenth century. It generally consists of two or even three melodies, interspersed with recitative.

CANTATRICE. A female vocalist.

CANTO. Literally a song, used as synonymous with *melody*.

CANTO-FERMO. A kind of composition where all the notes are of the same length, and the melody very simple.

CAPPELLA. The phrase *Alla Cappella* is was formerly used to signify a vocal performance without the aid of instruments; but now has reference to the movement, and indicates a considerable degree of rapidity.

CAPRICCIO. A term applied to every species of composition, written rather according to the whim of the composer, than the strict laws of unity of effect.

CARRAGE. Same as above. A CA- REZZO. Synonymous with *ad lib*, which see.

CAVATINA. A word used to designate a song consisting of a single movement, sometimes inserted in, or affixed to a *recitative*.

CHANT. A very simple harmonized melody, to which are sung portions of the Scriptures, though not in measure. There are several kinds of chants; as the *Plain Choral*, a simple unharmonized melody; the figurat chant, sung in parts; the Ambrosian chant, the Gregorian chant, &c.

CHE. An Italian word, sometimes used to signify *tham*, as *piu che lento*, more than slow, that is, slower than lento, &c.

CHOIR. This word has various significations, as follows: 1. The enclosed portion of a Cathedral, appropriated to the celebration of Divine Worship. 2. That part of the church appropriated to the singers; and lastly, the more general use of the word, any collection of singers.

CHORAL. A word derived from the Greek *Choros*, meaning originally, a dance, afterwards a dance accompanied by singing, and finally a company of singers alone. *Choral*, as an adjective, means that which relates to a choir, as a choral hymn; as a substantive, it is used to designate a species of music, of a peculiarly grave and solemn character, generally moving in notes of equal length. The phrase *Choral music* refers to music written in choral style, which should always be performed in a slow and dignified manner, without however drawing the time; this term also means music in parts, in distinction from *solo* or *verse* music.

CHORD. A term applied to any simultaneous combination of tones whatever.

CHORUS. From the Greek *Choros*. (See *choral*.) This word means, 1st, a collection of singers, and 2d, music written to be sung by a number of voices; the word is also used to distinguish such a piece of music from a solo, duet, trio or quartette. *Semi-chorus* means a small chorus.

CHROMATIC. A word applied to music which abounds in incidentals; also used as opposed to *diatonic*. (See Elementary Principles.)

CODA. Literally a *tail*. When a piece of music consists of several portions which are to be repeated, and is not of itself brought to a satisfactory close, it is usual to append a distinct portion, called the *Coda*, which serves to finish the piece in a complete manner.

COL, COLL, COLLA, COLLE, COI, COGLI. The Italian preposition *con*, (with,) combined with the definite article, meaning *with the*; as *Col arco*, with the bow; *Colla voce*, with the voice.

COME. As; *come prima*, as at first; *come sopra*, as above.

COMODO, or COMMODO. Used to indicate that a piece of music should be performed in a convenient grade of time.

CON, CO, COLLO. (See *Col, Coll*, &c.) Means *with, with the*, used in a great variety of connections, as *con fuoco*, with vehemence; *con lamo*, with the bass; *con gli strumenti*, with the instruments, &c.

CONCERTO. Union of voices and instruments.

CONDUCTOR. A term applied to one who has the general superintendence of a performance.

CORO. The Italian word for *chorus*.

COUNTERPOINT. A word of very extensive signification, applied not only to several distinct classes of composition in two or more parts, but also to every possible variety of harmony; the most general meaning is *harmony*, in all its different forms.

CRESCENDO. Abbreviated CRES, CR. A gradual increasing strength of sound. The sign for *crescendo* is ⟨.

D, DA, DAL, DALLA, DALLE, DALLO. *Da* is an Italian preposition meaning *from*, or *of*; combined with the definite article as above, it means *from the*, or *of the*; as *Da Capo*, from the beginning; *dal segno*, from the sign.

DA CAPO. *From the beginning.* A term used at the end of a piece of music, to direct the performer to commence the piece again, and go to the point marked FINE, *end.* This phrase is frequently abbreviated thus, D. C.

DECANI, a term used to distinguish the vocal priests of a Cathedral from the lay choristers, who are called *Cantoris*.

DECLAMANDO. In a speaking, rather than merely singing style.

DECRESCENDO. Synonymous with *Diminuendo*, which see.

DELICATO, DELICATAMENTE, CON DELICATEZZA; these all indicate a tasteful and delicate mode of performance.

DESCANT, or DISCANT. A musical composition in parts.

DIMINUENDO, implies a gradual diminution in the strength of the tones, the sign for the diminuendo ⟩. The union of the *crescendo* and *diminuendo*, ⟨⟩, is called a *swell*.

DI MOLTO. An Italian phrase, meaning *very, very much*; as *affetuso di molto*, with great feeling; *allegro di molto*, exceedingly quick and energetic.

DIRGE. A musical composition for funeral occasions.

DISCORD, DISSONANCE; a combination of tones, which being heard disconnectedly, sound disagreeably.

DICTIONARY OF MUSICAL TERMS.

DIVOTO. *Devoutly*, expressive of religious emotion.

DOLCE. With a soft, delicate expression; the superlative *dolcissimo*, is frequently found synonymous with *dolce*, and the less used words *dolcemente* and *dolcezza*.

DOLENTE, DOLOROSO, CON DUOLO, CON DOLORE; *with an expression of pain and distress.*

D. S., the abbreviation of *del segno*, which see.

DUETTO, or DUETT. A piece of music for two voices, whether with or without accompaniment.

DYNAMICS. (A Greek word.) Is used to a certain extent as applied to force, but may more properly be regarded as synonymous with power, the moving principle; which use had its origin either in the want of a knowledge of the real import of the word, or a clear sense of the idea to be conveyed.

E, before a vowel ED. An Italian conjunction meaning *and*.

ELEGANTE, ELEGANTAMENTE, CON ELEGANZA, *With grace*.

ELEGY, (Italian ELEGIA.) A vocal composition of a plaintive or mournful character.

ENCORE. A French adverb, meaning *again*. This has been for a long time used at musical performances, in calling for a repetition of a peculiarly striking or pleasing performance.

ENERGICO. *With vigor; with energy*.

ESPRESSIVO, or CON ESPRESSIONE. *With expression*; paying great attention to the dynamic and other signs which may occur.

EXPRESSION; such a performance as gives to music some designed, specific character, and makes it the powerfully expressive language of the soul. The dynamic signs, the *ritard*, and various Italian objectives are collectively termed *marks of expression*.

FANTASIA. Synonymous, or nearly so, with *Capriccio*, which see.

FEROCE. This word denotes a *wild, fierce mode of performance*.

FIERAMENTE; *Boldly*, full of *vigor* and *energy*.

FINALE; The close of a piece; as the *finale* of a symphony, or of an oratorio.

FINE; *The end*. A word generally used in the case of a *da capo* or *dal segno*, to indicate clearly where the piece closes.

FLEBILE. *Mournfully*, synonymous with *Lagrimoso*.

FORCE is that attribute of tone, the degree of which is indicated by the terms Piano, Pianissimo, Forte, &c.

FORTE. *Loud*; FORTISSIMO, superlative *very loud*, abbreviated *f*, and *ff*.

FORZA. *Force, power. Con tutta la forza*, as loud as possible.

FOLLANDO or RINFORZANDO, FORZATO or RINFORZATO. A very sudden increase of force, abbreviated *fz, rfz,* or >.

FUGUE, Italian FUGOA. A particular species of musical composition, where one part leads off, and seems to fly (hence its name) from the others, which pursue at certain distances, and according to certain rules.

FURIOSO, CON FUOCO, FURIBONDO, *with great energy and fury*.

GIOCHEVOLE, GIOCHEVOLMENTE, GIOCOSAMENTE, GIOCOLOSAMENTE, GIOCOSO GIOCANTE, GIUCHEVOLE; all mean *lightly, sportively, gaily*.

GIUSTO; *Just, exact*. A term used by composers in cases where they consider a steady and even performance especially important; also after a *tempo rubato*, which see.

GLEE. A species of composition in three or more parts, almost exclusively confined to England.

GLISBANDO. A *gliding* from one note to the next.

GLORIFICATION. Vocal adoration and praise to the Supreme Being.

GRANDIOSO. In an elevated style.

GRAVE. This word, when prefixed to a piece of music, indicates a very slow movement, with a peculiarly solemn and dignified method of performance.

GRAZIOSO, CON GRAZIA. *Gracefully, with elegance*.

H. The letter used by the Germans to denote our B natural; with them B is always understood to be B♭.

HARMONY. Any simultaneous combination of tones, whether a single chord, or a succession of chords; also used to denote the knowledge of the laws which regulate the succession of chords.

HYMN. This word originally meant any poem or song, but the use of the word has long been confined to short lyric poems for sacred purposes.

IMPETUOSO, CON IMPETO; *boisterously, noisily*.

INNOCENTE, INNOCENTAMENTE; this word indicates a simple, artless style of performance.

INTERLUDE. Any short intermediate instrumental performance.

LAGRIMOSO, LAGYIMANDO; indicates a sad, melancholy style.

LAMENTABILE, LAMENTOSO; nearly synonymous with the above.

LAMENTAVOLE; *plaintive, complaining*.

LANGUENDO, LANGUENTE, LANGUEMENTE; *languishing, pining*.

LARGO. This word designates the slowest grade of time; the diminutive, *larghetto*, indicates a movement between *adagio* and *largo*.

LEGATO; Very closely connected, joined together; superlative *legatissimo*.

LEGGIERO, LEGGERAMENTE; lightly, with elasticity.

LISTESSO, or LO STESSO. The same as *l'istesso tempo*, the same movement.

LUGUBRE. This word denotes a slow movement, combined with a mournful, gloomy, sad expression.

LUSINGANDO, LUSINGHIERO; in a flattering, insinuating manner.

LYRIC. A term applied to poetry intended especially to be sung.

MA. An Italian word meaning *but*, as *Allegro ma non troppo*, quick, but not too quick.

MAESTOSO. With dignity, with gravity; synonymous with this is the phrase *con Maestà*.

MARCANDO. This word denotes a very gradual diminution to the extreme degree of softness; nearly synonymous with this are the words *calando, morendo, perdendosi,* and *smorzando*.

MARCATO. In a distinct, prominent manner.

MASS. (Latin *missa*, Italian *messa*, German *messe*.) The service of celebrating the Lord's Supper in the Catholic Church; used also to denote the appropriate music for such an occasion.

MELODY. A regular and agreeable succession of tones, conveying some impression to the mind, either of joy or grief, agitation or calmness, &c., &c.

MENO. An Italian adverb, meaning *less*; it is used to qualify many of the adjectives, thus: *meno allegro*, less quick; *meno forte*, less loud; *meno vivace*, with less energy.

DICTIONARY OF MUSICAL TERMS.

MEZZO. Feminine *mezza, moderately*; thus, *mezza forte*, moderately loud; *mezzo piano*, moderately soft; abbreviated *mf*, *mp*.

MEZZA DI VOCE. A phrase signifying the middle of the voice.

MODERATO. Is used as a designation of the movement, and is thus often combined with other words, as *Allegro Moderato*; moderately fast.

MODULATION. A change of key in a piece of music.

MOLTO. *Very much*; synonymous with *assai*, as *molto vivace*, very lively.

MOSSO. An Italian participle, meaning *moved*. It is used to denote a quickened grade of time, when it is combined with the adverb *più*, thus, *più mosso*, quicker.

MOTETT. A sacred composition in parts; the words generally taken from the Scriptures.

MOTO. Unusually denotes an increase of movement, as *Andante con moto*, in the same style as *Andante*, but a little faster; *Con più moto*, faster.

MOVEMENT. Musical progression in general.

NEL, NELL', NELLA, NELLO. Compounds of the Italian definite article and the preposition *in*, meaning *in the*; as *Nello stesso tempo*, in the same time.

NON. This is both a Latin and Italian adverb, meaning *not*, as *non troppo allegro*, not too fast.

O, OD, OSIA. Italian conjunction meaning *or*; as *Soprano od alto*, the Soprano or alto, *Oboe osia clarinetto*, hautboy or clarinet.

OBLIGATO. An indispensable part, material to the intended effect of the piece.

consisting of solos, duetts, trios, quartetts and choruses.

ORCHESTRA. Means 1st, the space appropriated to the choir and instrumental performers, and 2d, the band of instrumental musicians themselves.

ORDINARIO. *In the usual manner*. *Tempo Ordinario*, in a moderate degree of time.

OTTAVA ALT. *An octave above*. OTTAVA BASSA. An octave below.

OVERTURE. An introductory symphony to a musical drama.

P. The abbreviation of the word *piano*, soft.

PASTORALE. A peculiar movement in 6-8 measure.

PATETICO. *Pathetic*, expressive of sad emotions.

PER. A Latin and Italian preposition, meaning *by, through, for*; as *Sonata per il violino*, a Sonata for the violin; *della voce*, for the voice.

PERDENDOSI. Means literally *vanishing away*; synonymous with *morendo, mancando*, &c.

PESANTE. Indicates that the notes are to be delivered in an *emphatic*, distinct manner.

PIACERE, and A PIACIMENTO. See *ad libitum*.

PIANO. Superlative *pianissimo*, abbreviated P, and PP, *soft* and *very soft*.

PIETOSO. Denotes a connected, slow and carefully accented mode of performance.

PIU. An Italian adverb, signifying *more*. It is used in connection with other words, as *più forte*, louder; *più allegro*, quicker.

POCO. An Italian adjective, signify-

faster, *crescendo poco a poco*, increasing little by little, or very gradually.

POMPOSO. *With majesty, and dignity*.

PORTAMENTO DI VOCE. Literally means *a carrying of the voice*; technically denotes the *melting* of one tone into another, in an extremely close and connected manner.

POSSIBILE. *Possible*; as *fortissimo quanto possibile*, as loud as possible, *presto quanto possibile*, as fast as possible.

PREGHIERA. Italian for *a prayer*.

PRESTO. An Italian word, signifying the quickest time used in music.

PRIMO. Feminine PRIMA; *the first*, or *most important*, as *Primo Violino, Primo Basso, Primo Volta*, the first time, &c.

QUARTETT; a composition in four parts, or for four voices.

QUASI; *as if, nearly, like*; as *Andante Quasi Allegretto*, &c.

QUINTETT; a piece of music in five parts, or for five voices.

RALLENTANDO, LENTANDO, or SLENTANDO; *retarding the time, gradually growing slower and slower*—synonymous with *Ritardando, Ritenuto*, and *Tardando*.

RECITANDO, RECITANTE; denotes a *speaking, declamatory* manner of performing vocal music.

RECITATIVO, or RECITATIVE; a species of vocal music, which differs very materially both in rhythm and melody from the singing style, and very nearly resembles declamation.

RELIGIOSO; in a devout, serious style.

RISOLUTO. *With firmness and energy*.

RITARDANDO, or RITARD. See *Rallentando*.

RUBATO; literally *robbed*; used to designate an arbitrary disregard of the regular time.

tion of an opera or other dramatic performance, including generally a recitative and cavatina.

SCHERZANDO; in a playful, gay manner.

SEMPLICE. This word denotes that the music is to be performed in a perfectly simple manner, without any ornamental notes, or capricious dragging of the time, &c.

SEMPRE; *always*, or *continually*,—as *sempre pianissimo*, very soft throughout.

SENZA; *without*,—as *senza organo*, without the organ.

SESTETTO, or SIXTETT; a composition in six parts, or for six voices.

SICILIANO; a piece of music in 6-8 measure, of a slow movement.

SIGNATURE; the sharps or flats placed immediately after the clef to determine the key. (See *Elements*.)

SINO; an Italian preposition, meaning *as far as*; as *sino al segno*, as far as the sign.

SMANIOSA, CON SMANIA. Expressing madness and phrenzy.

SOAVE, SOAVEMENTE; same as *Dolce*, which see.

SOLO; plural SOLI. An Italian adjective, meaning *alone*; it is used to denote a composition for a single voice or instrument, with or without accompaniment. When the word occurs in the middle of a chorus, it means that only one voice should sing the part.

SONATA. A short piece of music written especially as an exercise or study for an instrument.

SOPRA. An Italian preposition meaning *above, over*, and *beyond*, as *come sopra*, as above; *ottave sopra*, the octave above.

SOPRANO. A term applied to the highest part of composition, which gene-

57

DICTIONARY OF MUSICAL TERMS.

SOSTENUTO. Indicates that the tones are to be performed in a sustained, continuous manner, being held out to their full value, and closely joined to each other.

SOTTO, means *under*, *beneath*; as *sotto voce*, under voice, or with a suppressed voice; *ottava sotto*, the octave below.

STACCATO. This term is used in music to denote a short, detached, distinct method of performance, exactly the opposite of *legato*, or sustained, connected style.

STREPITOSO, CON STREPITO. A *bustling*, *noisy* style of performance.

STRINGENDO, STRETTO, denotes an *acceleration of time*, and is nearly synonymous with *accelerando*.

SUBITO. In a *quick*, *hasty manner*, as *volti subito*, or V. S., turn over quickly; *attacca subito*, commence immediately.

SUBJECT. This word, in music, means a musical idea, or form of melody.

SVEGLIATO. *Brisk, lively, animated.*

SYMPHONY, (Italian, *Sinfonia*, French, *Symphonie*.) This word, which is of Greek origin, primarily meant a concordance of tones, any music in general, but of late years is used only with reference to compositions intended for instruments alone, without voices.

TACE, SI TACCIA, (Latin, *Tacet*, *Taceant*.) A phrase placed over any individual part of a composition, to supersede the necessity of rests, when a prolonged silence is to be indicated.

TASTO. An Italian word, meaning *the touch*, and hence *anything touched*, the key of a piano-forte or organ. The phrase *Tasto Solo*, abbreviated *T. S.* or simply the word *Tasto*, denotes that in passages thus marked, the Bass only is to be played without any accompanying chords.

TEMPERAMENT. The systematic adjustment of the tuning of keyed instruments, with reference to the different relations of tones.

TEMPO. This Italian word is used merely to denote the *movement*, i. e. the quickness or slowness of the beat; a measured, symmetrical time.

TENERO, TENERAMENTE, CON TENEREZZA. *With delicacy and tenderness*, nearly synonymous with *Dolce*.

TENUTO. Synonymous with *Sostenuto*, which see.

TERZETTO. A vocal composition for three voices.

THEMA, (Italian and French *Tema*.) Greek and Latin for *Subject*.

THOROUGH BASS. The system of representing chords by figures, sometimes incorrectly used as synonymous with *harmony*.

TIMOROSO, designates a style of performance that indicates a state of mind agitated by *fear* or *hesitation*.

TOSTO. An Italian word, meaning *quick*, *soon*; but in connection with *piu*, it means *rather*, as *Andante, piu tosto Allegretto, Andante, or rather Allegretto.*

TRANQUILLAMENTE, CON TRANQUILITA. In a calm, composed manner.

TRE. Italian for *three*; as *a tre voci*, for three voices.

TREMOLO, TREMANDO, TREMULANDO. Italian words denoting a tremulous, wavy style of performance.

TRIO. An instrumental composition in three parts; this word is sometimes incorrectly applied to vocal compositions. (See *Terzetto*.)

TROPPO. An Italian adverb, signifying *too much*, *excessive*; as *non troppo Presto*, not too fast.

TUTTI, feminine TUTTE. Italian adjective meaning *all*, in opposition to *solo* or *soli*; as *tutti bassi*, all the basses.

UN. *One*, or *a*; thus, *un poco piu allegro*, a little faster.

VELOCE, CON VELOCITA, *with rapidity*, *velocity*.

VERSE. Synonymous with *soli*; one voice on each part.

VESPERS. The evening service of the Catholic Church, consisting mainly of certain Chants, with the *magnificat*, and often diversified by various anthems, motetts, &c.

VIBRATO. A sudden, violent, darting method of striking a tone, nearly synonymous with *Forzando*.

VIGOROSO. *With energy, vigorously.* See *risoluto*.

VIVACE, VIVO. Words used to indicate a high degree of animation and spirit in performance.

VOCE. Italian for *voice*. *A mezza voce*, with a moderate degree of force. *Voce di petto*, the chest voice; *voce di testa*, the head voice, called in males, the *falsetto*.

VOLTA. Means in addition to various significations, a *time*, as *prima volta*, the first time; *seconda volta*, the second time.

VOLUNTARY. This word, formerly used to designate any extemporaneous performance, is now only employed with reference to certain pieces played before service, or on other occasions, and selected at the will of the performer.

WALTZ. A German word, meaning 1st, a particular kind of dance, and 2d, a piece of music of a peculiar style, written in 3-4 or 3-8 measure, and performed *Allegro*.

ZELOSO. *With earnestness, and animation.*

THE CHORAL HARMONY.

No. 1.   OLD HUNDRED. L. M.

CHORAL.

1. Be thou, O God, ex-alt-ed high, And as thy glo-ry fills the sky; So let it be on earth displayed, Till thou art here, as there, obeyed.
2. From all that dwell be-low the skies, Let the Cre-a-tor's praise a-rise; Let the Redeemer's name be sung, Thro' eve-ry land, by eve-ry tongue.
3. Praise God, from whom all blessings flow; Praise him, all creatures here be-low; Praise him a-bove, ye heavenly host, Praise Father, Son, and Ho-ly Ghost.

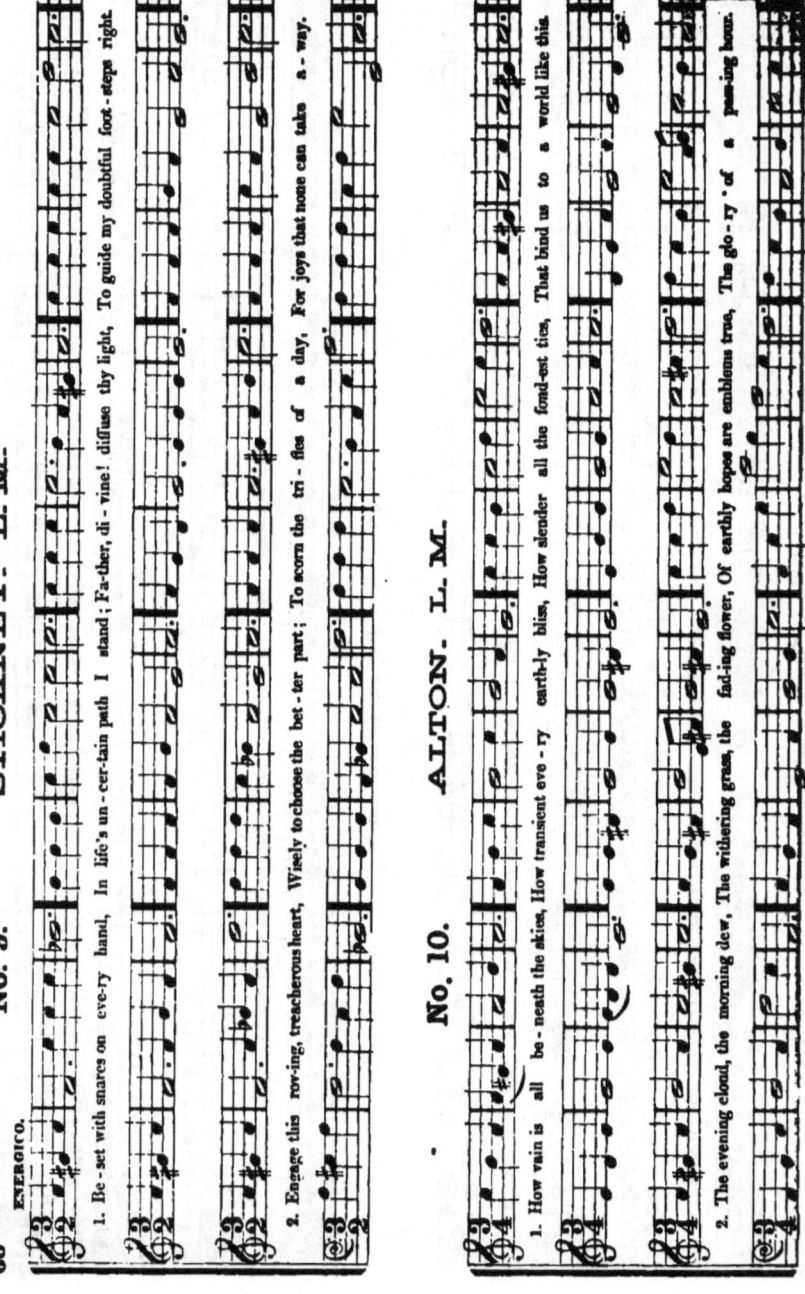

No. 15. BERLIN. L. M.

LENTO.

1. When Power Divine, in mortal form, Hushed with a word the rag-ing storm, In soothing accents Je-sus said, "Lo, it is I! be not a-fraid."
2. So, when in si-lence na-ture sleeps, And his lone watch the mourn-er keeps, One thought shall every pang re-move—Trust, feeble man, thy Maker's love.

No. 16. HASTINGS. L. M.

ANDANTE.

1. Heaven is a place of rest from sin; But all who hope to enter there, Must here that ho-ly course begin, Which shall their souls for rest prepare.
2. Clean hearts, O God, in us cre-ate, Right spir-its, Lord, in us re-new; Commence we now that higher state, Now do thy will as angels do.

69

No. 17. DUNHAM. L. M.

1. E-ter-nal and im-mor-tal King! Thy peerless splendors none can bear; But darkness veils so-raptic eyes, When God with all his glo-ry's there.

2. Yet faith can pierce the aw-ful gloom; The great In-vis-i-ble can see; And with its trembling mingle joy, In fixed regards, great God! on thee.

No. 18. CHORAL HYMN. L. M.

MAESTOSO.

1. Great Framer of unnumbered worlds! And whom unnumbered worlds adore, Whose goodness all thy creatures share, While nature trembles at thy power!

2. Thine is the hand that moves the spheres, That wakes the wind, and lifts the sea; And man who moves, the lord of earth, Acts but the part assigned by thee.

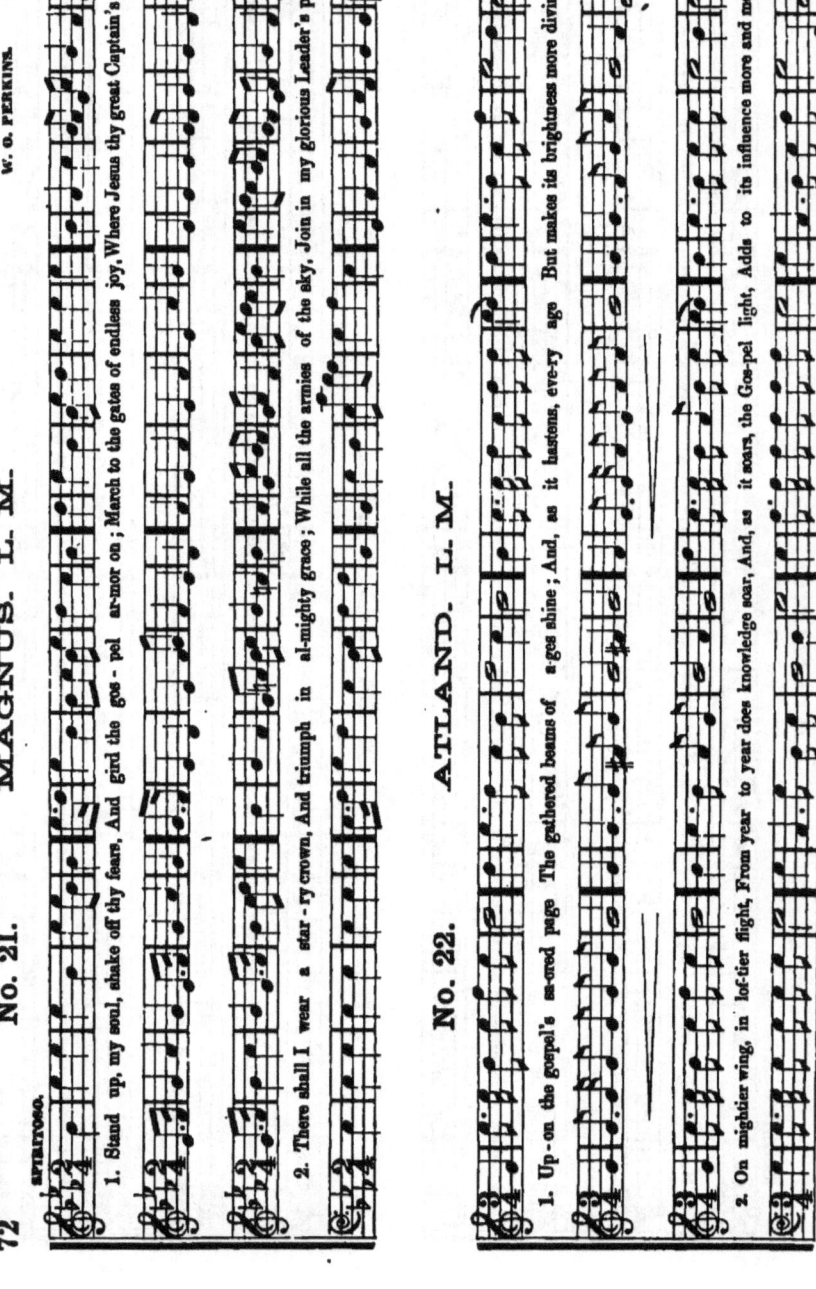

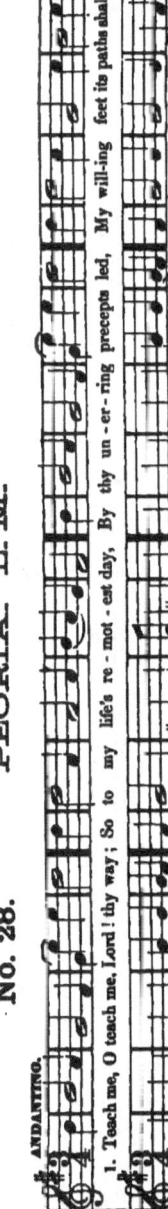

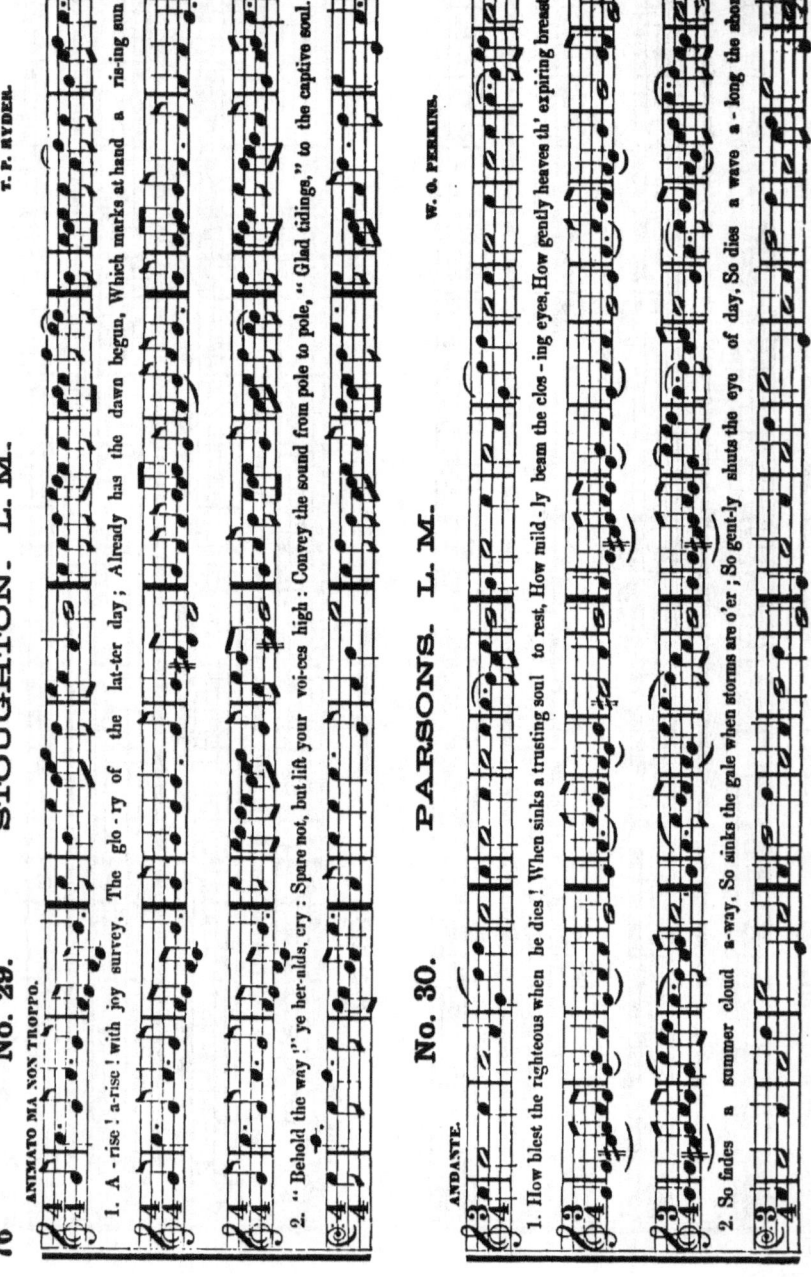

77

No. 31. FOX HOW. L. M.
F. F. HEARD.

1. O God, whose presence glows in all, With-in, a-round us, and above! Thy word we bless, thy name we call, Whose word is Truth, whose name is Love.
2. That truth be with the heart believed Of all who seek this sa-cred place; With power proclaimed, In peace received, Our spirits' light, thy Spirit's grace.

No. 32. TRENTON. L. M.
LARGHETTO.

1. 'Tis finished! so the Saviour cried, And meekly bowed his head and died; 'Tis fin-ished! yes, the race is run, The battle fought, the victory won.
2. 'Tis finished! all that heaven decreed, And all the ancient prophets said, is now ful-fill'd as was designed, In me, the Saviour of mankind.

80

No. 37. MANOAH. L. M.

MAESTOSO MA NON TROPPO.

1. Let one loud song of praise a - rise, To God, whose goodness ceaseless flows; Who dwells enthroned above the skies, And life and breath on all bestows.
2. Let all of good this bo - som fires To him, sole good, give praise due; Let all the truth himself in - spires, U - nite to sing him on - ly true.

No. 38. BEAVERS. L. M.

CANTABILE.

1. O Lord, thy heavenly grace im-part, And fix my frail, in-constant heart; Henceforth my chief desire shall be To ded - i - cate my-self to thee.
2. Whate'er pur-suits my time em-ploy, One thought shall fill my soul with joy; That silent, secret thought shall be, That all my hopes are fixed on thee.

82

No. 41. SEAVER. L. M.

CANTABILE.

1. So let our lips and lives express, The ho-ly Gos-pel we pro-fess; So let our works and vir-tues shine, To prove the doctrine all di-vine.
2. Thus shall we best pro-claim a-broad, The honors of our Saviour, God, When the sal-va-tion reigns within, And grace subdues the power of sin.
3. Re-li-gion bears our spir-its up, While we ex-pect that blessed hope, The bright ap-pear-ance of the Lord, And faith stands leaning on his word.

No. 42. CHESTERVILLE. L. M.

A. S. RIGGS.

ANDANTE CANTABILE.

1. Come hith-er, all ye wea-ry souls, Ye hea-vy la-den sin-ners, come; I'll give you rest from all your toils, And raise you to my heavenly home.
2. They shall find rest, who learn of me; I'm of a meek and low-ly mind; But pas-sion rag-es like the sea, And pride is rest-less as the wind.

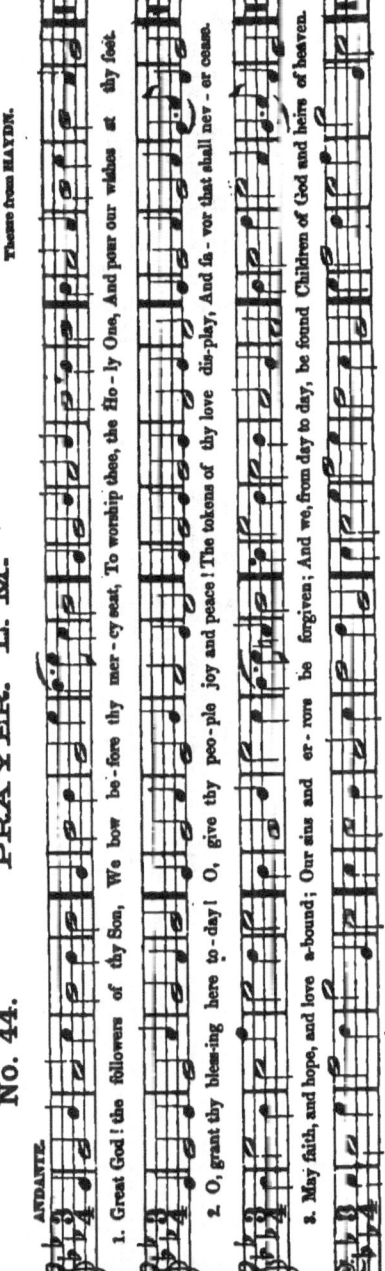

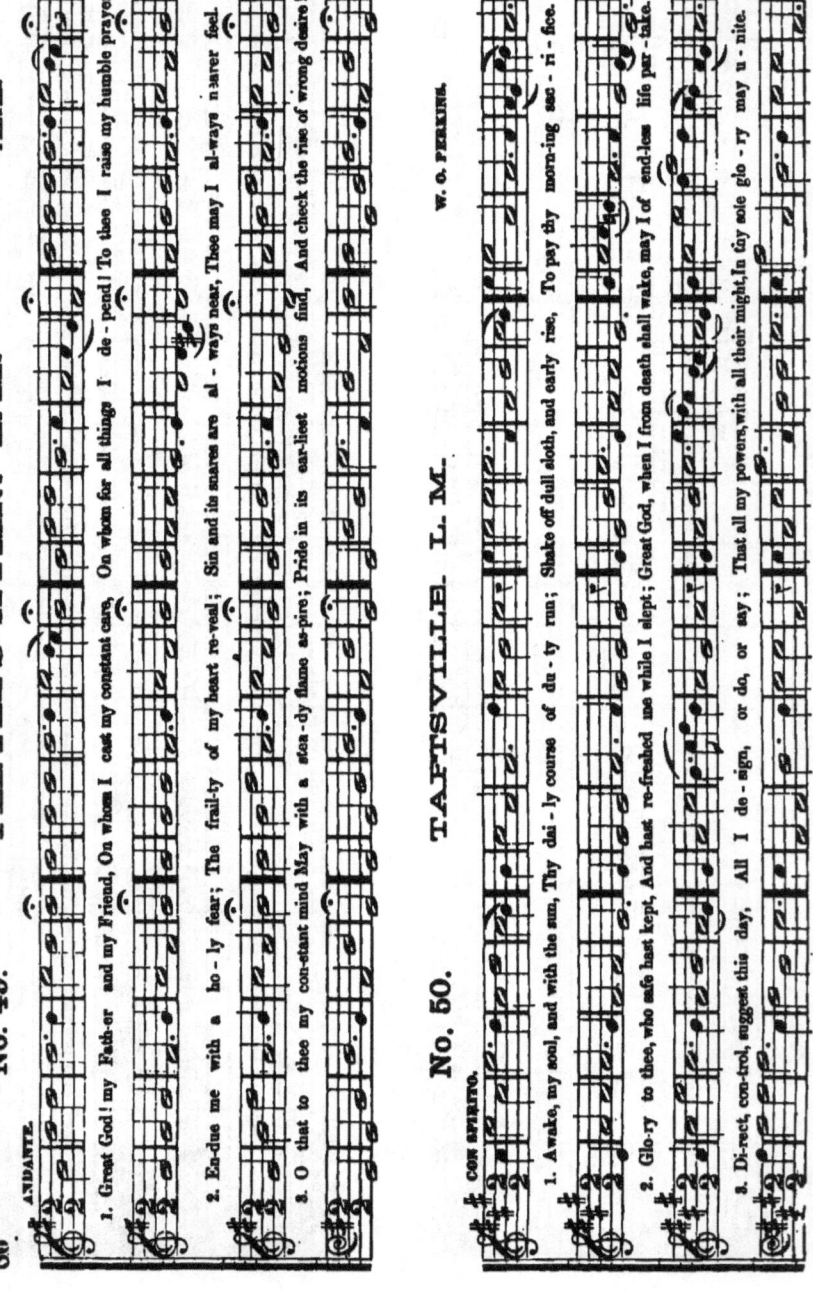

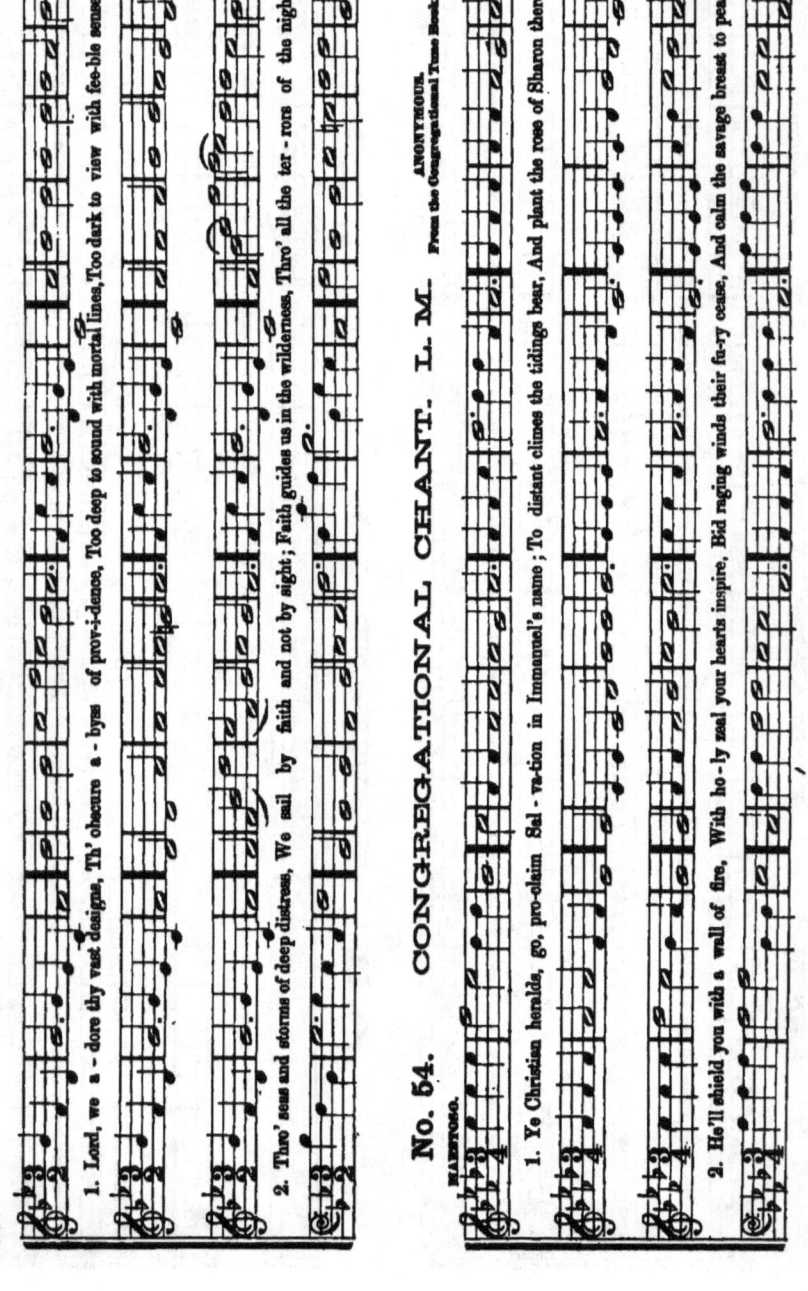

No. 55. VERDURE. L. M.

ANDANTE E LEGATO.

Arranged from HAYDN
By W. O. PERKINS.

1. Great Source of good, from thee proceed The copious drops of gen-ial rain, Which o'er the hill, and thro' the mead, Revive the grass and swell the grain,

2. The flowe-ry spring at thy command, Perfumes the air and paints the land; The summer rays with vigor shine, To deck the earth, and cheer the vine,

Re-vive the grass and swell the grain.

To deck the earth and cheer the vine.

No. 56. OVID. L. M.

This tune may be sung Congregationally.

1. E-ter-nal God, al-migh-ty cause
Of earth, and seas, and worlds un-known; } All things are sub-ject to thy laws;
All things de-pend on thee a-lone.

2. Wor-ship to thee a-lone be-longs;
Wor-ship to thee a-lone we give; } Thine be our hearts, and thine our songs,
And to thy glo-ry may we live.

No. 57. FRANKLIN. L. M.

ANDANTE.

1. Come, gracious Spirit, heavenly Dove, With light and comfort from a-bove; Be thou our Guardian, thou our Guide, O'er every thought and step preside.

2. The light of truth to us dis-play, And make us know and choose thy way; Plant ho-ly fear in eve-ry heart, That we from God may not de-part.

No. 58. LEWIS. L. M.

1. What shall the dy-ing sin-ner do, Who seeks re-lief for all his woe? Where shall the guilty sufferer find A balm to soothe his anguished mind?

2. In vain we search, in vain we try, Till Jesus brings his gos-pel nigh; 'Tis there we find a sure re-lief, A soothing balm for inward grief.

No. 61. AMPHION. L. M.

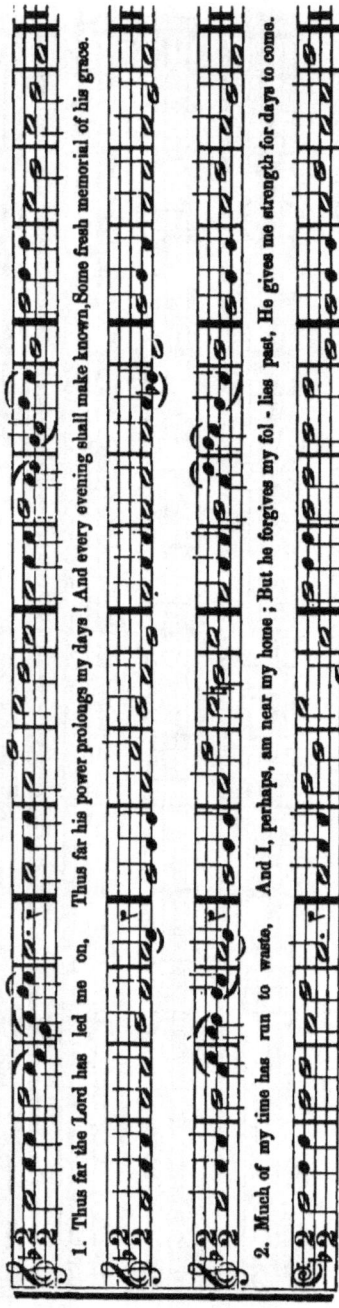

1. Thus far the Lord has led me on, Thus far his power prolongs my days! And every evening shall make known, Some fresh memorial of his grace.

2. Much of my time has run to waste, And I, perhaps, am near my home; But he forgives my fol-lies past, He gives me strength for days to come.

No. 62. MONMOUTH. L. M.
LUTHER.

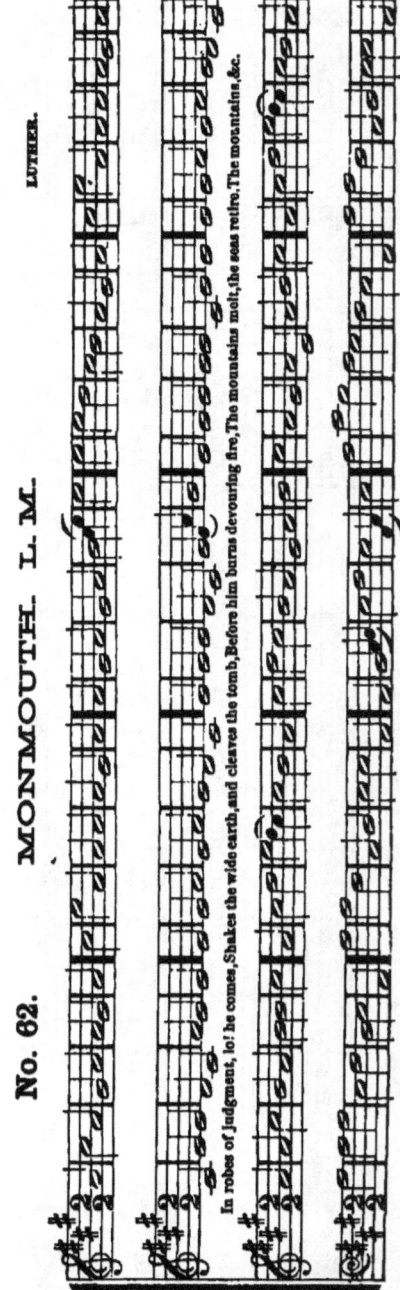

In robes of judgment, lo! he comes, Shakes the wide earth, and cleaves the tomb, Before him burns devouring fire, The mountains melt, the seas retire, The mountains, &c.

No. 63. QUINTETTE. L. M.

MODERATO E LEGATO.
SOPRANO OBLIGATO.

W. O. PERKINS.

93

1. There is a stream whose gen - tle flow, Sup - plies the ci - ty of our God; Life, love, and joy, still
2. That sa - cred stream whose ho - ly fount, Does all our rag - ing fears con - trol; Sweet peace thy prom - is -

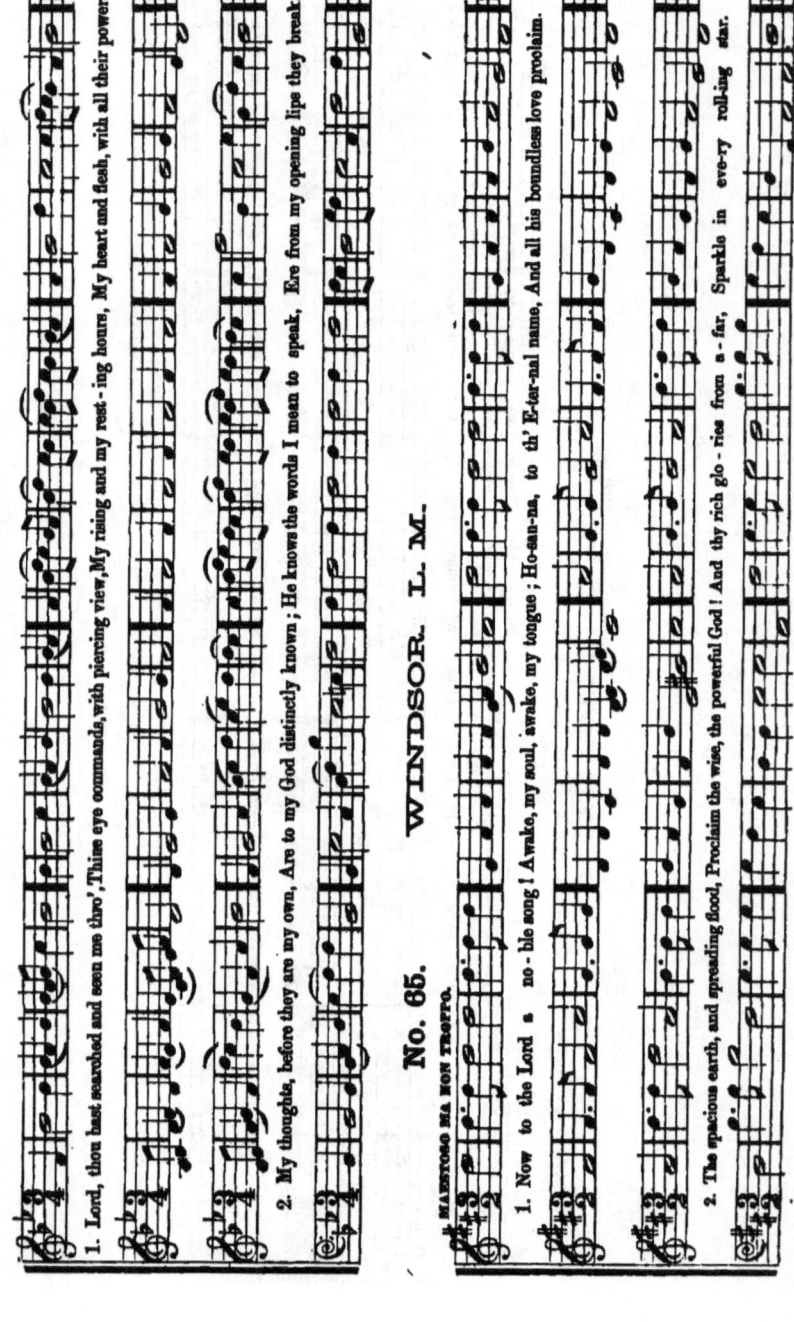

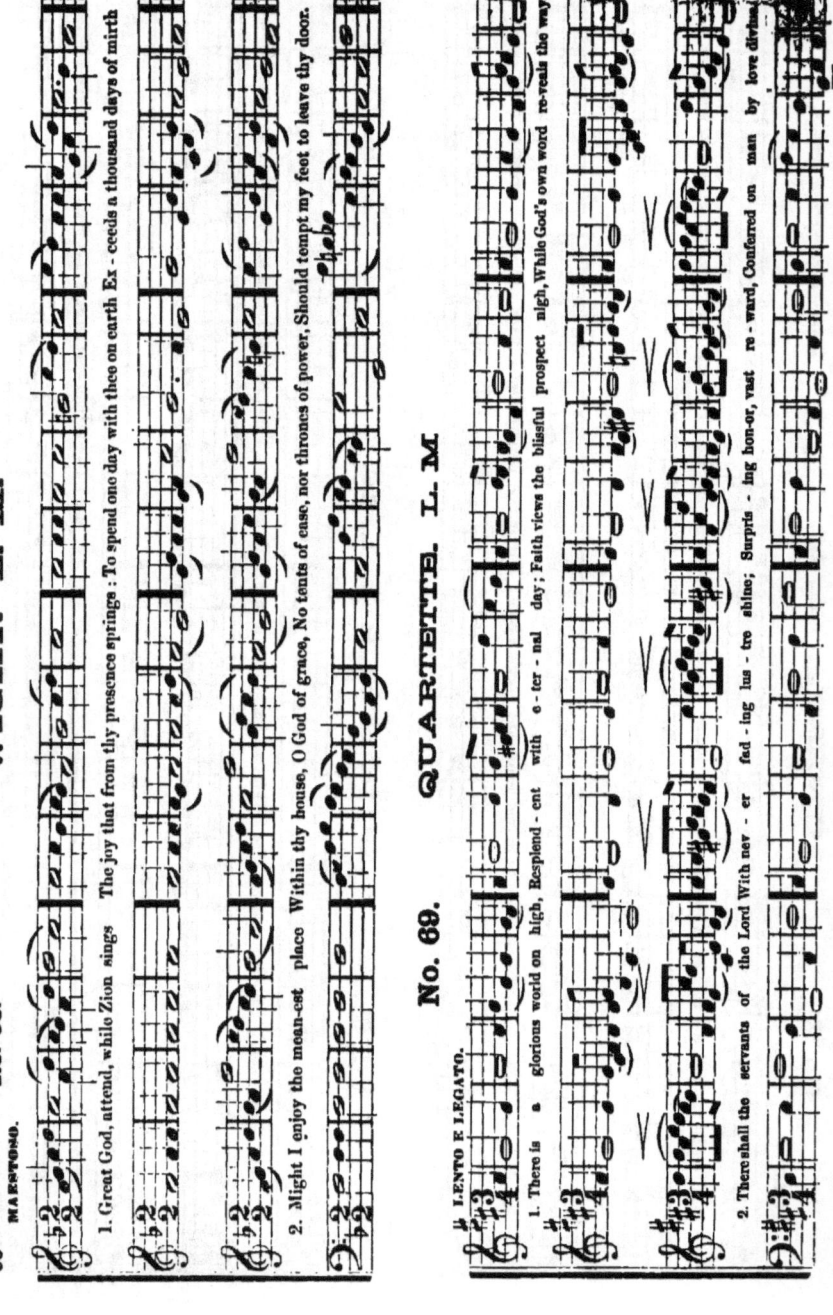

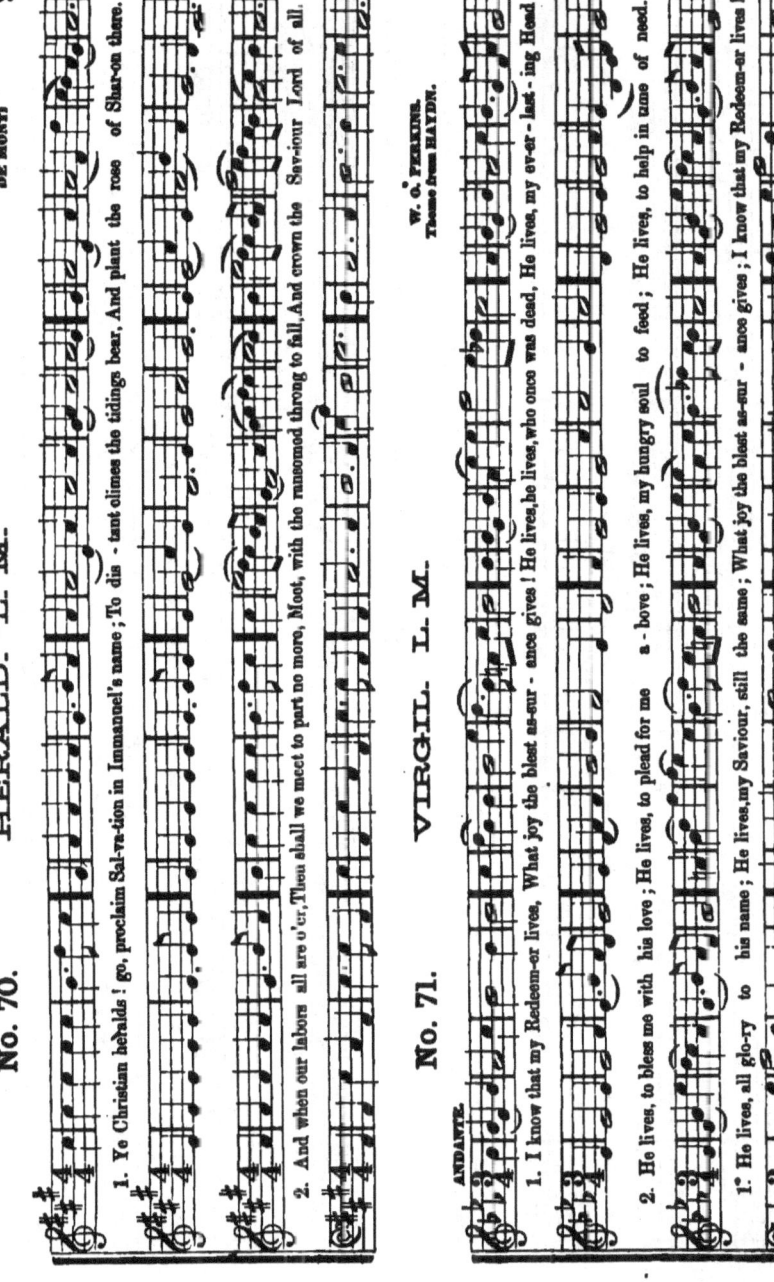

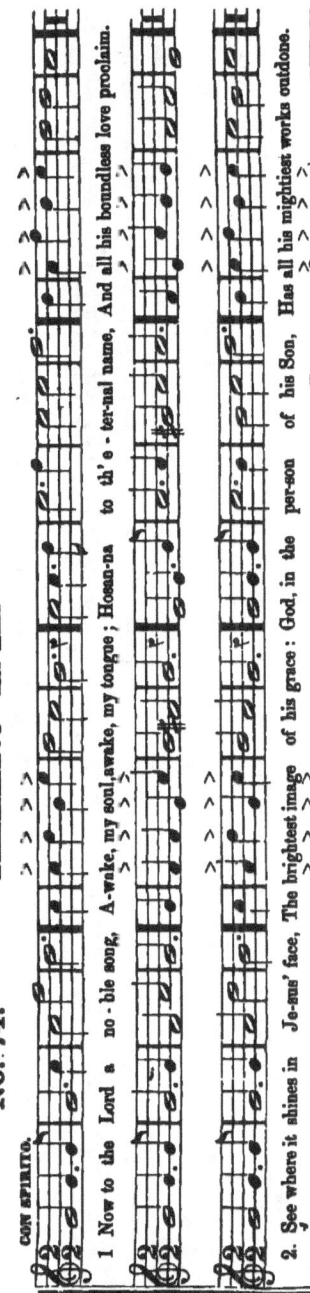

No. 75. HOMER. L. M. For Men's Voices.

MAESTOSO NON TROPPO.

1. Join, all who love the Saviour's name, To sing his ev-er-last-ing fame; Great God, prepare each heart and voice, In him for-ev-er to rejoice.
2. Praise him in cheerful, grateful songs, To him your highest praise belongs! Bless him, who doth your heav'n prepare; And whom you'll praise forever there.

No. 76. MONTPELIER. L. M. For Men's Voices.

LARGHETTO. Ritard.

1. Come, weary souls, with sin distressed, Come, and accept the promised rest; The Saviour's gracious call o-bey, And cast your gloomy fears a-way.
2. Here mercy's boundless ocean flows, To cleanse your guilt and heal your woes; Pardon, and life, and endless peace, How rich the gift! how free the grace!

No. 77. ASYLUM. L. M. For Men's Voices.

ANDANTINO.

1. Come, gracious Spir-it, heavenly Dove, With light and comfort from a-bove; Be thou our Guardian, thou our Guide, O'er every tho't and step preside.
2. The light of truth to us display, And make us know and choose thy way; Plant ho-ly fear in every heart, That we from God may not depart.

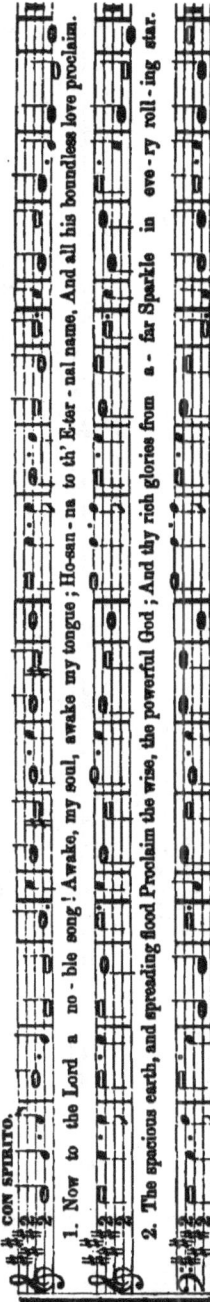
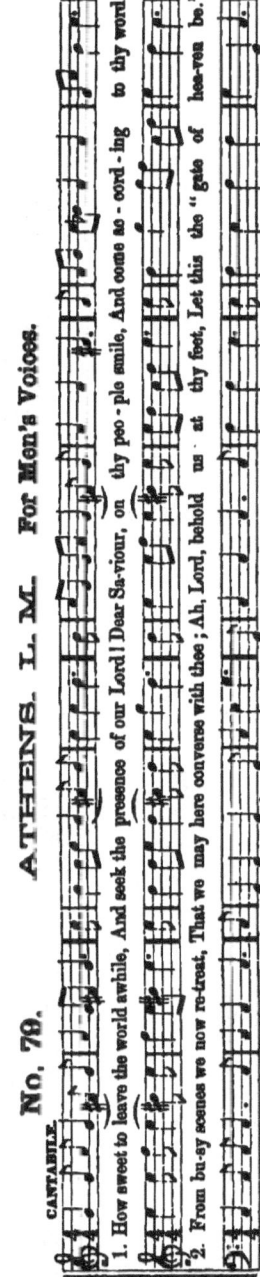
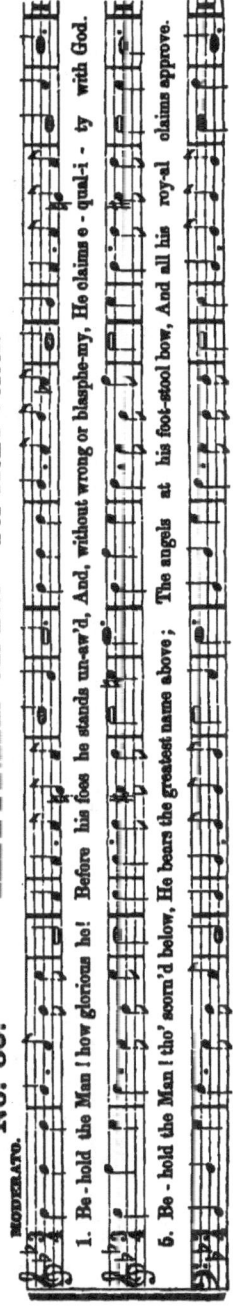

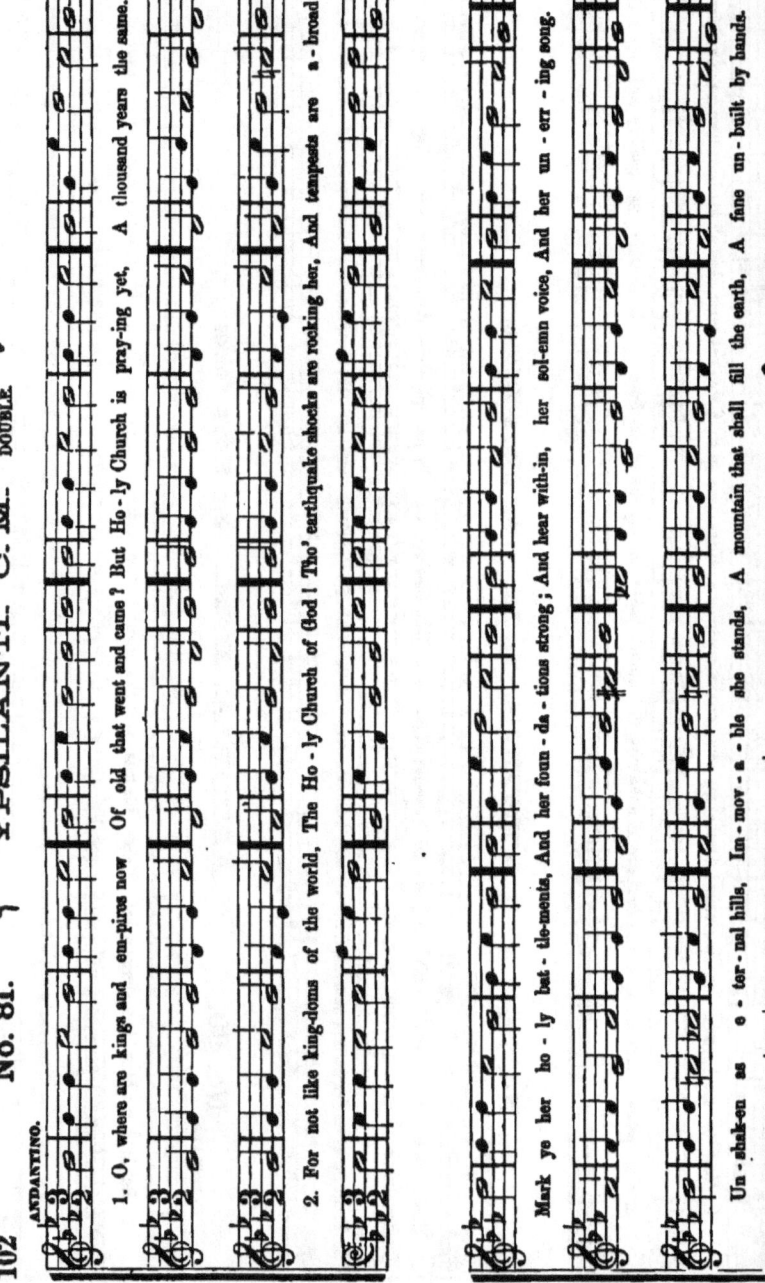

No. 83. KELLER. C. M. 6 LINES.

WARFORD.

1. Be - yond, be - yond that bound-less sea, A - bove that dome of sky, Far - ther than thought it - self can flee,
Thy dwell - ing is on high; Yet dear the aw - ful thought to me, That thou, my God, art nigh.

2. We hear thy voice when thun - ders roll Through the wide fields of air; The waves o - bey thy dread con - trol;
Yet still thou art not there: Where shall I find Him, O my soul, Who yet is eve - ry - where?

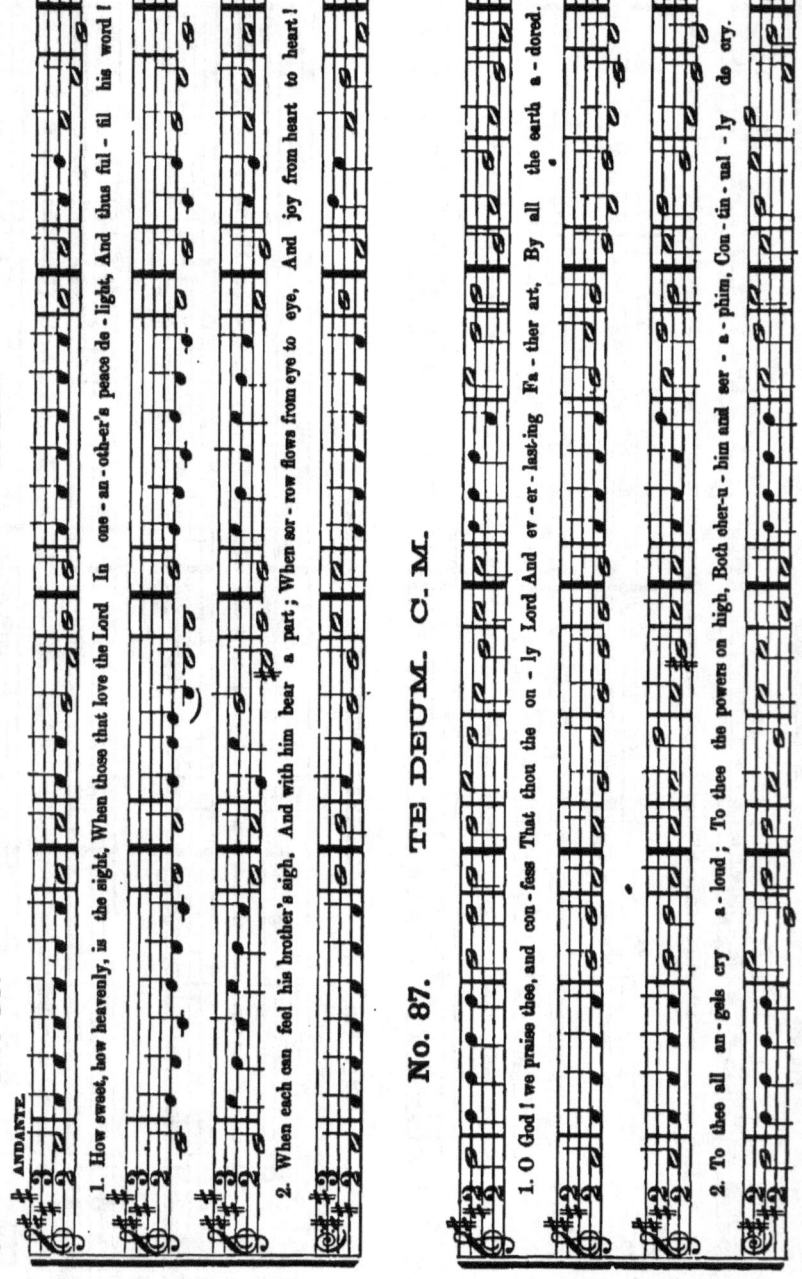

109

No. 92. MARTIN. C. M.

1. By cool Si-lo-am's sha-dy rill, How fair the li-ly grows! How sweet the breath beneath the hill, Of Shar-on's dew-y rose!

2. By cool Si-lo-am's sha-dy rill The li-ly must de-cay; The rose that blooms be-neath the hill, Must short-ly fade a-way.

No. 93. HOWARD. C. M.

Lord, hear the voice of my complaint; Ac-cept my se-cret prayer; To thee a-lone, my King, my God, Will I for help re-pair.

111

No. 95. JULIUS. C. M.

ANDANTE.

1. Speak gent-ly, it is bet-ter far To rule by love than fear; Speak gent-ly, let no harsh word mar, The good we may do here

2. Speak gent-ly to the young, for they Will have e-nough to bear; Pass thro' this life as best they may, 'Tis full of anx-ious care.

No. 96. DIXON. C. M.

No. 97. LYRA. C. M.

ESPIRITUSO.

1. Mor-tals, a-wake, with an-gels join, And chant the cheer-ful lay; Joy, love, and grat-i-tude com-bine, To hail th' aus-pi-cious morn.

2. Swift thro' the vast expanse it flew, And loud the ech-o roll'd; The theme, the song, the joy was new, 'Twas more than heaven could hold.

No. 98. DUNDEE. C. M.

Let not de-spair, nor fell re-venge, Be to my bo-som known; Oh, give me tears for oth-ers' wo, And patience for my own.

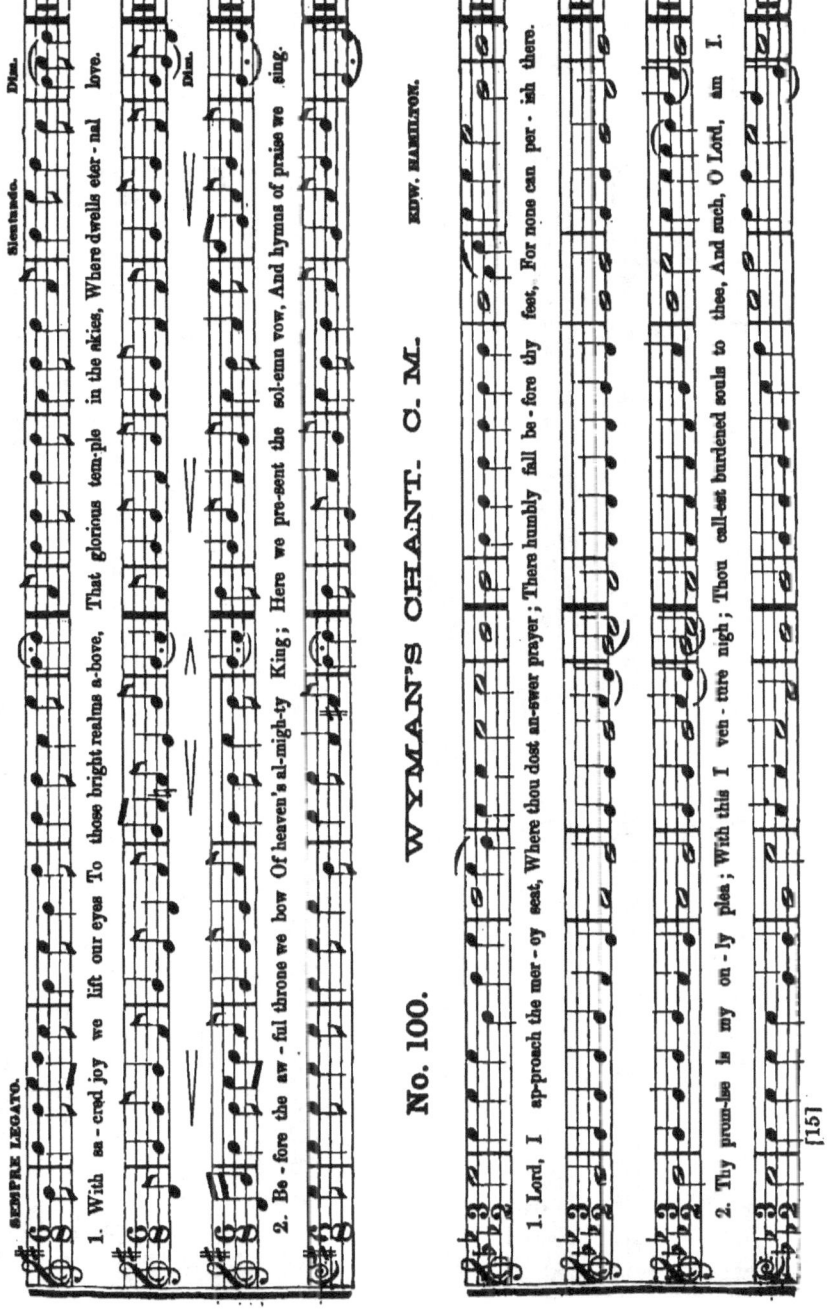

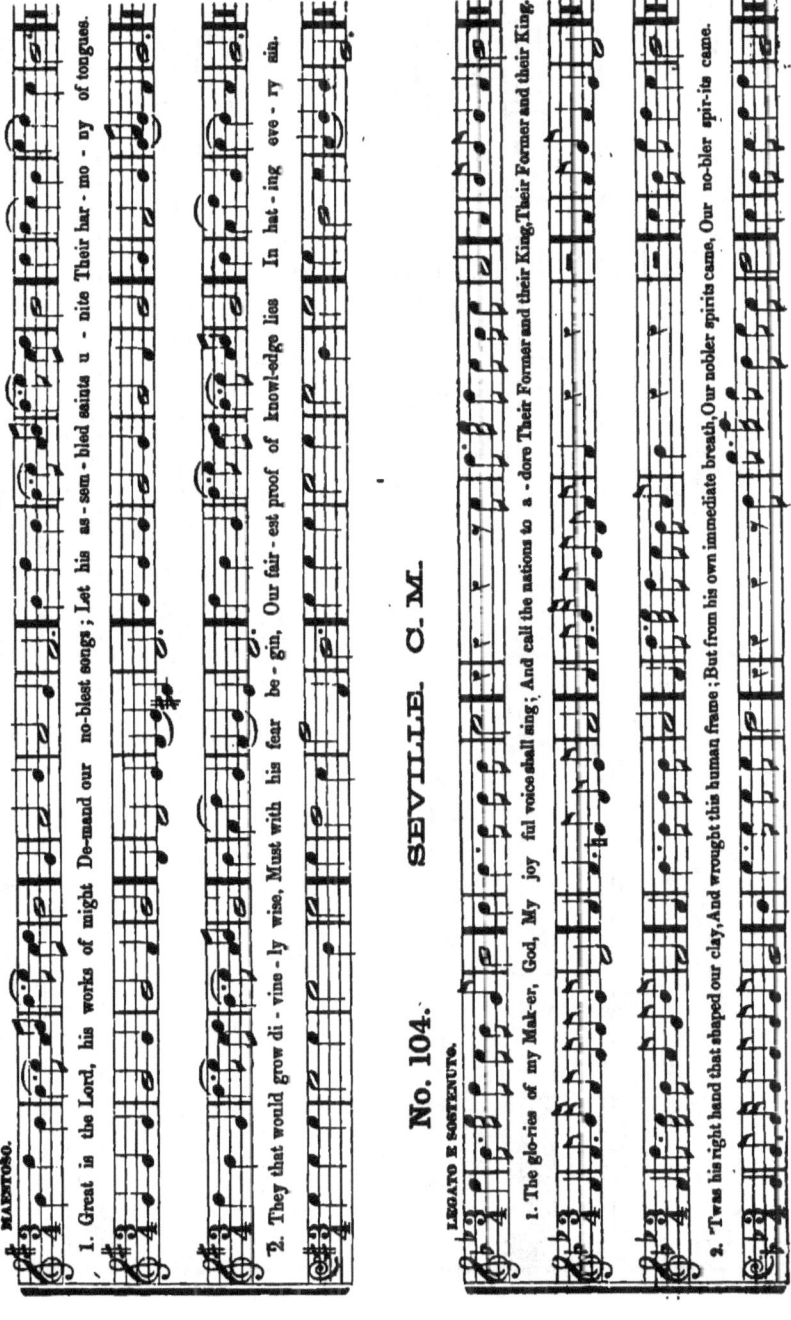

No. 105. CHRISTMAS. C. M.
HANDEL.

1. A-wake, my soul, stretch eve-ry nerve, And press with vig-or on; A heaven-ly
race de-mands thy zeal, And an im-mor-tal crown, And an im-mor-tal crown.

2. A cloud of wit-ness-es a-round, Hold thee in full sur-vey; For-get the
steps al-rea-dy trod, And on-ward urge thy way, And on-ward urge thy way.

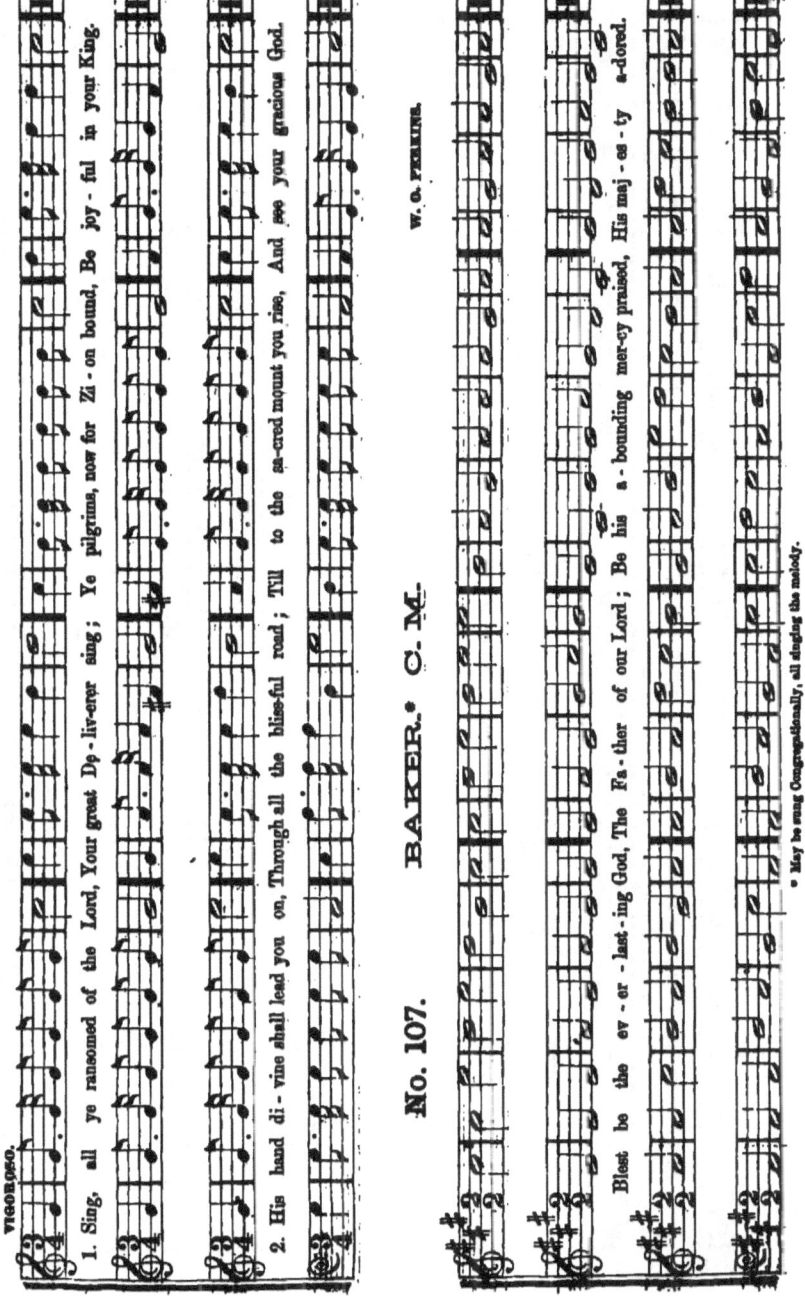

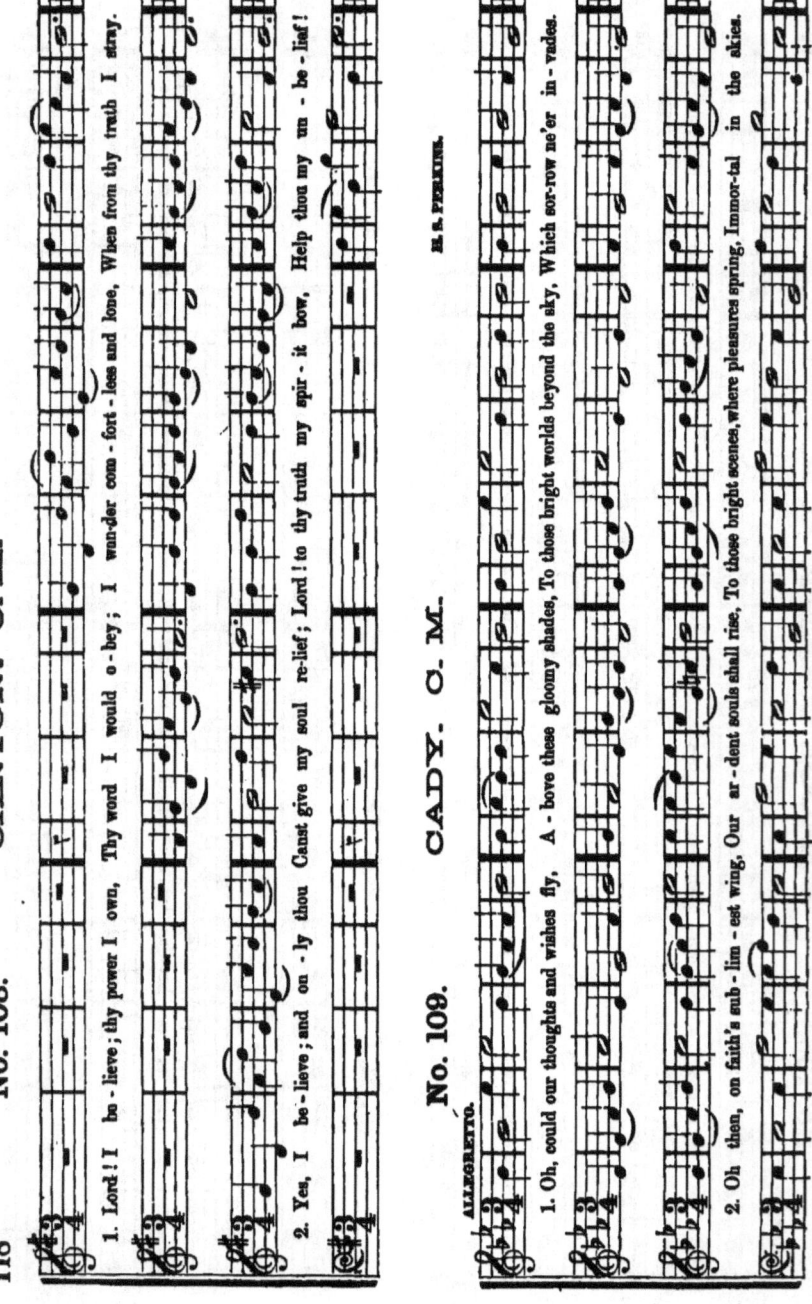

No. 110. CHINA. C. M.

1. Why do we mourn de-part-ing friends, Or shake at death's a-larms? 'Tis but the voice that Je-sus sends, To call them to his arms.
2. Are we not tend-ing up-ward too, To heaven's desired a - bode? Why should we wish the hours more slow, Which keep us from our God.

No. 111. HARDWICK. C. M.

ANDANTE E SOSTENUTO.

1. O here, if ev - er, God of love! Let strife and ha-tred cease; And eve-ry thought har - mo-nious move, And every heart be peace.
2. Not here, where met to think on him, Whose la - test thoughts were ours, Shall mor-tal pas - sions come to dim The prayer de-vo - tion pours.

119

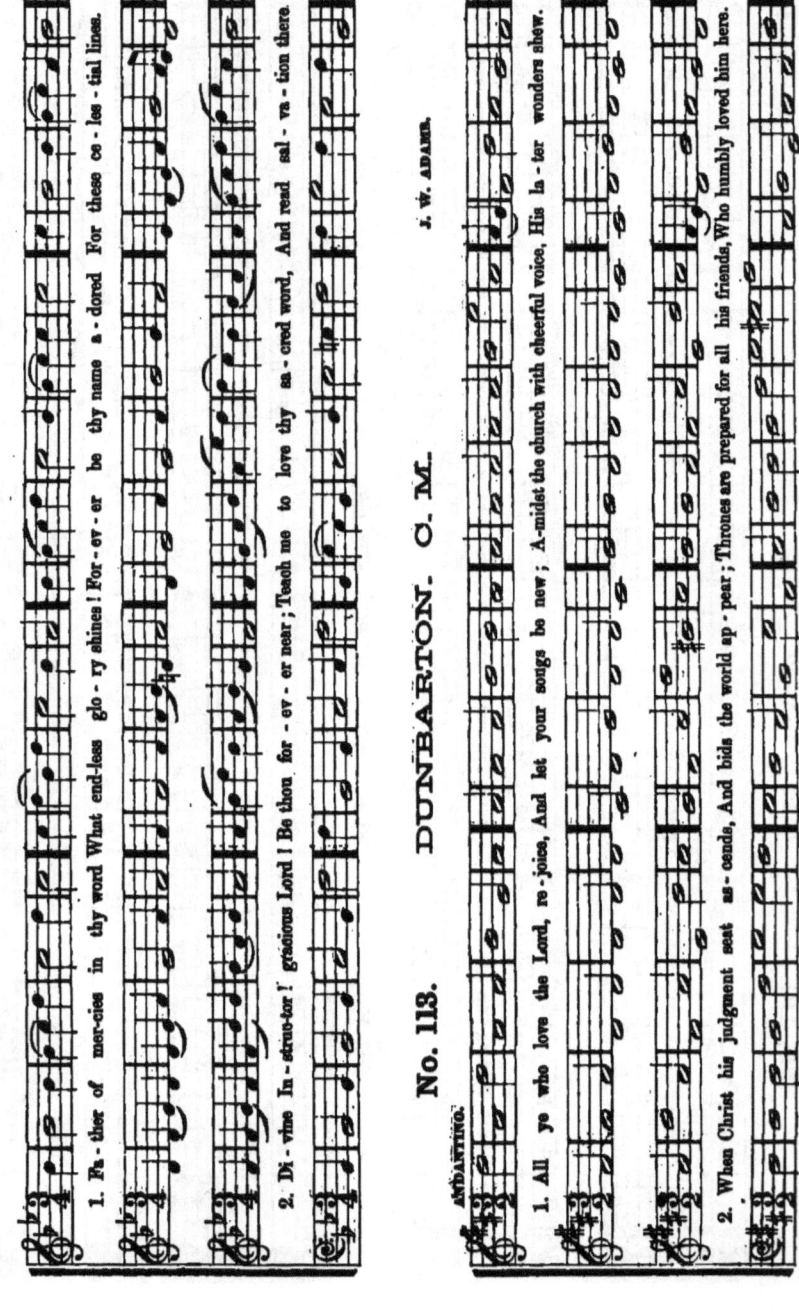

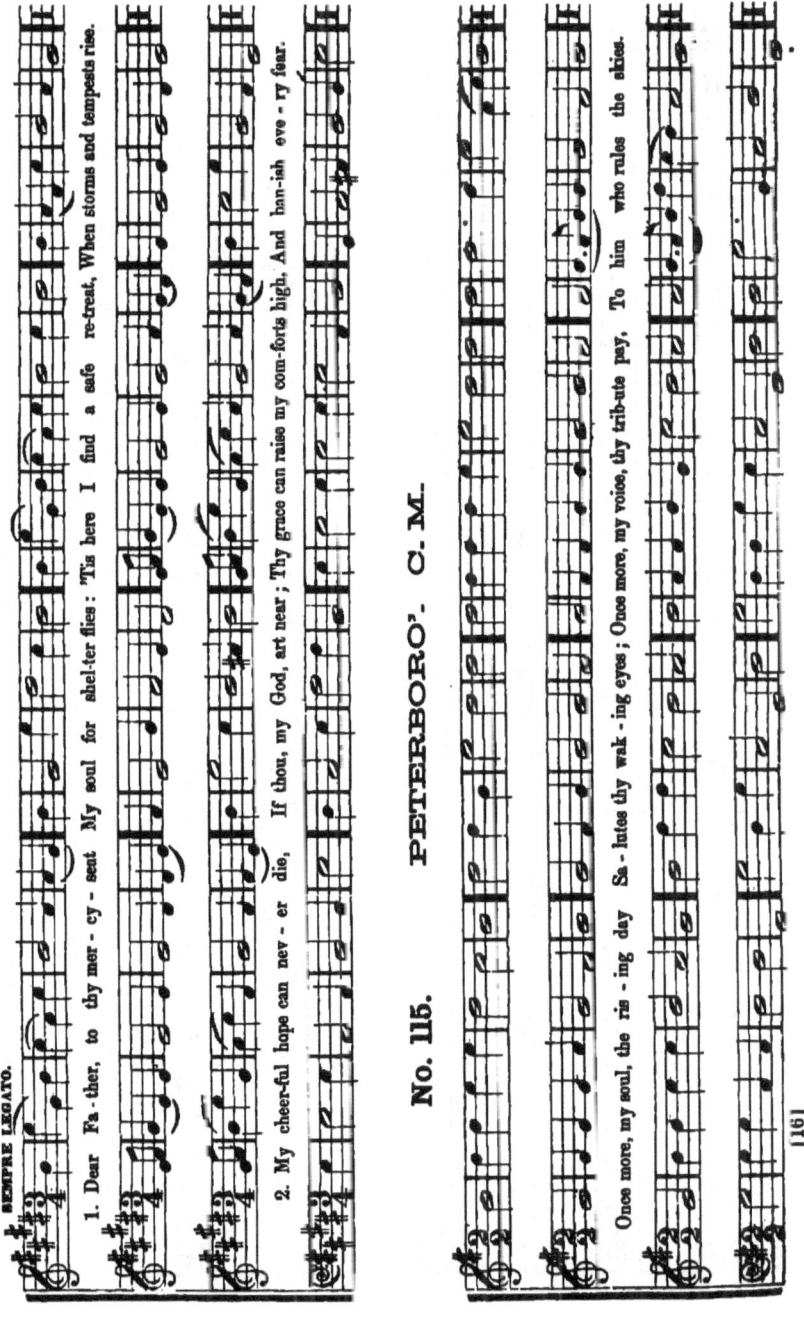

No. 119. BARSTOW. C. M.

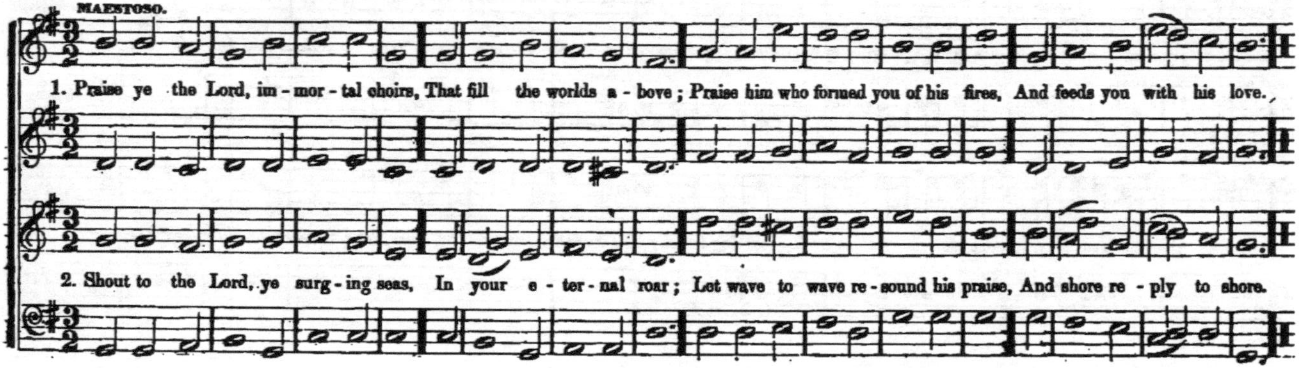

MAESTOSO.

1. Praise ye the Lord, im-mor-tal choirs, That fill the worlds a-bove; Praise him who formed you of his fires, And feeds you with his love.
2. Shout to the Lord, ye surg-ing seas, In your e-ter-nal roar; Let wave to wave re-sound his praise, And shore re-ply to shore.

No. 120. LYME. C. M.

VOGLER.

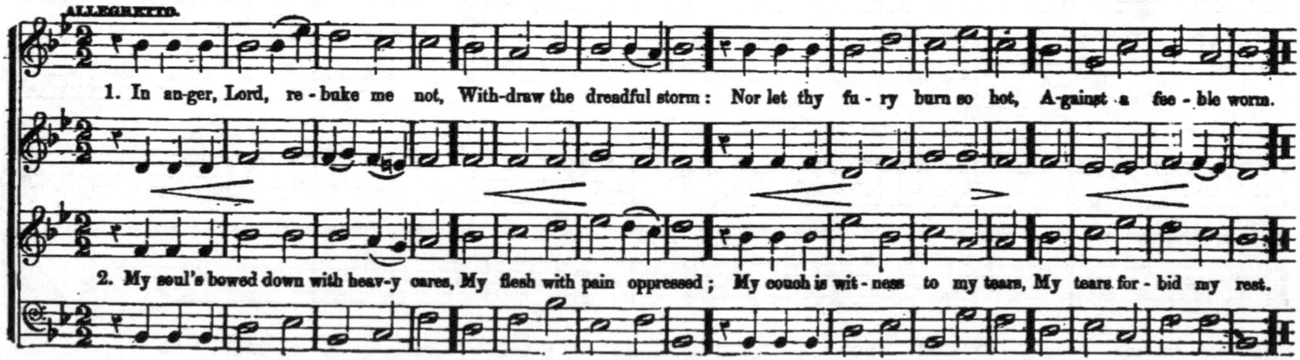

ALLEGRETTO.

1. In an-ger, Lord, re-buke me not, With-draw the dreadful storm: Nor let thy fu-ry burn so hot, A-gainst a fee-ble worm.
2. My soul's bowed down with heav-y cares, My flesh with pain oppressed; My couch is wit-ness to my tears, My tears for-bid my rest.

125

No. 121. BURFORD. C. M.

1. Lord, thou hast scourged our guilty hand; Be-hold thy poo-ple mourn; Shall vengeance ev-er guide thy hand, And mer-cy ne'er re-turn?
2. Our Zi-on trembles at thy stroke, And dreads thy lift-ed hand; Oh heal the people thou hast broke, And spare our guil-ty land.

No. 122. CAMBRIDGE. C. M. DR. RANDALL.

1. Come, Ho-ly Spirit, heavenly Dove, With all thy quickening power, Kindle a flame of sacred love, In these cold hearts of ours, In these, &c.
2. Look! how we grovel here be-low, Fond of these trifling toys! Our souls can neither fly nor go, To reach e-ter-nal joys, To reach eternal joys, To reach e-ter-nal joys.

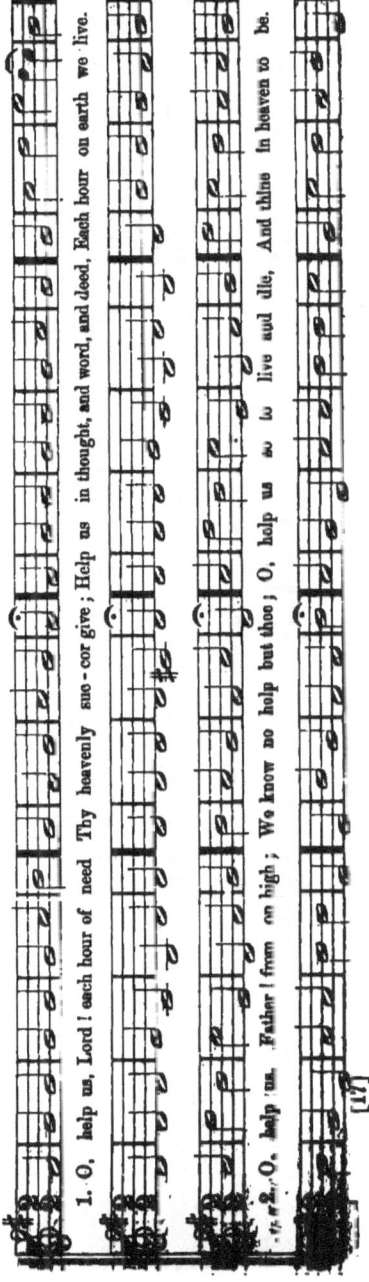

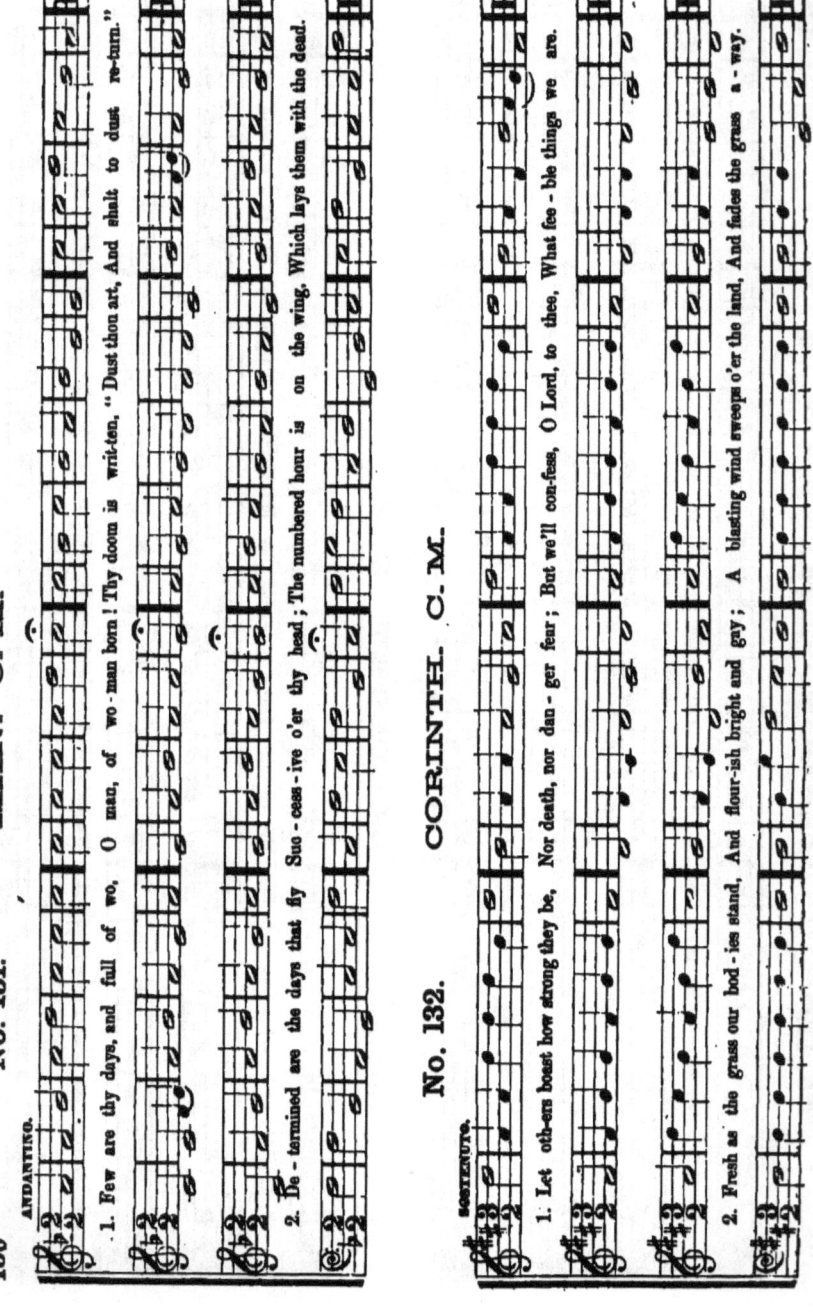

No. 133. HAZEN. C. M.

1. Our Father, God, who art in heaven, All hal-lowed be thy name; Thy kingdom come, thy will be done, In heaven and earth the same.
2. Give us this day our dai - ly bread; And as we those for - give, Who sin a-gainst us, so may we For - giv - ing grace re-ceive
3. In - to temp-ta - tion lead us not; From e - vil set us free; And thine the kingdom, thine the power, And glo - ry ev - er be.

No. 134. MALONE. C. M.

MODERATO.

1. Great Ru - ler of all na-ture's frame, We own thy power di-vine; We hear thy breath in eve - ry storm, For all the winds are thine.
2. Wide as they sweep their sound-ing way, They work thy sovereign will; And, awed by thy ma - jes - tic voice, Con - fu - sion shall be still.

No. 135. ZION. C. M. DOUBLE.

J. A. GOULD

1. How did my heart re-joice to hear My friends de-vout-ly say, "In Zi-on let us all ap-pear, And keep the fes-ti-val day!"
2. Up to her courts, with joy un-known, The ho-ly tribes re-pair; The Son of Da-vid holds his throne, And sits in judgment there.

I love her gates, I love the road; The church a-dorned with grace, Stands like a pal-ace built for God, To show his mild-er face.

He hears our prais-es and complaints, And while his aw-ful voice Di-vides the sin-ners from the saints, We trem-ble and re-joice.

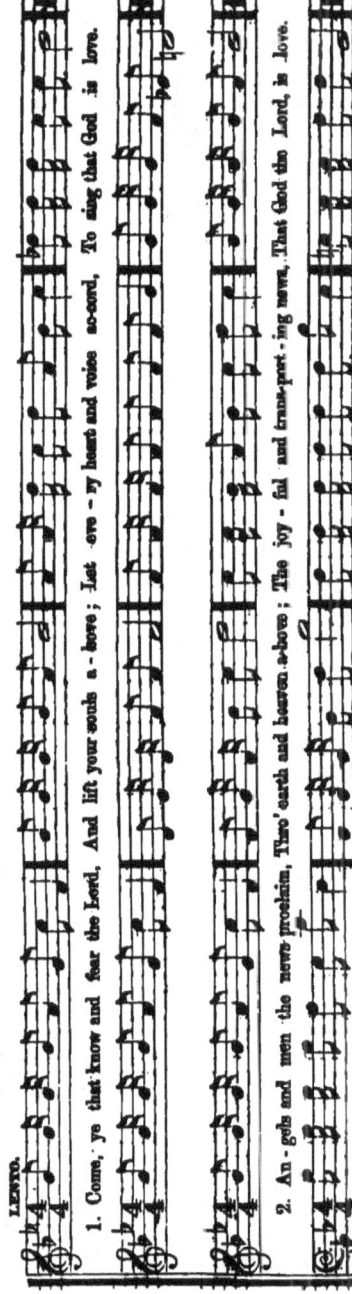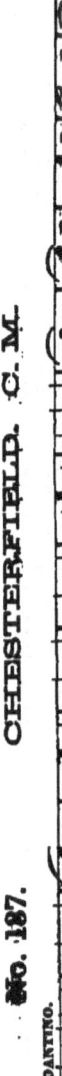

135

No. 140. CHARLESTOWN. C. M.

MODERATO.

1. O all ye na-tions, praise the Lord, Each with a different tongue; In eve-ry language learn his word, And let his name be sung.

2. His mer-cy reigns through eve-ry land, Pro-claim his grace a-broad; For-ev-er firm his truth shall stand, Praise ye the faith-ful God.

No. 141. AUGUSTA. C. M.

W. A. PERKINS.

1. Sweet is the prayer whose ho-ly stream, In ear-nest plead-ing flows; De-vo-tion dwells up-on the theme, And warm and warm-er glows.

2. Faith grasps the blessings she de-sires; Hope points the up-ward gaze; And Love, ce-les-tial Love, in-spires, The el-o-quence of praise.

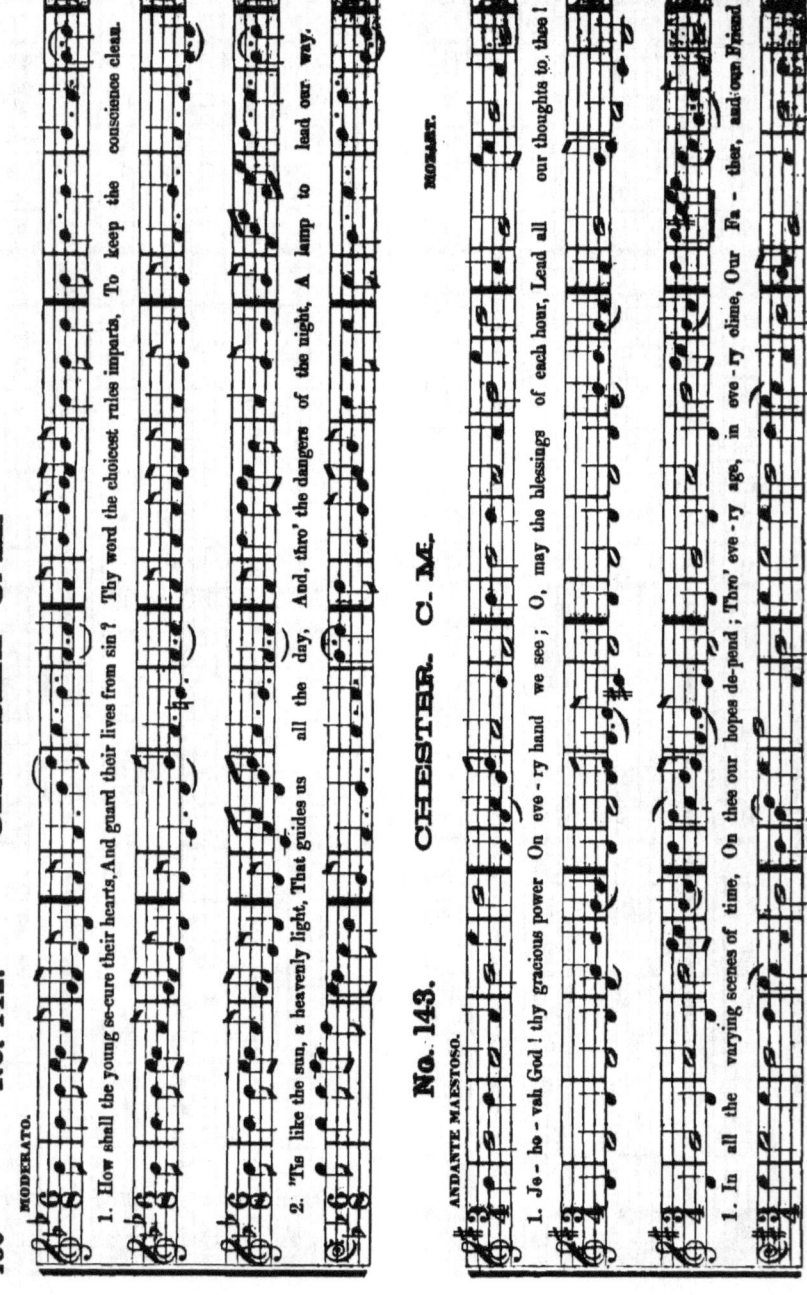

No. 146. ORLAND. C. M.

1. Long as I live, I'll bless thy name, My King, my God of love; My work and joy shall be the same, In brighter worlds a-bove.
2. Great is the Lord, his power unknown, Oh let his praise be great; I'll sing the hon-ors of thy throne, Thy works of grace re-peat.

No. 147. ORTONVILLE. C. M.

DR. THOS. HASTINGS.
By Permission.

1. Ma-jes-tic sweetness sits enthroned On my Redeemer's brow; His head with radiant glories crowned, His lips with grace o'erflow, His lips with grace o'erflow.
2. No mor-tal can with him compare A-mong the sons of men: Fair-er is he than all the fair That fill the heavenly train, That fill the heavenly train.

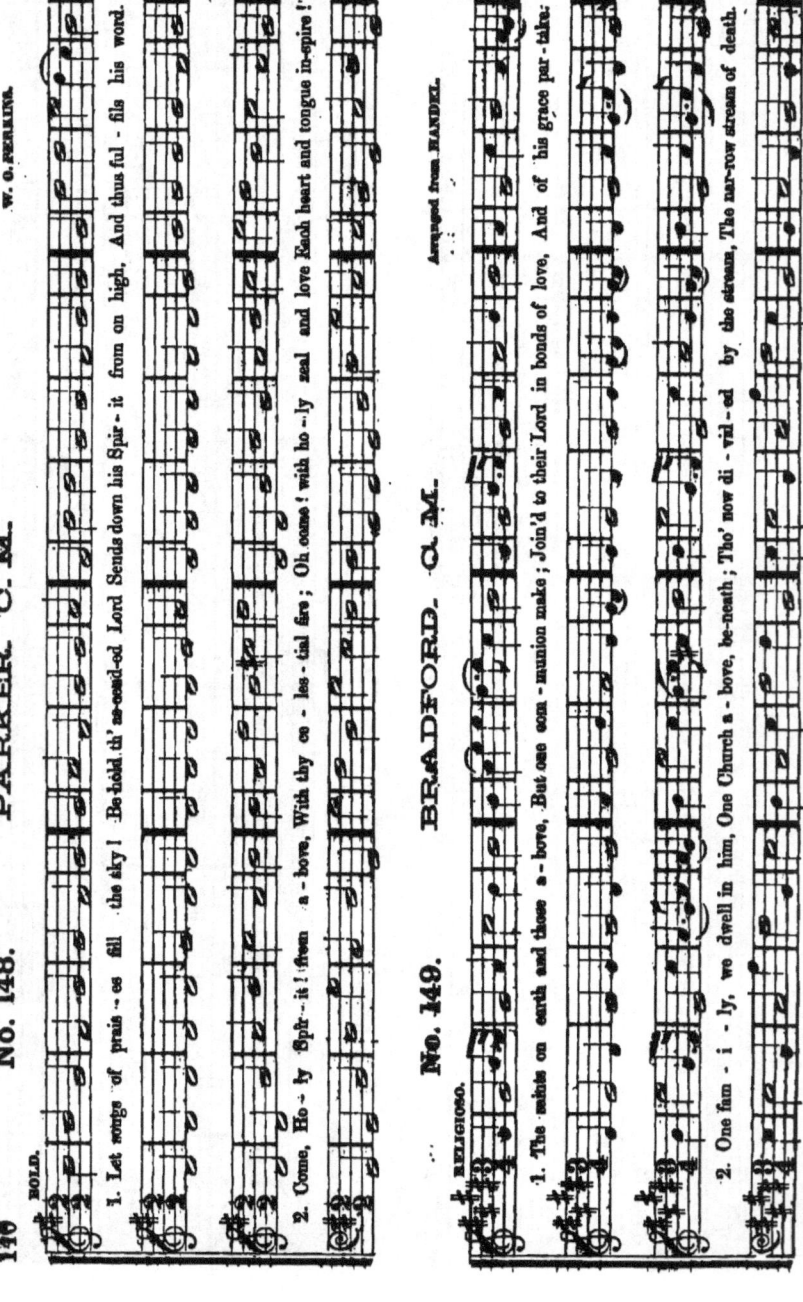

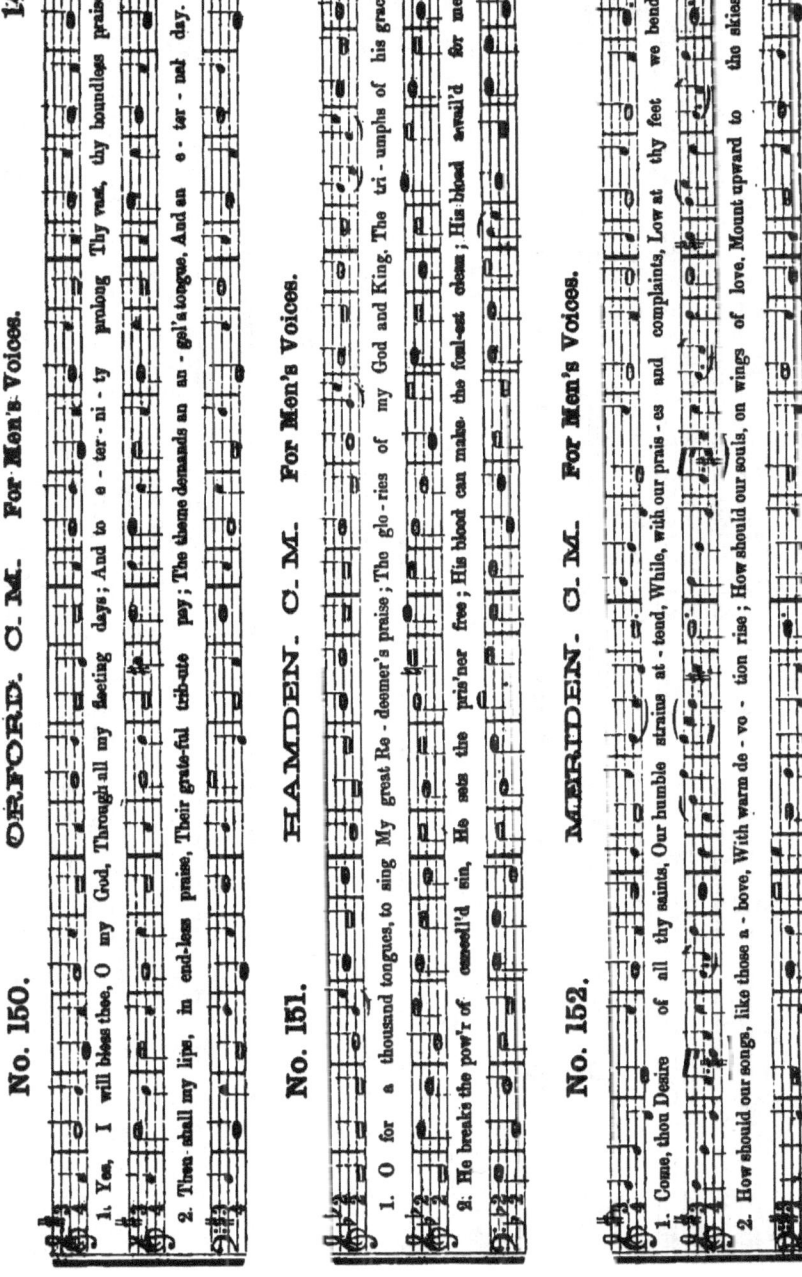

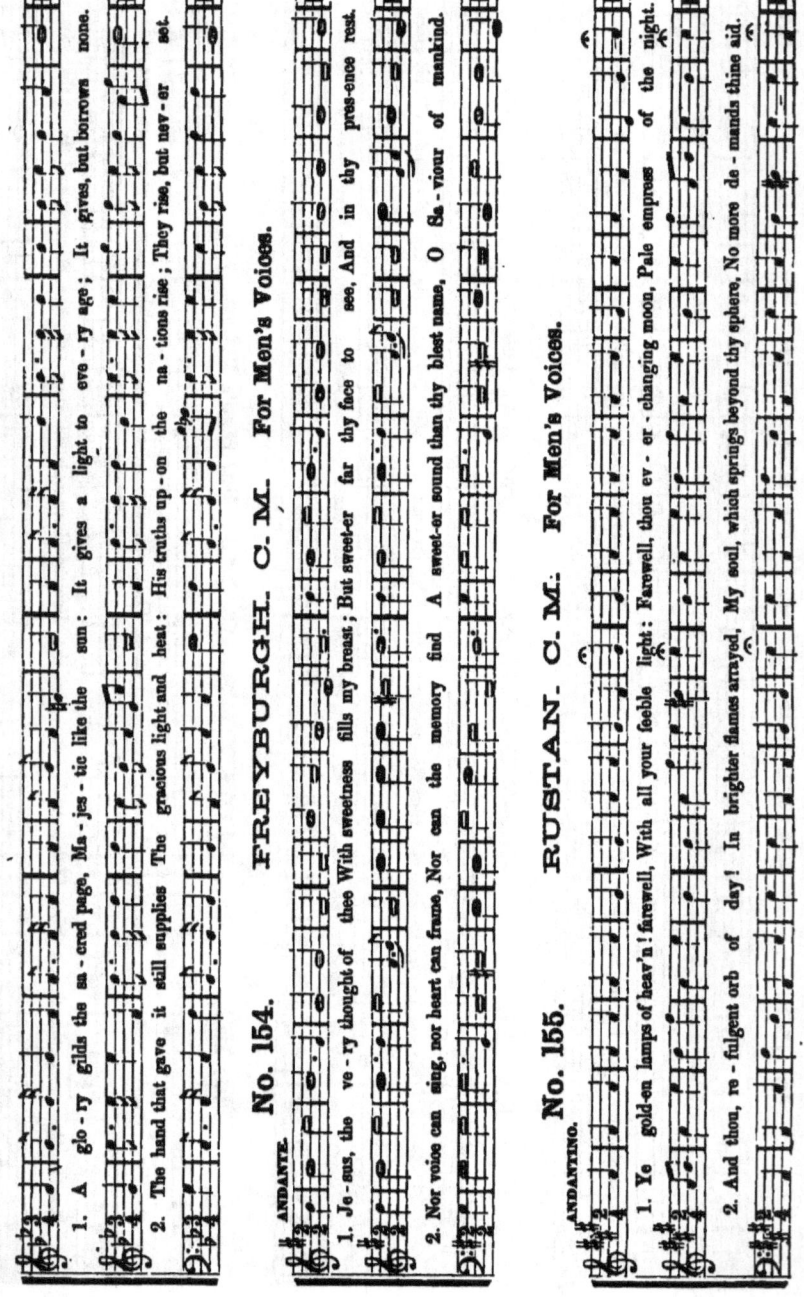

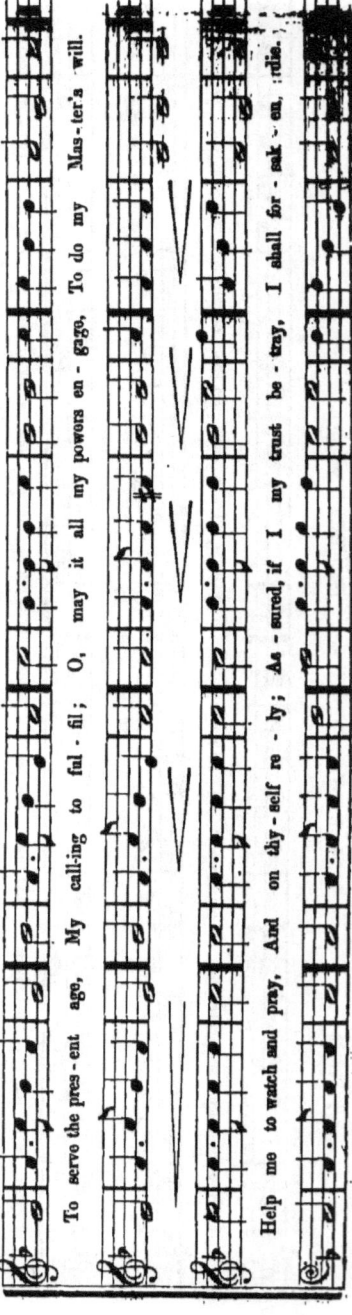

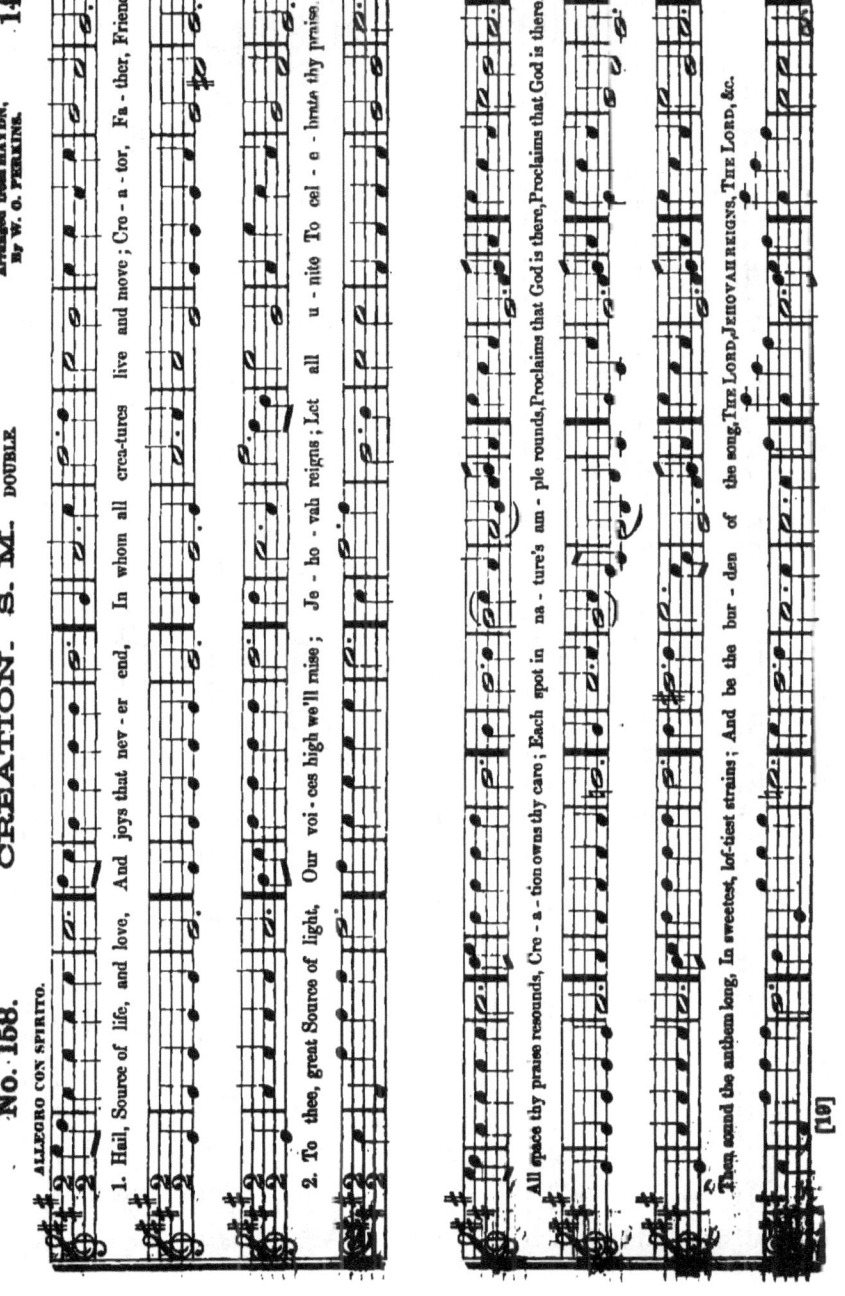

No. 161. ROCKFORD. S. M.

No. 162. ORSON. S. M.

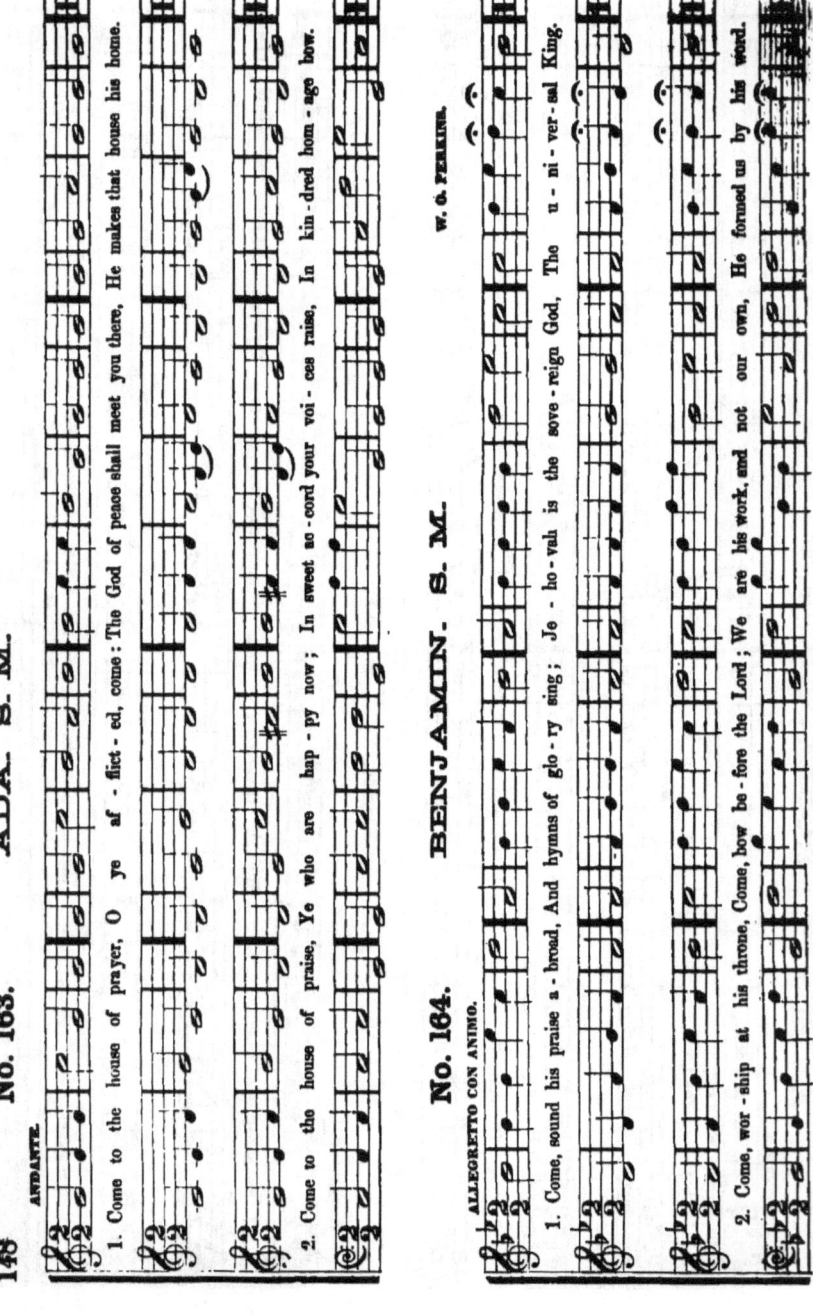

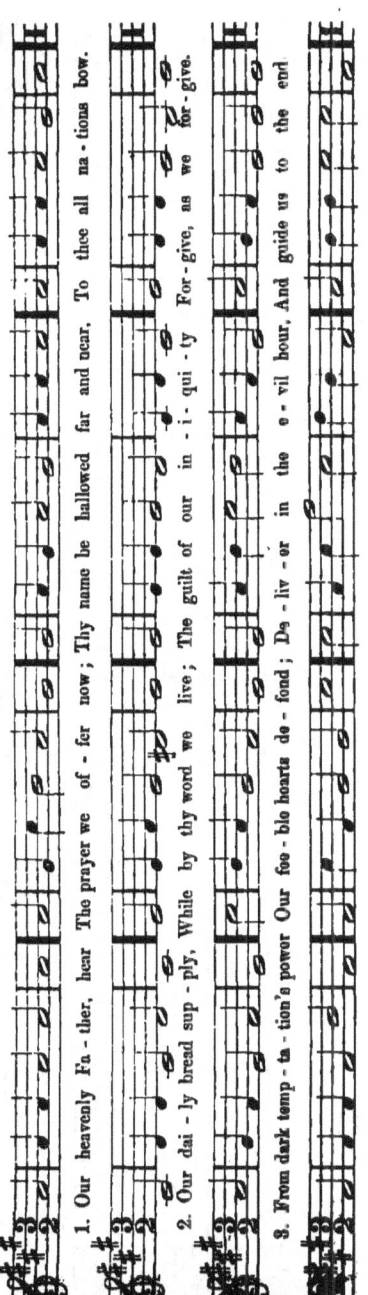

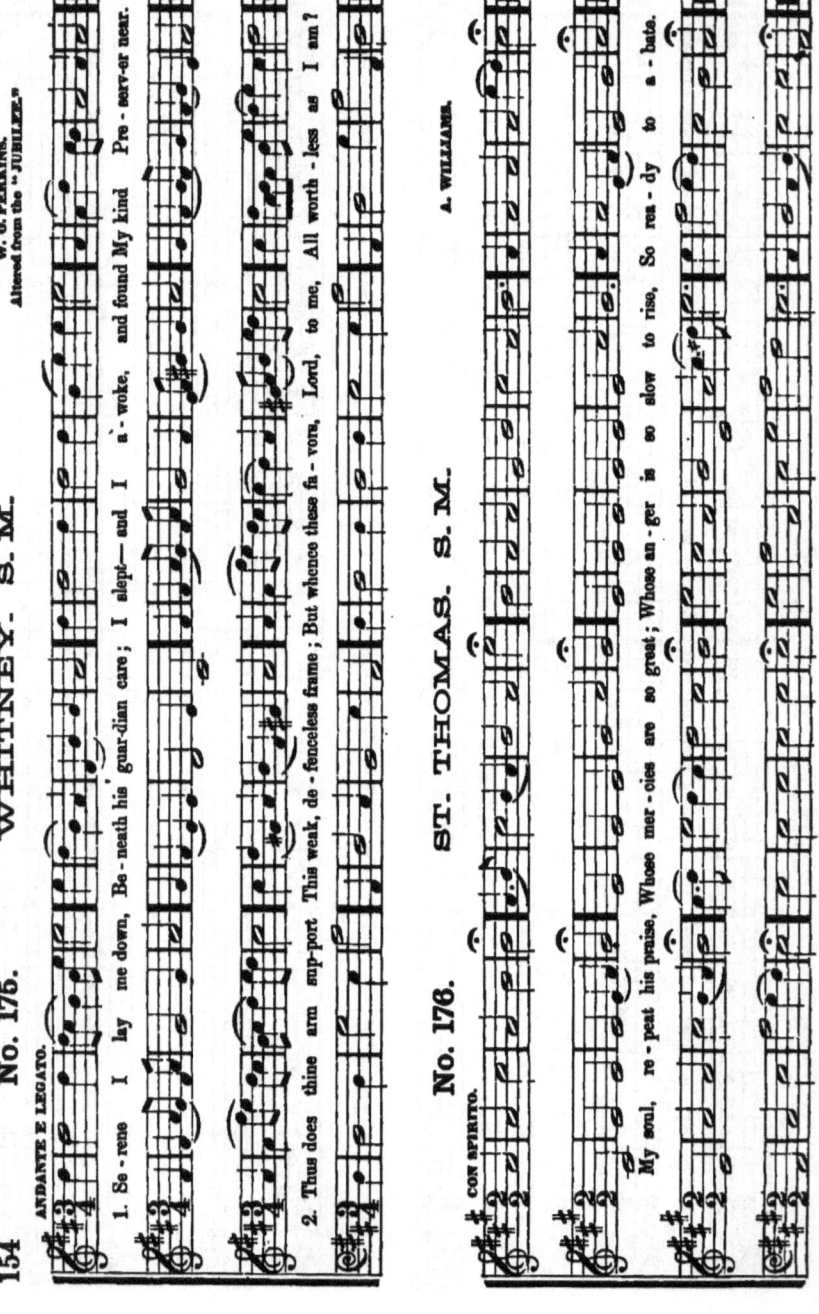

155

No. 177. SACO. S. M.

ALLEGRETTO SOSTENUTO.
1. O Lord our heavenly King, Thy name is all di-vine: Thy glories round the earth are spread, And o'er the heavens they shine, And o'er the heavens they shine.
2. When to thy works on high, I raise my wondering eyes, And see the moon, complete in light, A-dorn the darksome skies, A-dorn the darksome skies.

No. 178. WESTBORO'. S. M.

LEGATO.
1. O, where shall rest be found, Rest for the wea--ry soul? "Twere vain the o-cean depths to sound, Or pierce to ei-ther pole.
2. The world can nev-er give The bliss for which we sigh; 'Tis not the whole of life to live, Nor all of death to die.

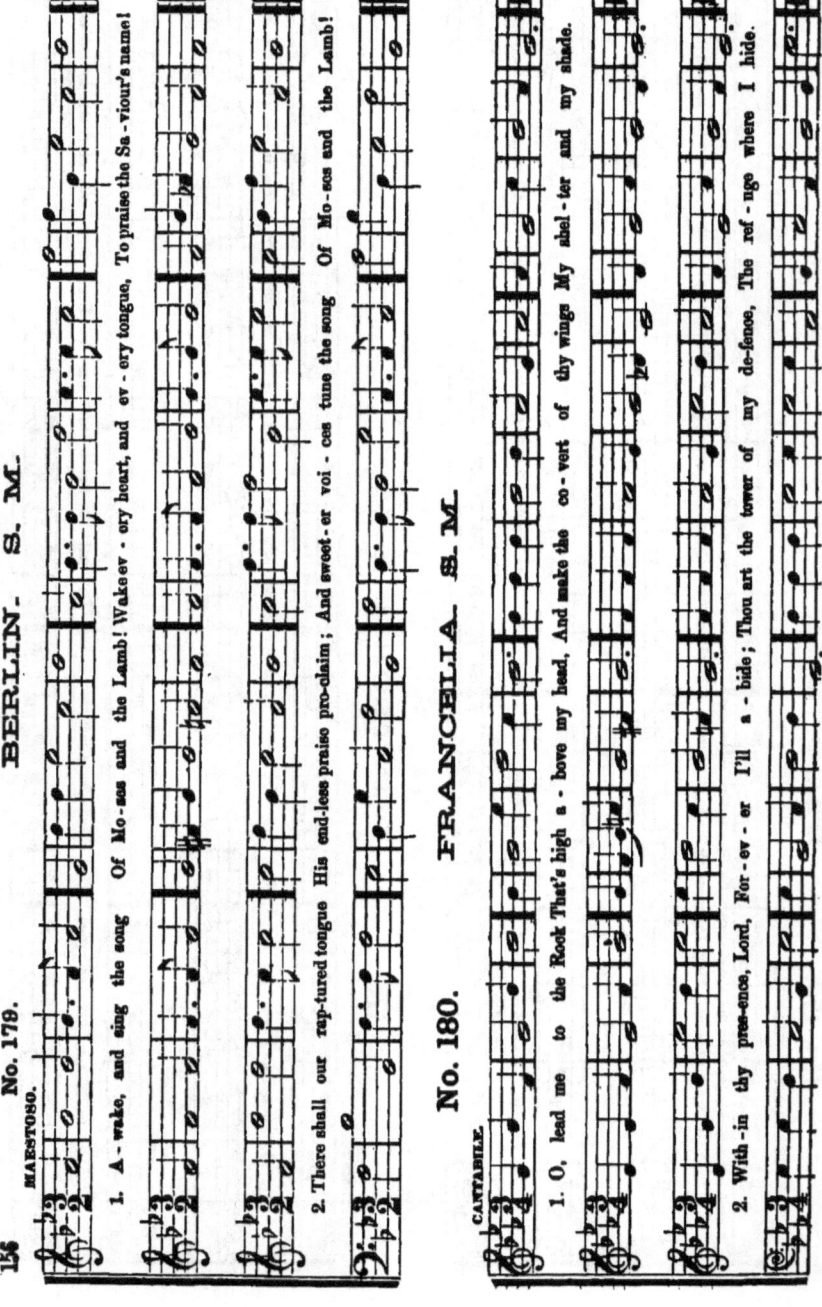

No. 185. PACIFIC. S. M.

1. O, bless the Lord, my soul, Let all with-in me join, And aid my tongue to bless his name, Whose fa-vors are di-vine.
2. O bless the Lord, my soul! Nor let his mer-cies lie For-got-ten in un-thank-ful-ness, And with-out prais-es die.

No. 186. CHAMBERLAIN. S. M.
H. S. PERKINS.

1. I lift my soul to God, My trust is in his name; Let not my foes, that seek my blood, Still tri-umph in my shame.
2. From ear-ly dawn-ing light, Till eve-ning shades a-rise, For thy sal-va-tion, Lord, I wait, With ev-er-long-ing eyes.

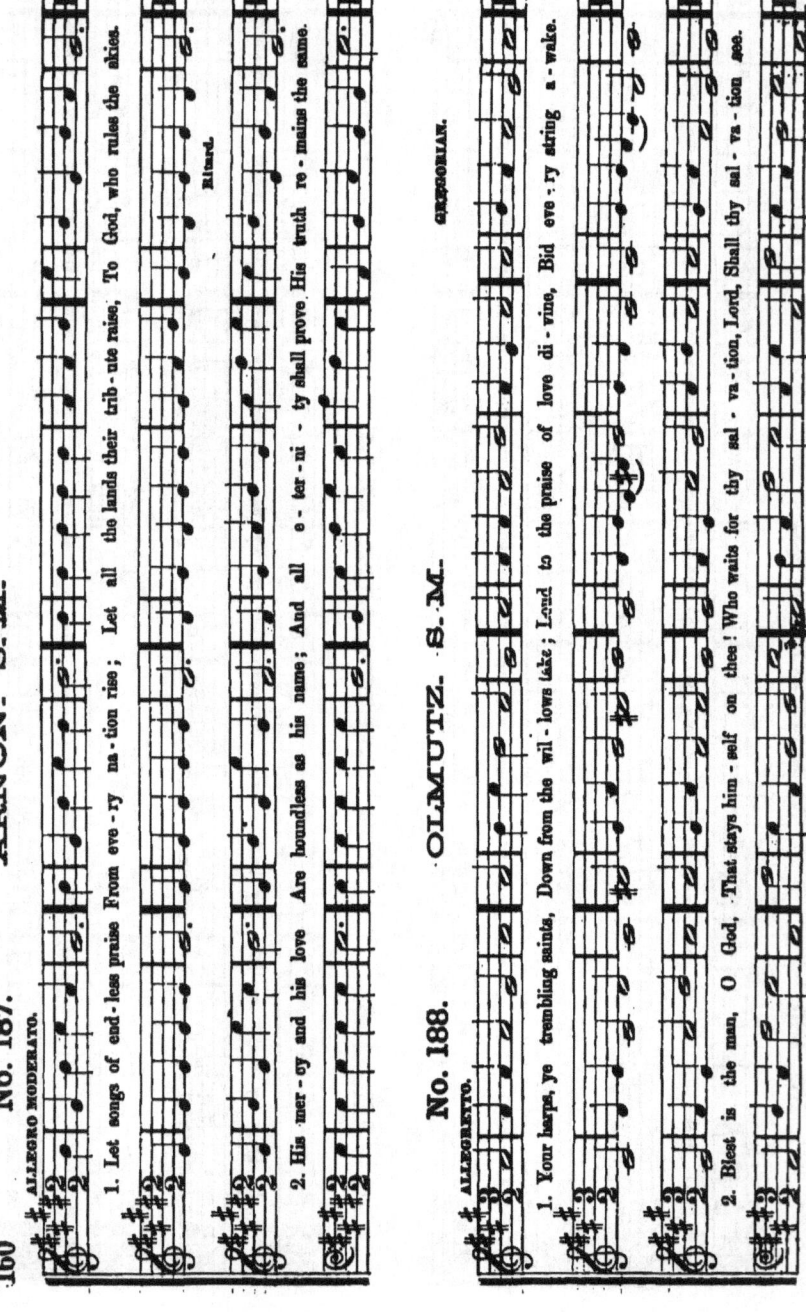

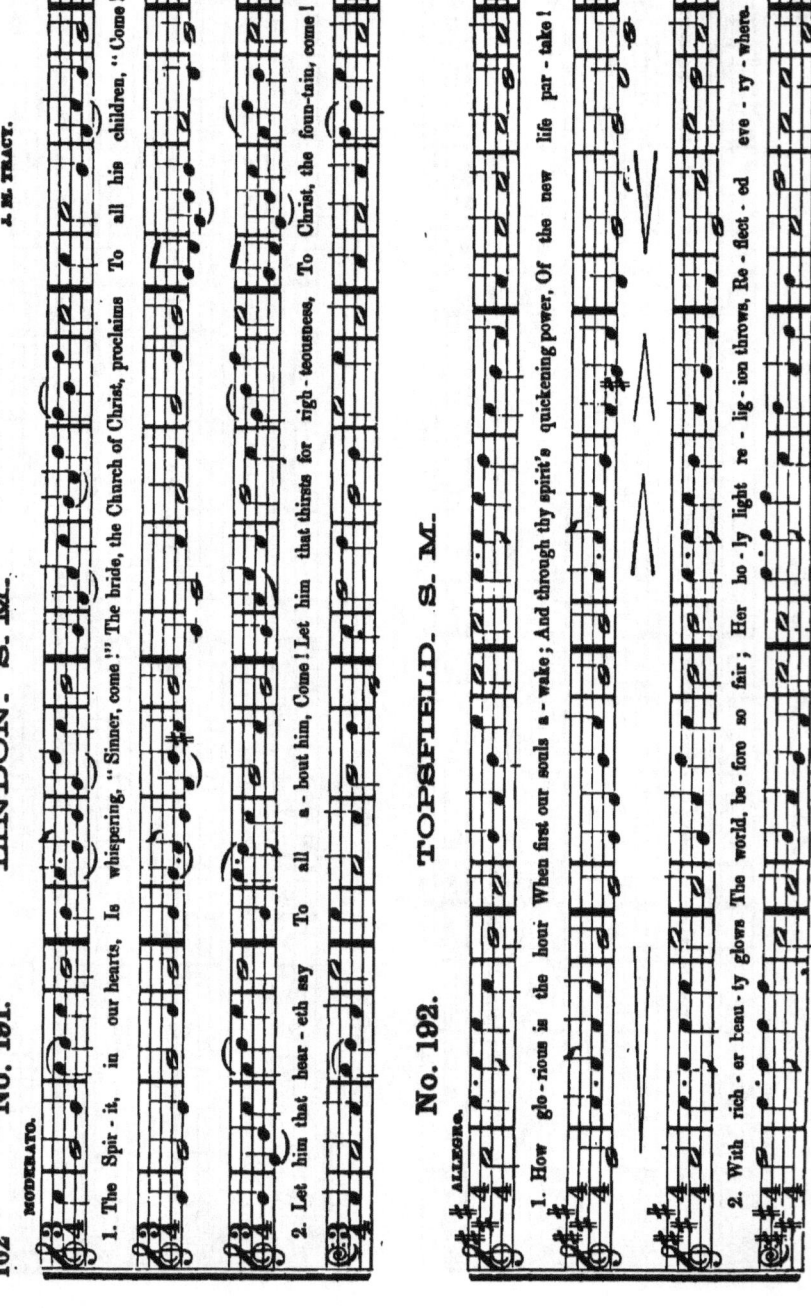

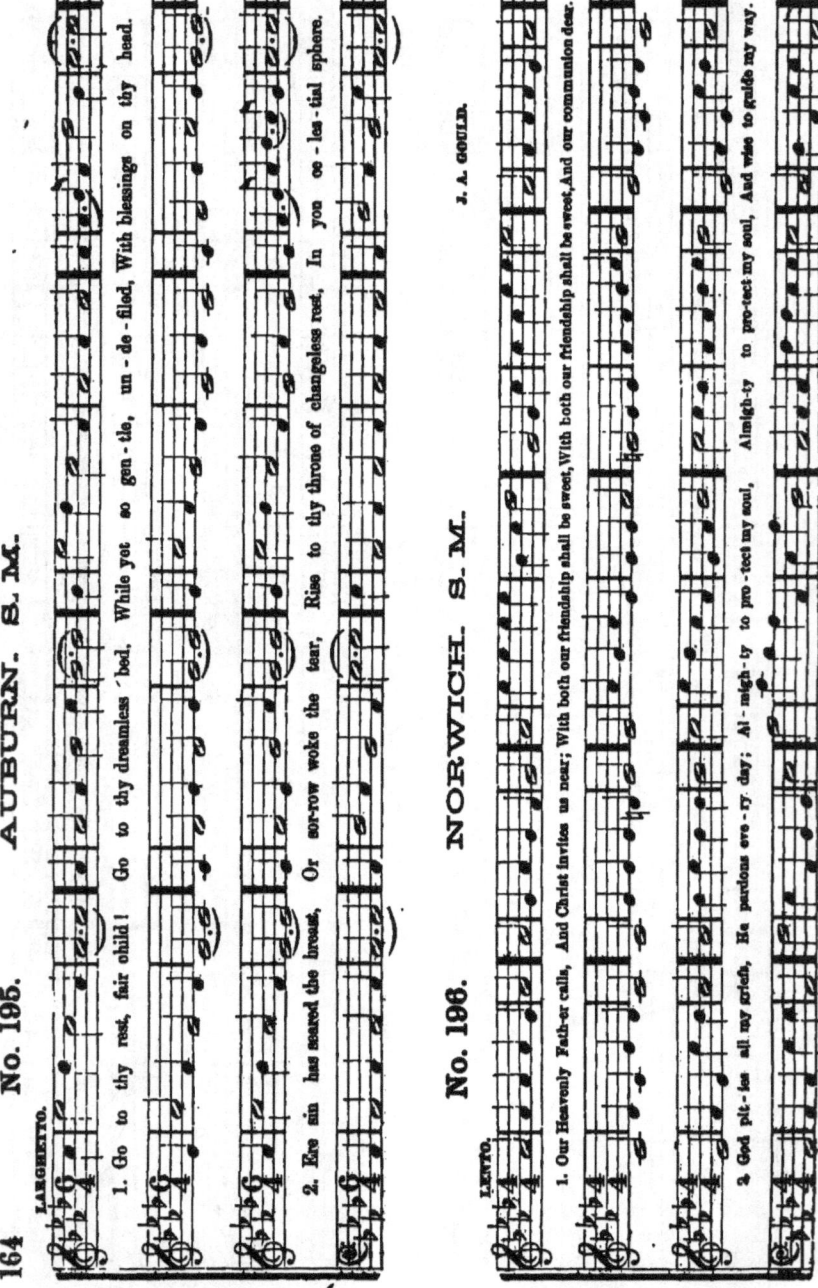

No. 201. CRANBROOK. S. M. THOMAS CLARK.

Grace! 'tis a charm-ing sound! Har-mo-nious to the ear! Heaven with the ech-o shall re-sound, Heaven with the ech-o shall re-

Heaven with the ech-o shall re-sound, And all the earth shall hear, And all the earth shall hear, And all the earth shall hear.

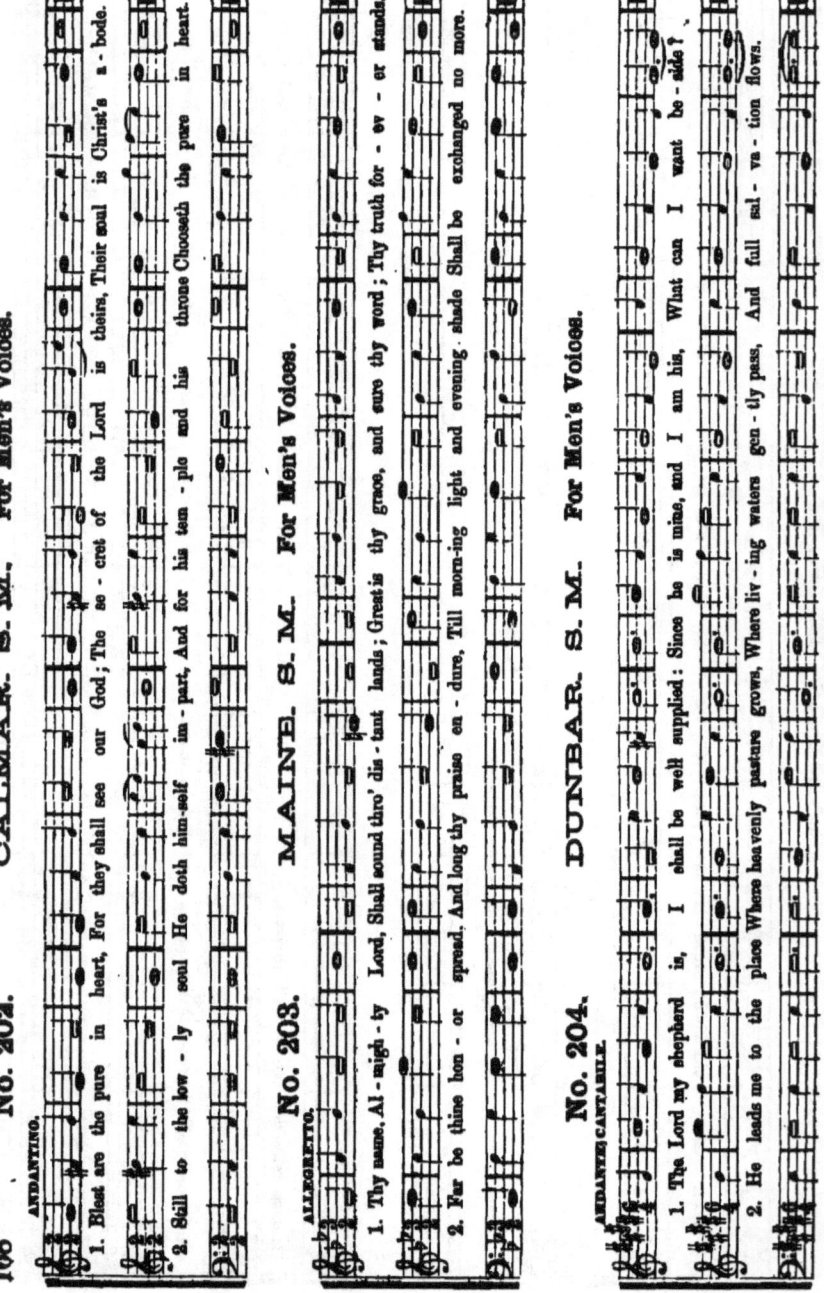

170　No. 206.　　RUSSEL. L. P. M.

VIGOROSO.

1. Let all the earth their voi-ces raise, To sing a psalm of no-bler praise, To sing and bless Je-ho-vah's name;
2. Oh! haste the day—the glo-rious hour, When earth shall feel his sav-ing power, And barb'rous na-tions fear his name:

His glo-ry let the hea-then know, His won-ders to the na-tions show, And all his sav-ing works pro-claim.

Then shall the race of man con-fess, The beau-ty of his ho-li-ness, And in his courts his grace pro-claim.

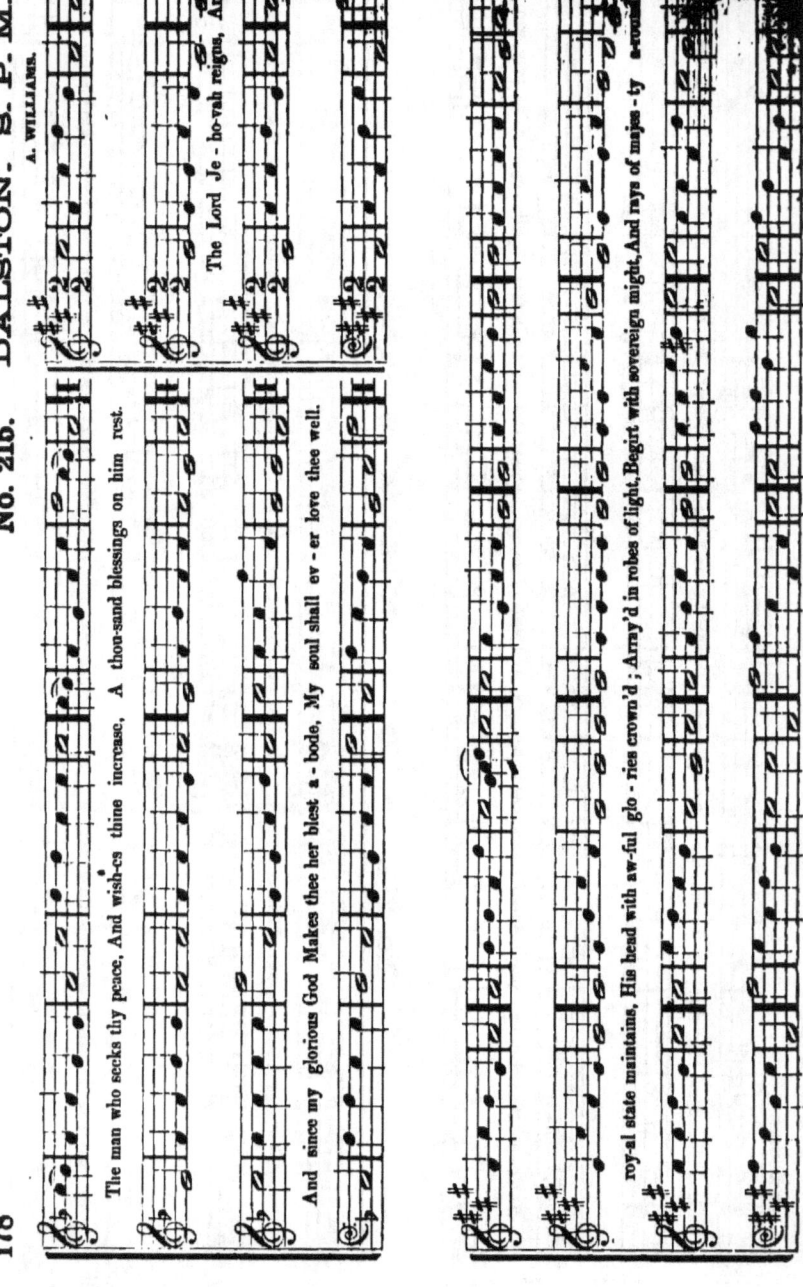

No. 217. HARDING. H. M.

Lord of the worlds a-bove, How pleasant and how fair, The dwellings of thy love, Thine earthly temples, are! To thine a-bode.......

No. 218. LEANDER. H. M. W. O. PERKINS.

1. Give thanks to God most high, The u-ni-ver-sal Lord; my heart as-pires, With warm desires to see my God.

2. How might-y is his hand! What wonders he hath done;

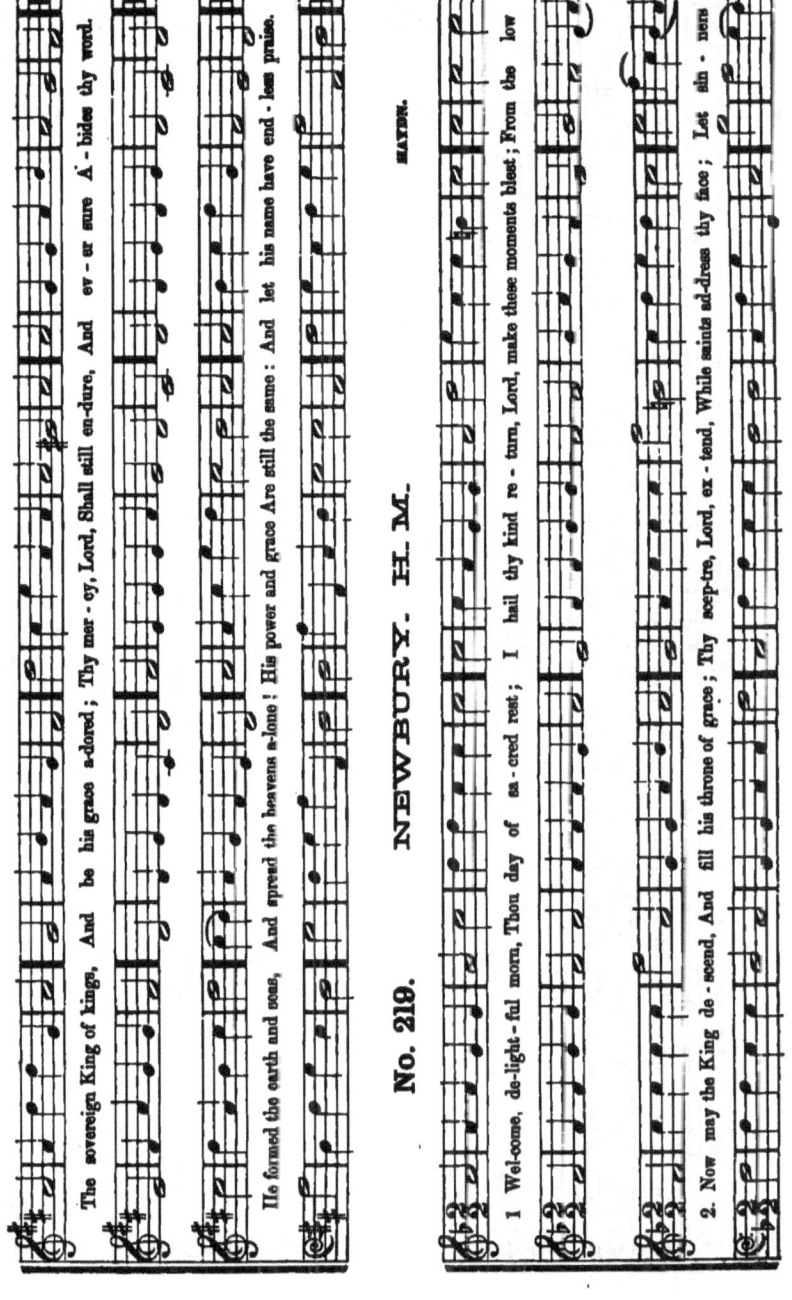

No. 221.   PRAGUE. H. M.   183

1. The Lord Jehovah reigns, His throne is built on high; The garments he assumes, Are light and majesty; His glories shine With beams so bright, No mortal eye Can bear the sight.

2. And can this mighty King Of glory condescend? And will he write his name, My Father and my Friend? I love his name, I love his word; Join all my powers, And praise the Lord.

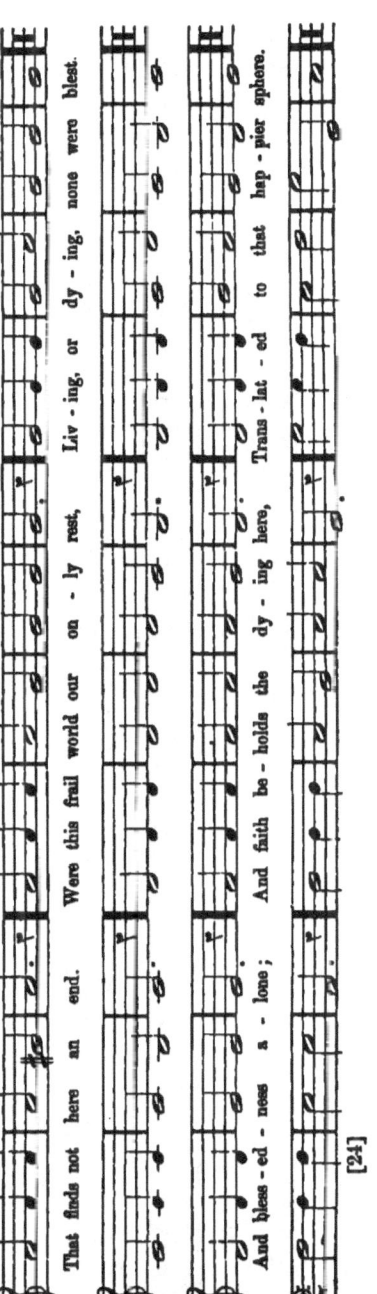

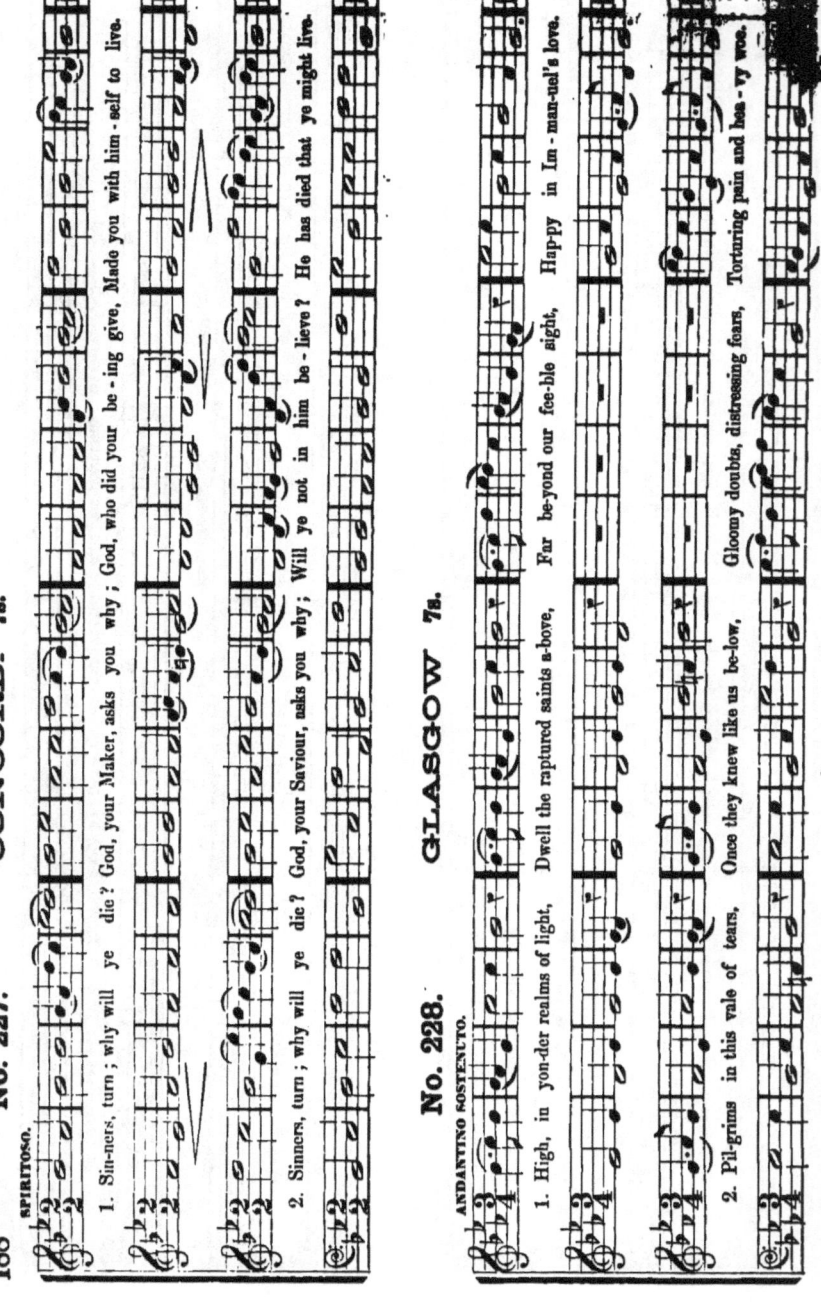

No. 229. KEOKUCK.* 7s. 6 LINES. 189

LEGATO.

1. Rock of A - ges, cleft for me, Let me hide my-self in thee! Let the wa - ter and the blood,
2. Not the la - bors of my hands Can ful - fil thy law's de - mands; Could my zeal no re-spite know,

From thy riv - en side which flowed, Be of sin the dou - ble cure, Cleanse me from its guilt and power.
Could my tears for - ev - er flow, All for sin would not a - tone, Thou must save, and thou a - lone.

No. 242. DANVERS. 7s.

CON SPIRITO.

1. Hail! all hail the joy-ful morn! Tell it forth from earth to heaven, That to us a child is born, That to us a son is given.

2. An-gels bend-ing from the sky, Chant-ed at the won-drous birth; "Glo-ry be to God on high, Glo-ry be to God on high, Peace, good will to man on

No. 243. LINDLEY. 7s.

CANTABILE.

1. Gracious Spirit, Love divine! Let thy light within me shine; All my guilty fears remove, Fill me with thy heavenly love.
2. Let me never from thee stray, Keep me in the narrow way; Fill my soul with joy divine, Keep me, Lord, for-ever thine.

No. 244. GRANNIS. 7s.

W. G. PERKINS.
From the "JUBILATE," by permission.

PIANO E LEGATO.

1. Gently falls the dews of eve, Raising still the languid flowers; Sweetly flow the tears that grieve, O'er a mourner's stricken hours.
2. Blessed tears and dews that yet Lift us nearer un-to heaven! Let us still his praise repeat, Who in mercy all hath given.

197

No. 247. NASHVILLE. 7s.

S. B. BALL.

No. 248. EDES. 7s.

MOZART.

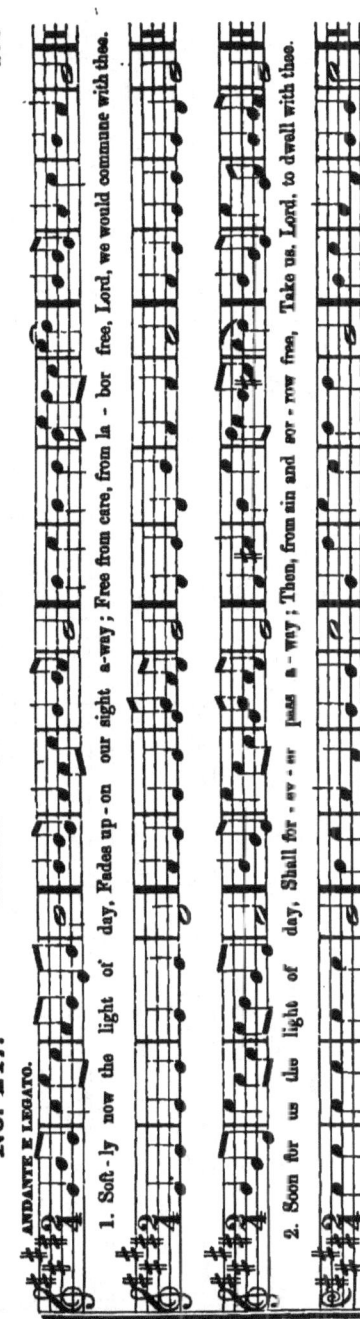

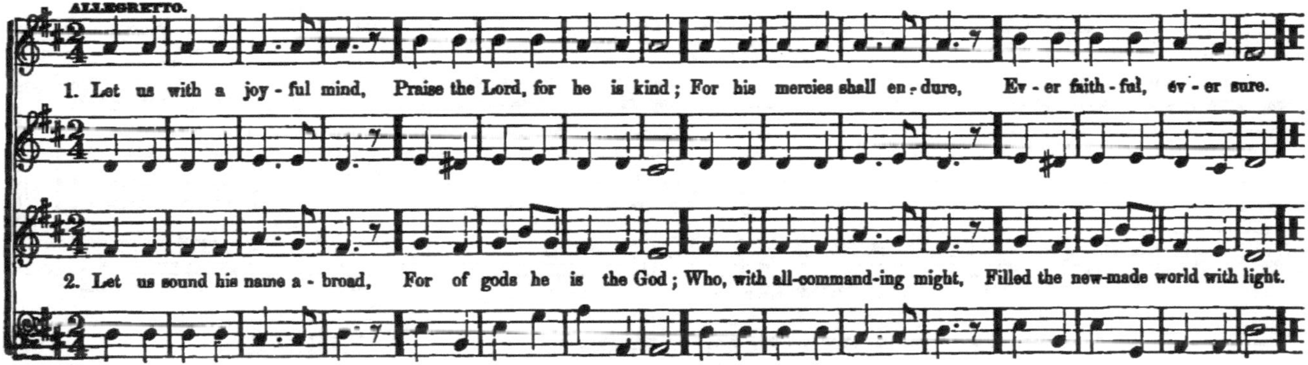

No. 255. DOANE. 8s & 7s. DOUBLE.

1. Hark! what mean those holy voices, Sweetly sounding thro' the skies? Lo! th' angelic host rejoices, Heavenly hallelujahs rise; Hear them tell the wondrous story, Hear them chant in hymns of joy, Glory in the highest, glory, Glory be to God on high.

2. Haste, ye mortals, to adore him; Learn his name and taste his joy; Till in heaven ye sing before him, Glory be to God most high. Haste, ye mortals, to adore him; Learn his name, and taste his joy; Till in heav'n ye sing before him, Glory be to God most high.

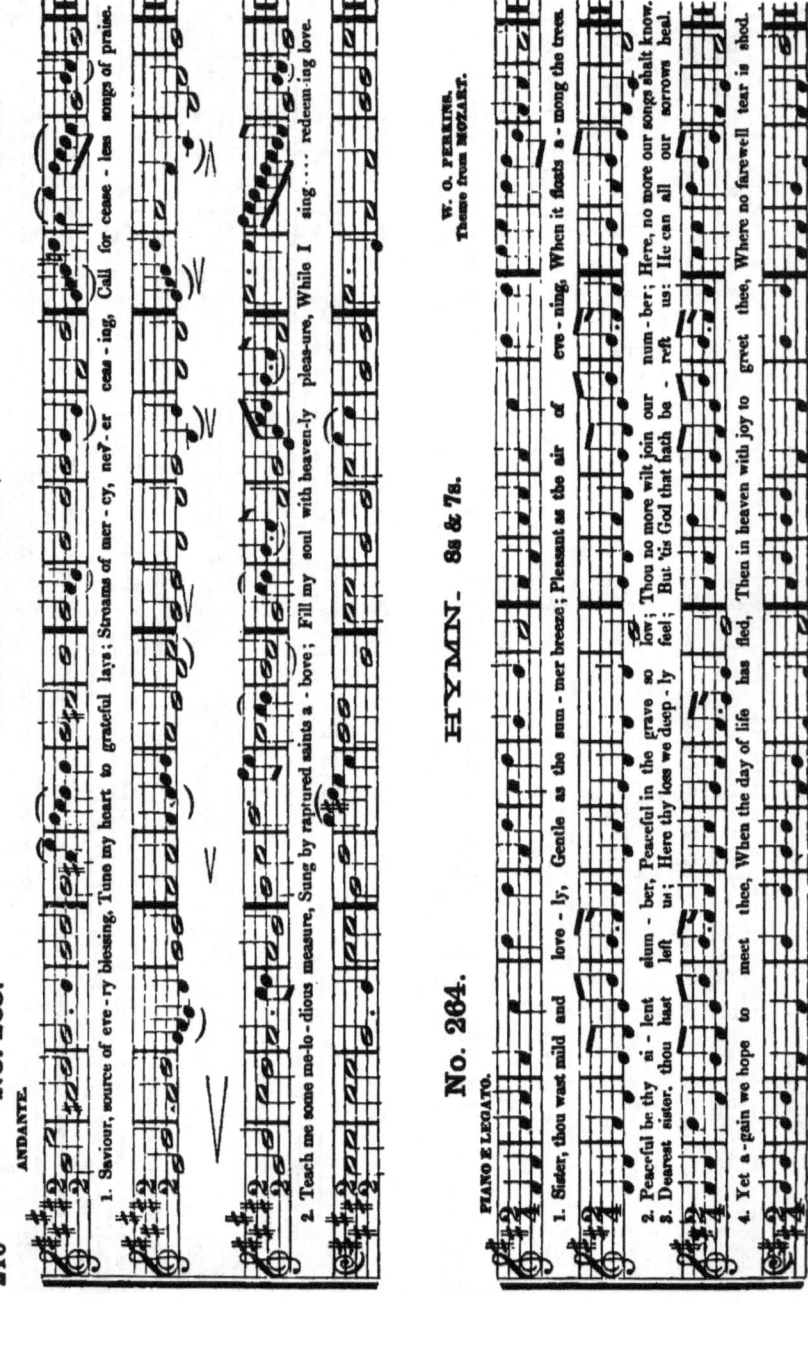

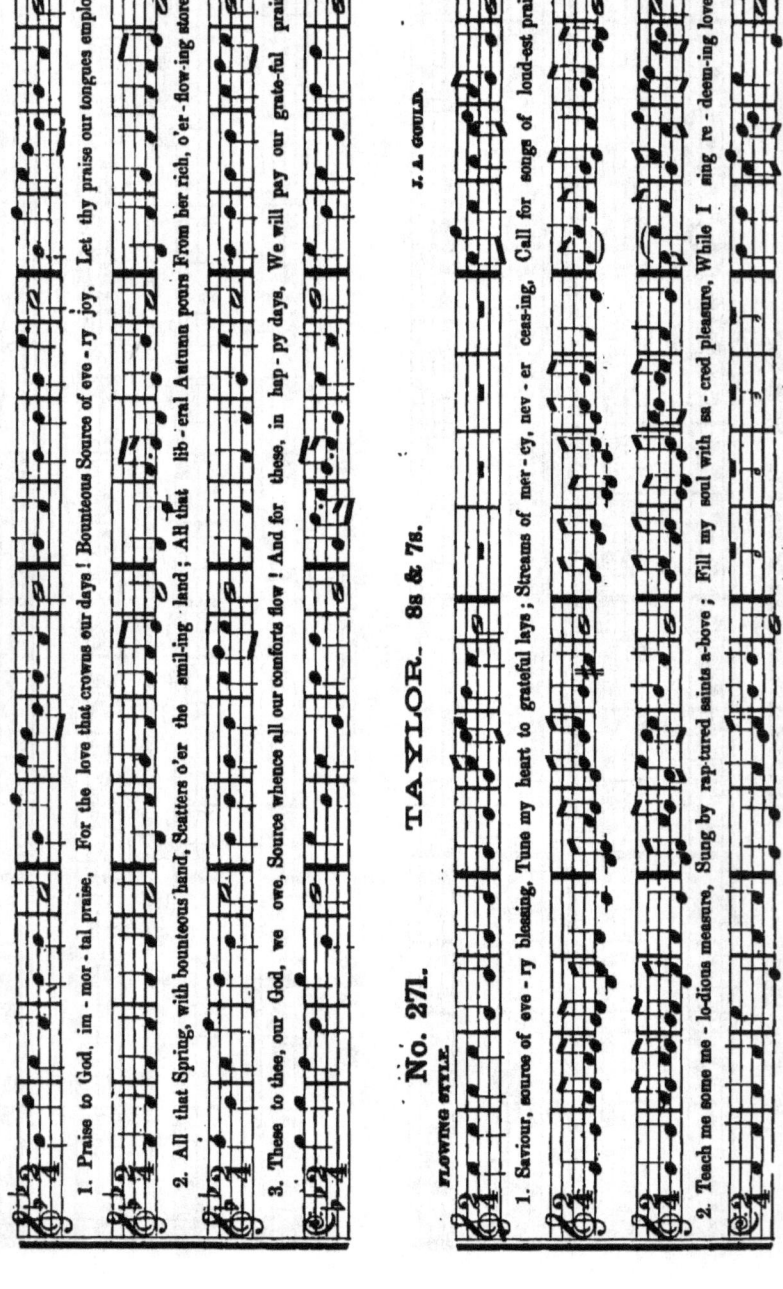

216. No. 274. O, LAND OF REST. 8s & 6s. DOUBLE. ORSON PERKINS.

1. Oh! land of rest, for thee I sigh, When will the moment come, When I shall lay my ar-mor by, And dwell with Christ at home.
2. No tran-quil joys on earth I know, No peace-ful, sheltering dome; This world's a wil-der-ness of wo, This world is not my home.
3. To Je-sus Christ I sought for rest, He bade me cease to roam; And fly for ref-uge to his breast, And he'd con-duct me home.
4. When by af-flic-tions sharp-ly tried, I view the gap-ing tomb; Al-though I dread death's chill-ing flood, Yet still I sigh for home.
5. Wea-ry of wandering round and round, This vale of sin and gloom; I long to leave th' unhallowed ground, And dwell with Christ at home.

And dwell with Christ at home, And dwell with Christ at home, When I shall lay my ar-mor by, And dwell with Christ at home.
This world is not my home, This world is not my home, This world's a wil-der-ness of wo, This world is not my home.
And he'd conduct me home, And he'd conduct me home, And fly for ref-uge to his breast, And he'd conduct me home.
Yet still I sigh for home, Yet still I sigh for home, Al-though I dread death's chilling flood, Yet still I sigh for home.
And dwell with Christ at home, And dwell with Christ at home, I long to leave th' unhallowed ground, And dwell with Christ at home.

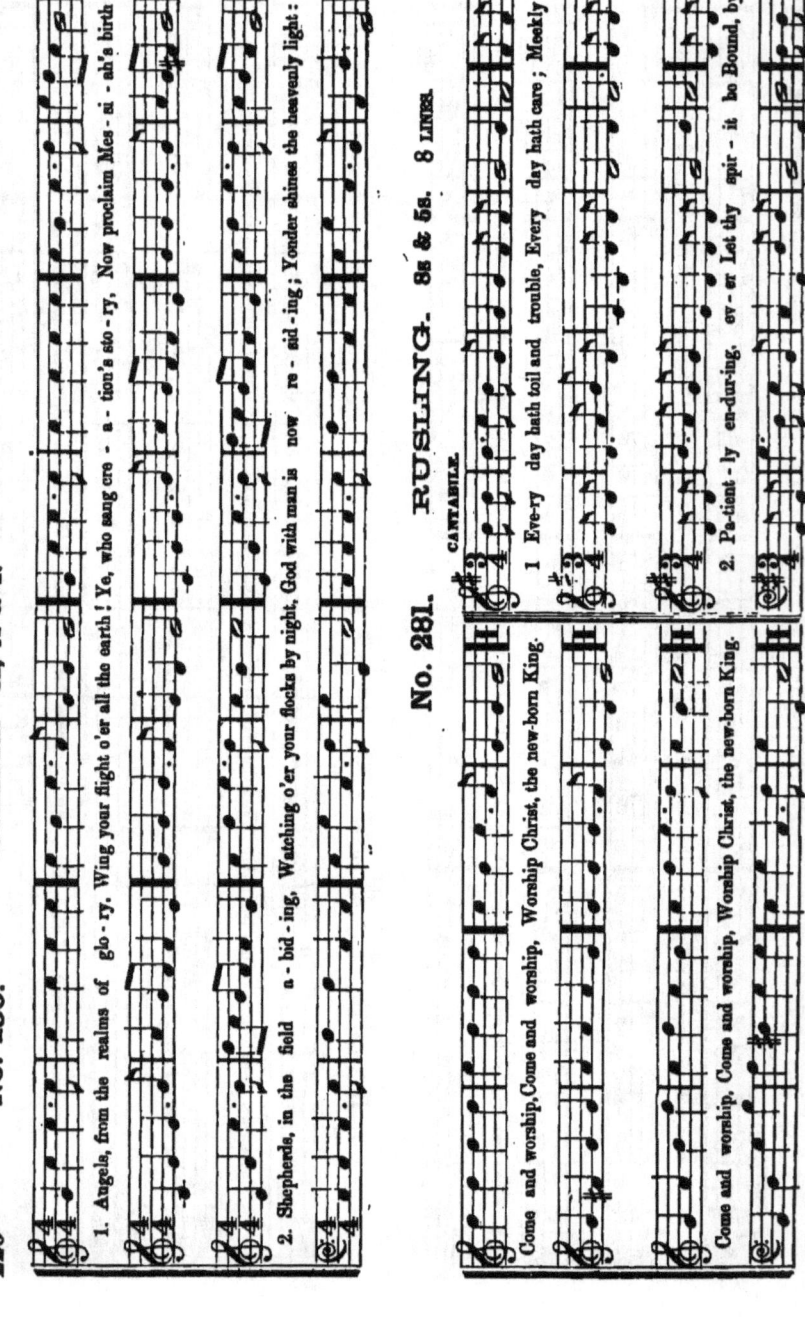

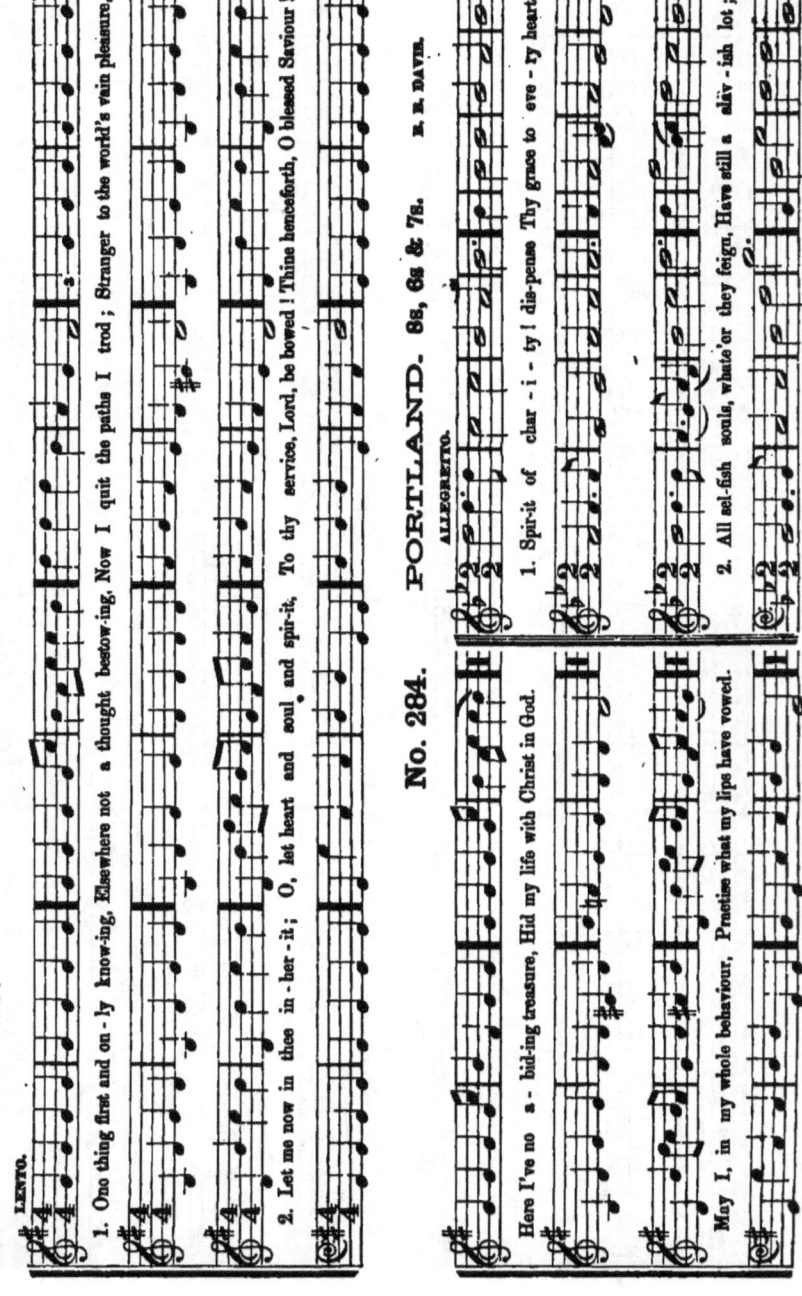

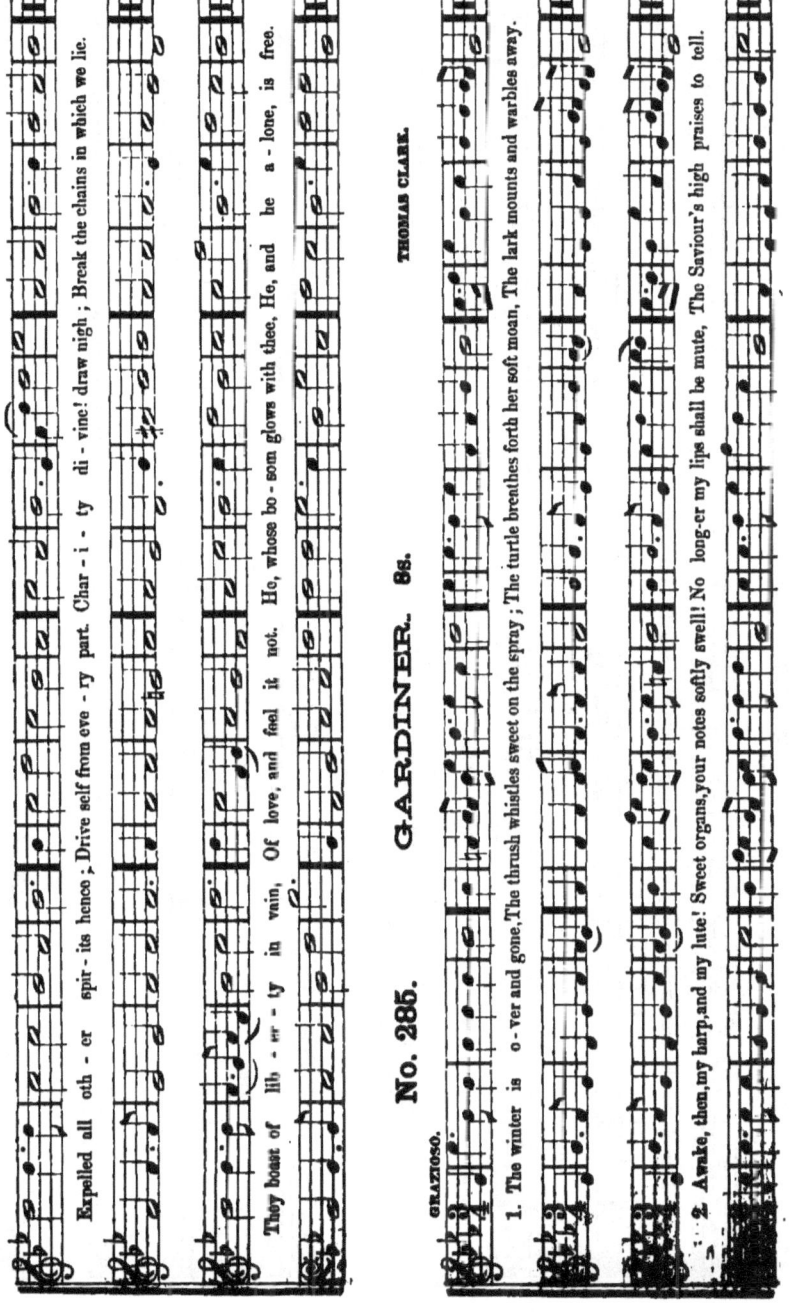

224 No. 286. STRATTON. 8s. DOUBLE.

1. Blessed be thy name for-ev-er, Thou of life the Guard and Giver! Thou canst guard thy creatures sleeping, Heal the heart long broke with weeping:

God of stillness and of motion, Of the desert and the ocean, Of the mountain, rock, and riv-er, Blessed be thy name for-ev-er!

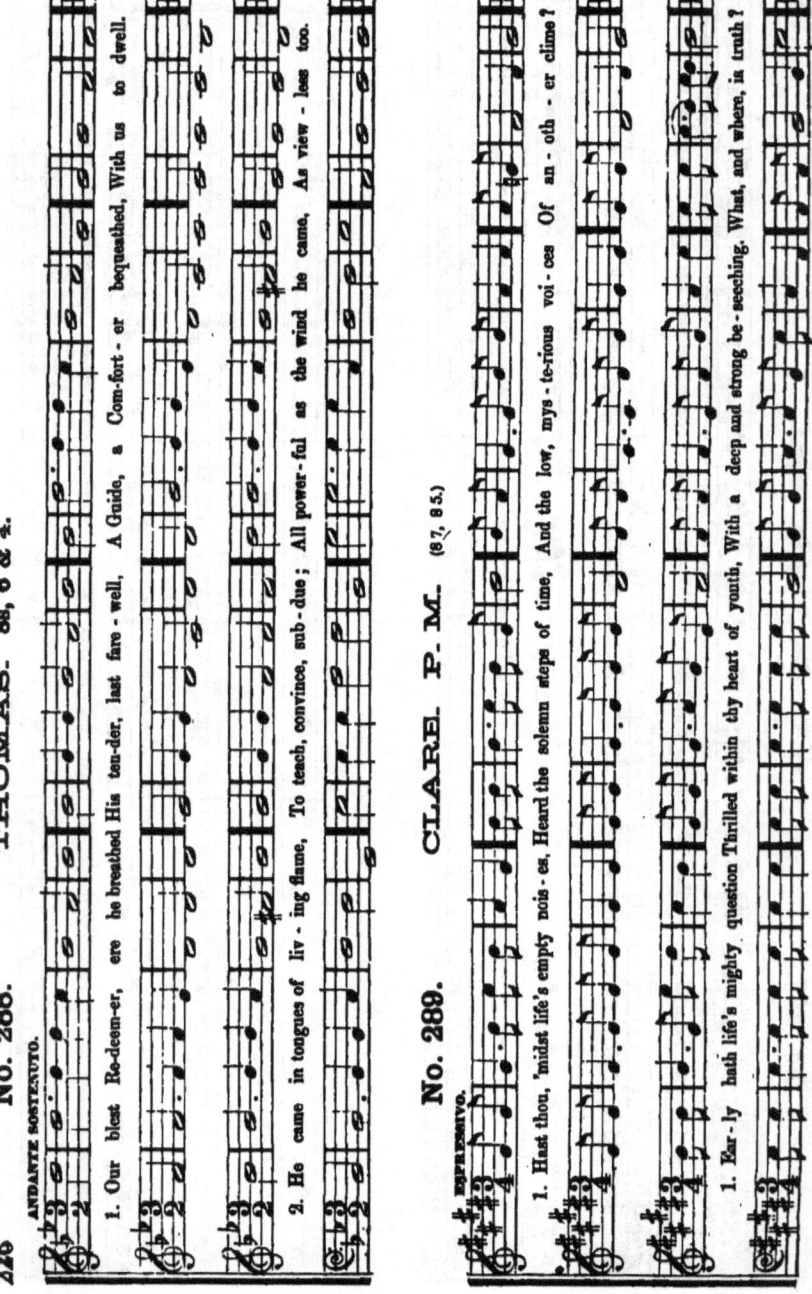

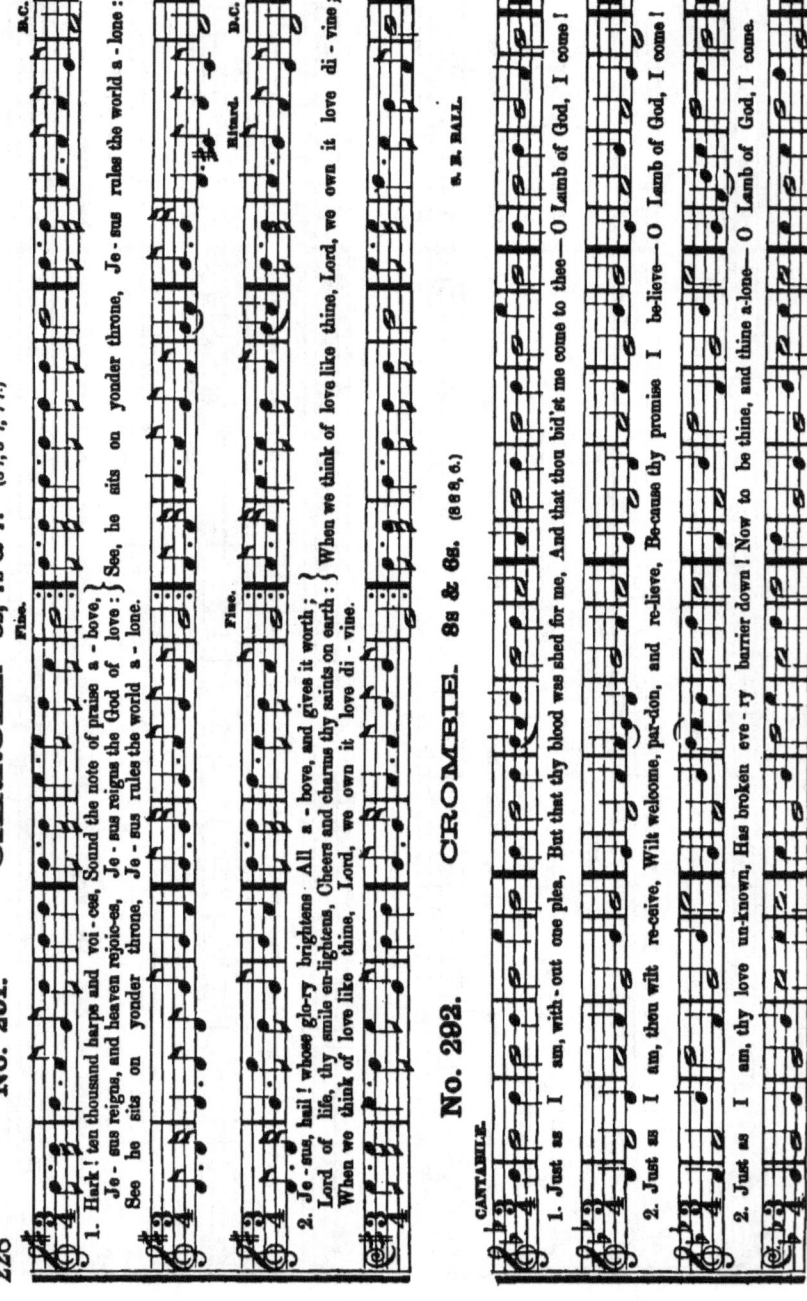

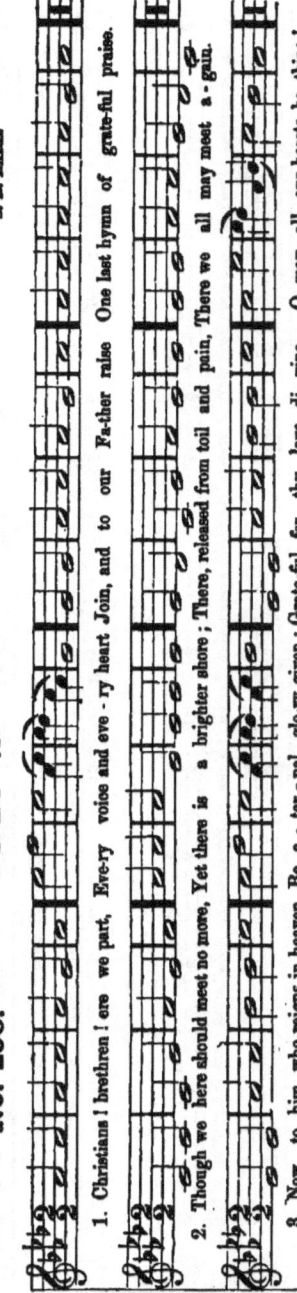

No. 297.   CHICKERING. 8s, 6s & 10s. 7 Lines.   231

VIGOROSO.

1. God is our ref-uge and de-fence, Our shield his dread om-nip-o-tence. Earth may be-neath us shrink, The an-cient

2. There is a riv-er calm and pure, Whose streams re-fresh and well so-cure The dwell-ing-place of God. Blest ai - ty,

moun-tains hoar Down in the deep tide sink,— Let the wild del-uge roar, Je - ho-vah is our ref-uge and de-fence!

fair and bright, His fa-vored saints' a-bode, Where the Lord reigns in light,— No foe can shake his strong foun-da-tions sure.

232

No. 298. ALL IS WELL. 8s & 3s.

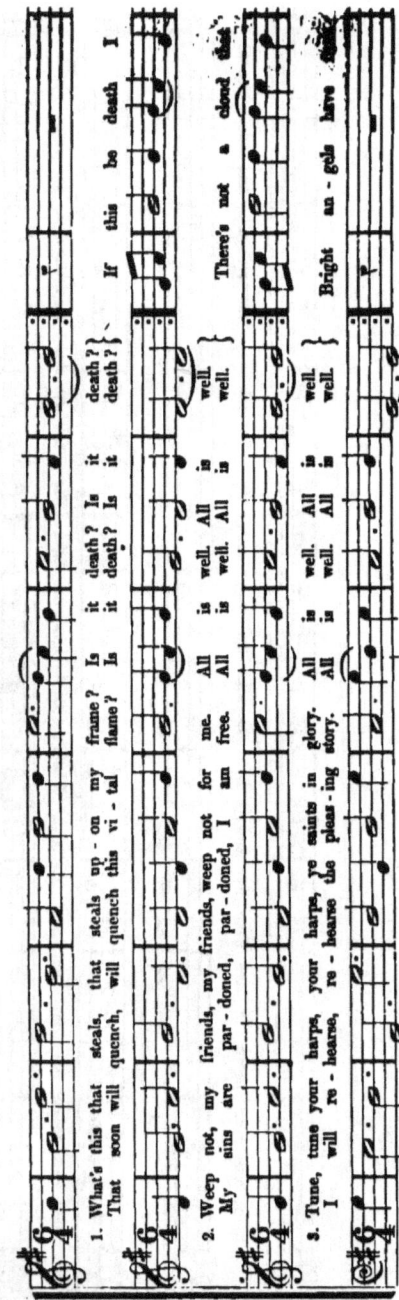

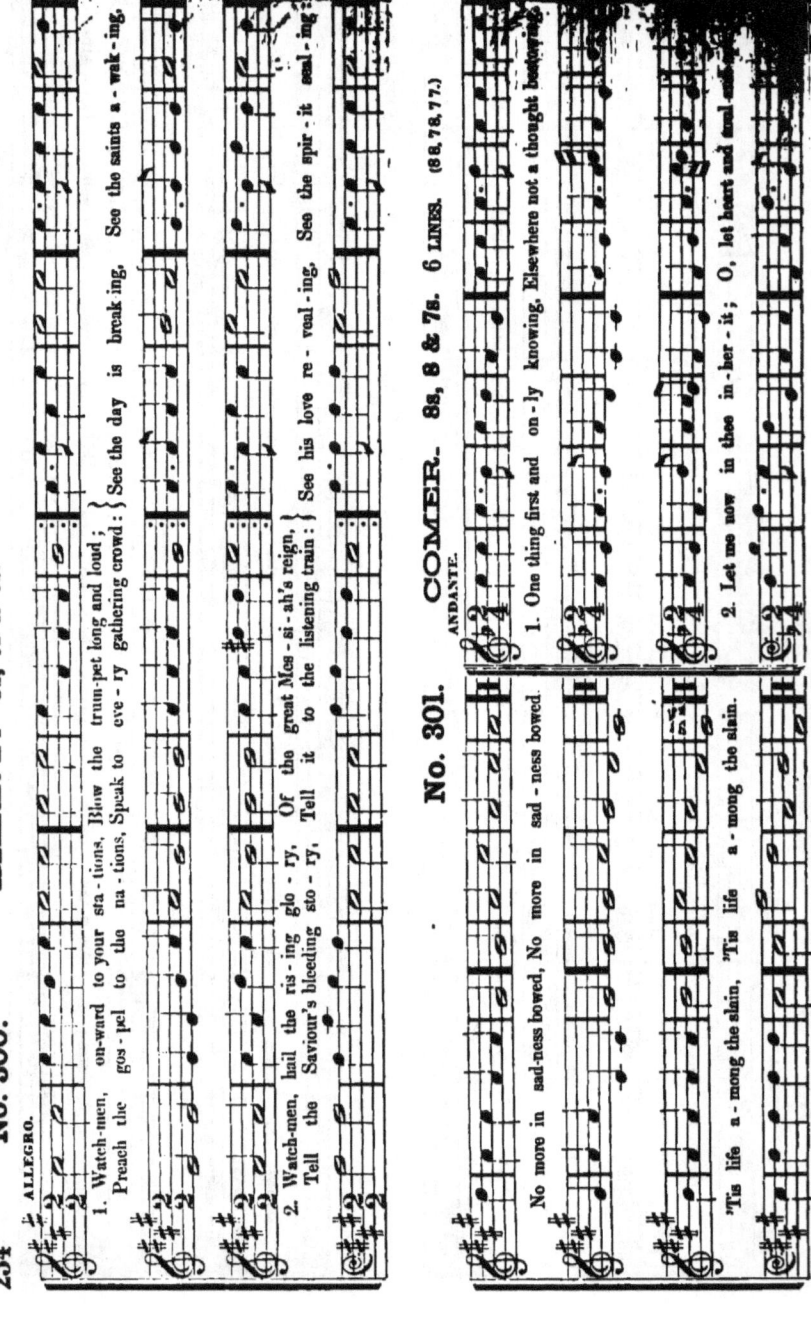

236

No. 303.   COMMUNION. P. M.   (8 6, 8 & 8 6,)

1. Blest is the hour when cares depart, And earthly scenes are far,— When tears of woe forget to start, And gently dawns upon the heart Devotion's holy star.

2. Blest is the place where angels bend To hear our worship rise, Where kindred thoughts their musings blend, And all the soul's affections tend Beyond the veiling skies.

No. 304.   NILE.   8s & 8s.

1. A little child, in bulrush ark, Came floating on the Nile's broad water; That child made Egypt's glory dark, And freed his tribe from bonds and slaughter.

No. 308. CONSOLATION. 6s & 5s.

1. Where the mourn-er weep - ing, Sheds the se - cret tear, God his watch is keep - ing, Though none else is near.
2. God will nev - er leave thee, All thy wants he known, Feels the pains that grieve thee, Sees thy cares and woes.

No. 309. NEWCASTLE. 5s & 6s.

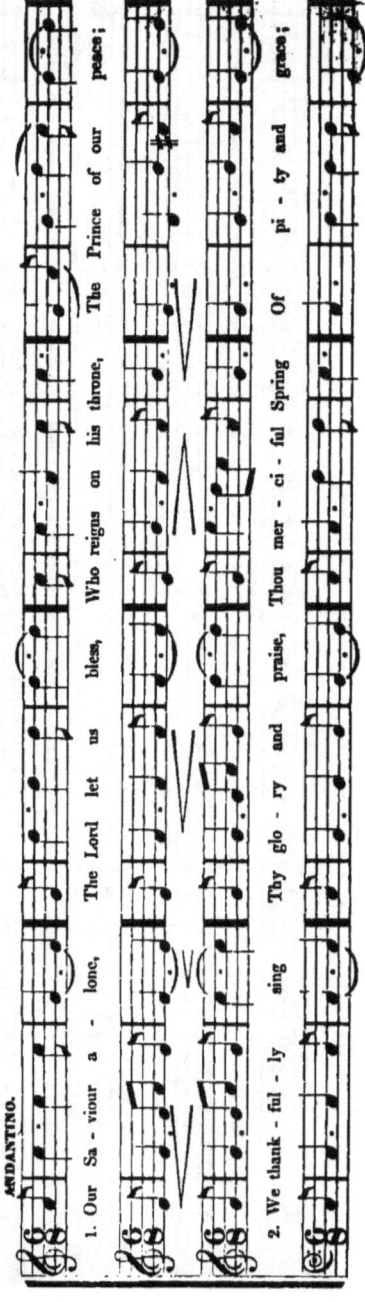

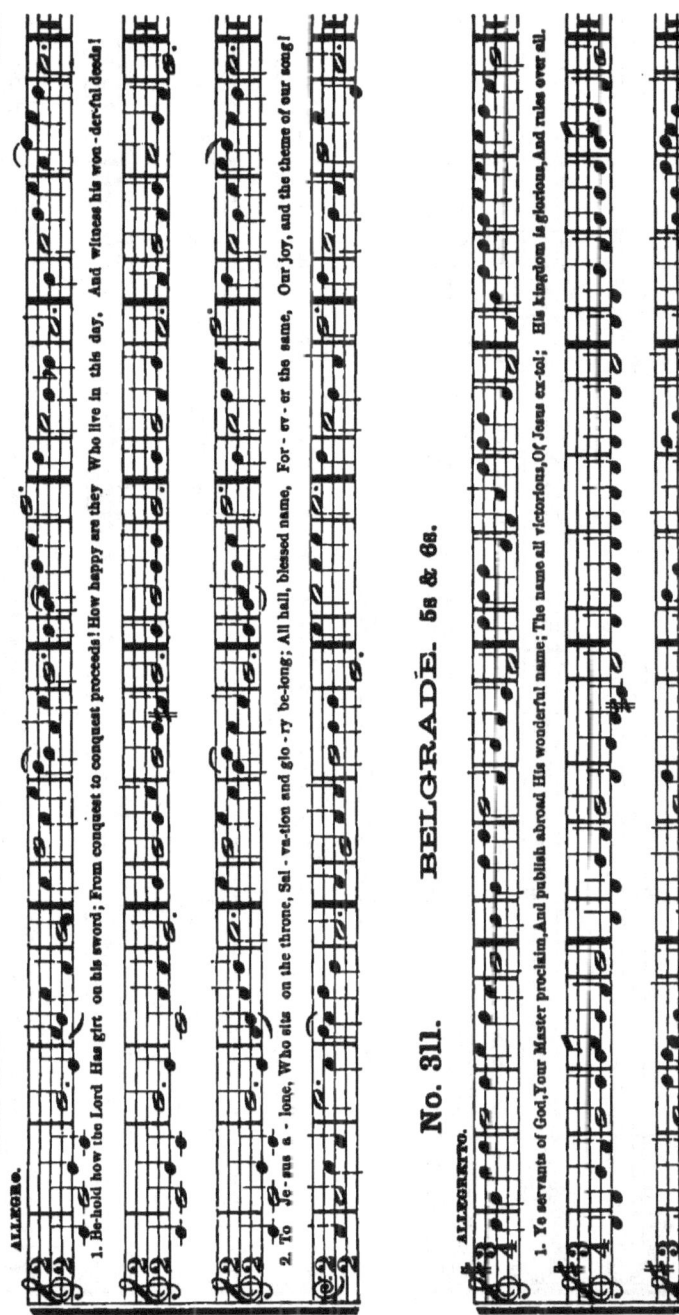

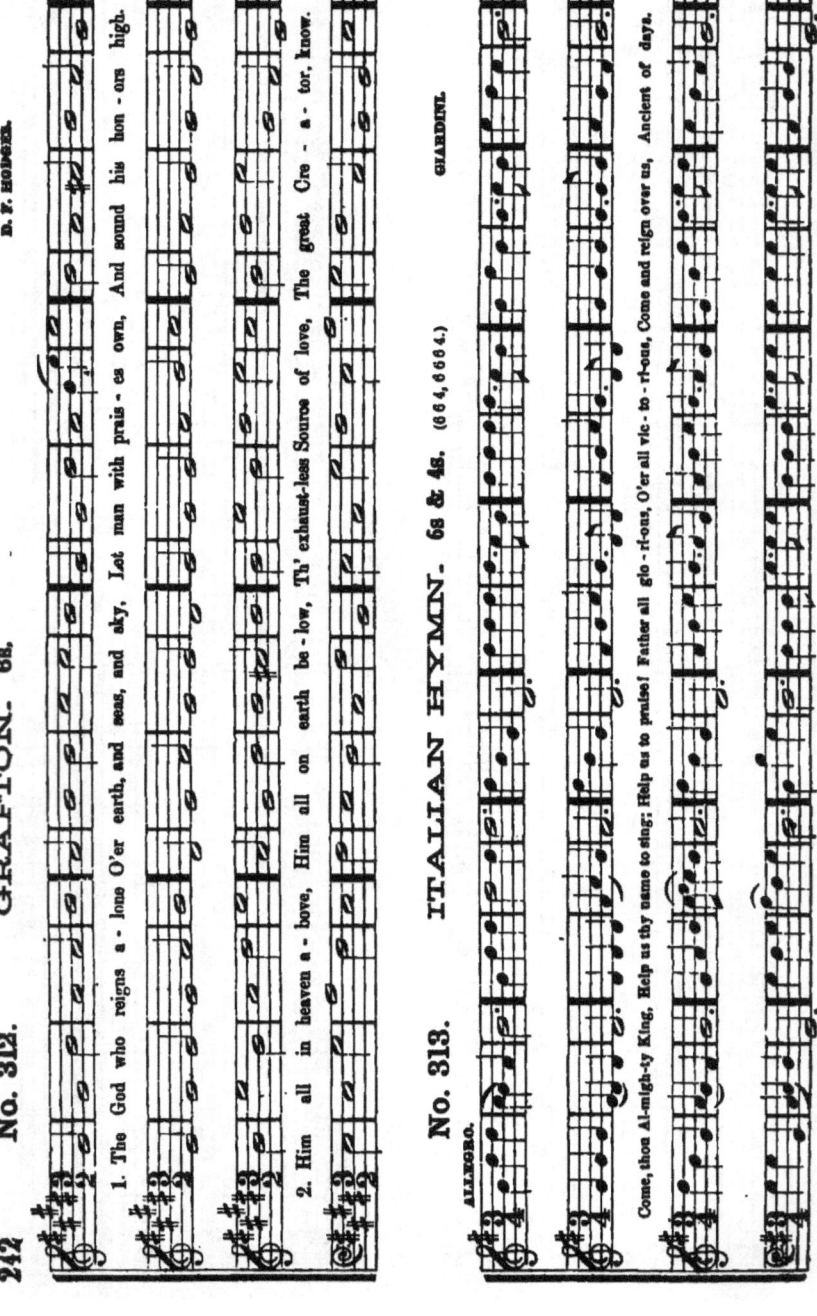

No. 314.   PARTING. 6s & 5s. Peculiar. (8 5, 8 5, 8 6 5.)   W. O. PERKINS.

243

1. When shall we meet a - gain? Meet ne'er to sev - er? When will peace wreathe her chain Round us for - ev - er?
2. Up to that world of light, Take us, dear Sav-iour; May we all there u - nite, Hap - py for - ev - er;
3. Soon shall we meet a - gain, Meet ne'er to sev - er; Soon shall peace wreathe her chain, Round us for - ev - er;

Our hearts will ne'er re - pose, Safe from each blast that blows, In this dark vale of woes— Nev - er,— no, nev - er!
Where kin - dred spir - its dwell, There may our mu - sic swell, And time our joys dis - pel, Nev - er,— no, nev - er!
Our hearts will then re - pose, Se - cure from fears or woes; Our songs of praise shall close Nev - er,— no, nev - er!

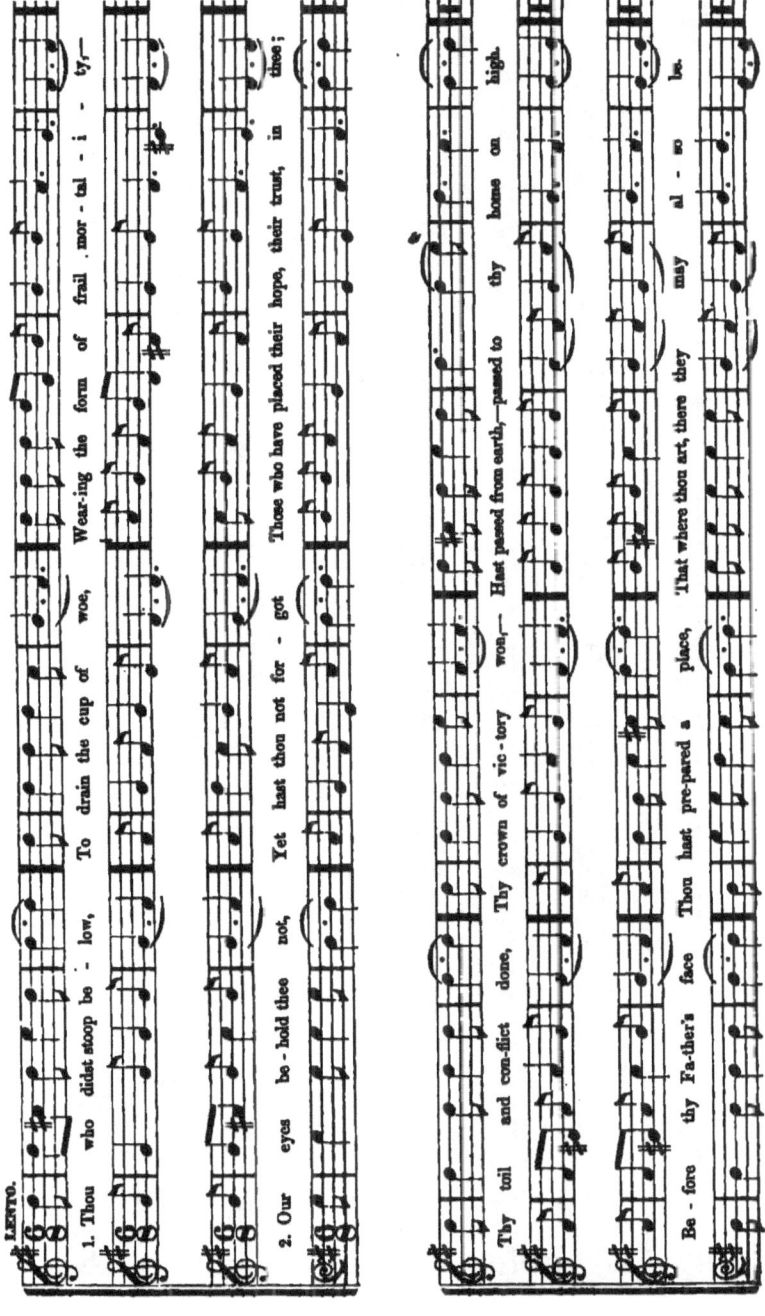

246

No. 317. BRITAIN. 6s & 4s. (664,6664.)

1. Glad hearts to thee we bring; With joy thy name we sing, Father a-bove; Creation praises thee; Thy bounty's full and free; In all a-round we see Em-blems of love.

2. Thou who in heav-en art, To us that grace impart, Our Saviour knew: May we his truth re-ceive; Aid us like him to live, To thee our hearts to give, Thou on-ly true.

No. 318. LINTON. 6s.

SOSTENUTO.

1. I feel with-in a want For ev-er burn-ing there; What I so thirst for, grant, O thou who hear-est pray'r.

2. This is the thing I crave, A like-ness to thy Son; This would I rath-er have, Than call the world my own.

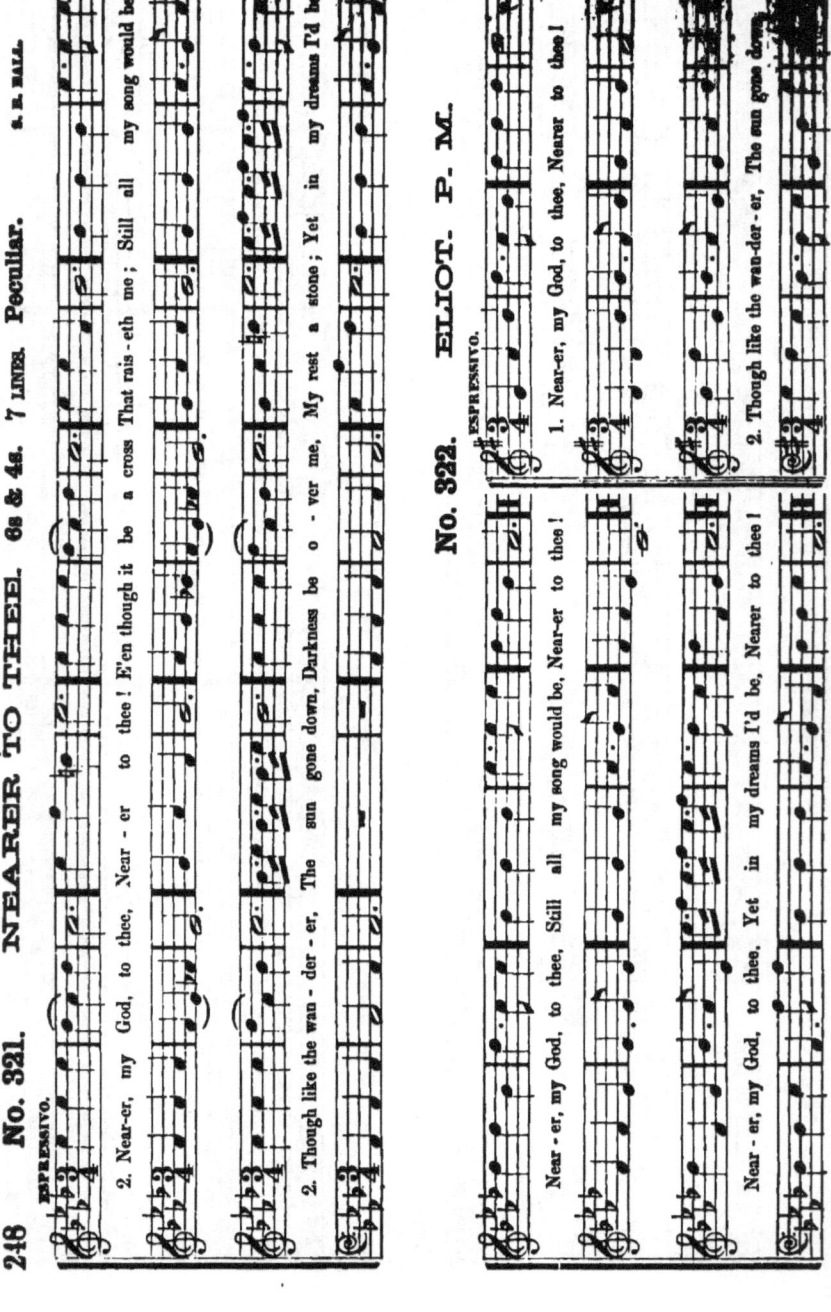

251

No. 326. CORYDON. 6s & 10s.

No. 329. AUDIO. 6s & 4s. (6 4, 6 4, 4 4, 6 4.)

SIMEON FULLER,
Of the "Boston Music School."

Child of sin and sor-row, Filled with dis-may, Wait not for the mor-row, Yield thee to-day;
Heaven bids thee come, While yet there's room, Child of sin and sor-row, Hear and o-bey.

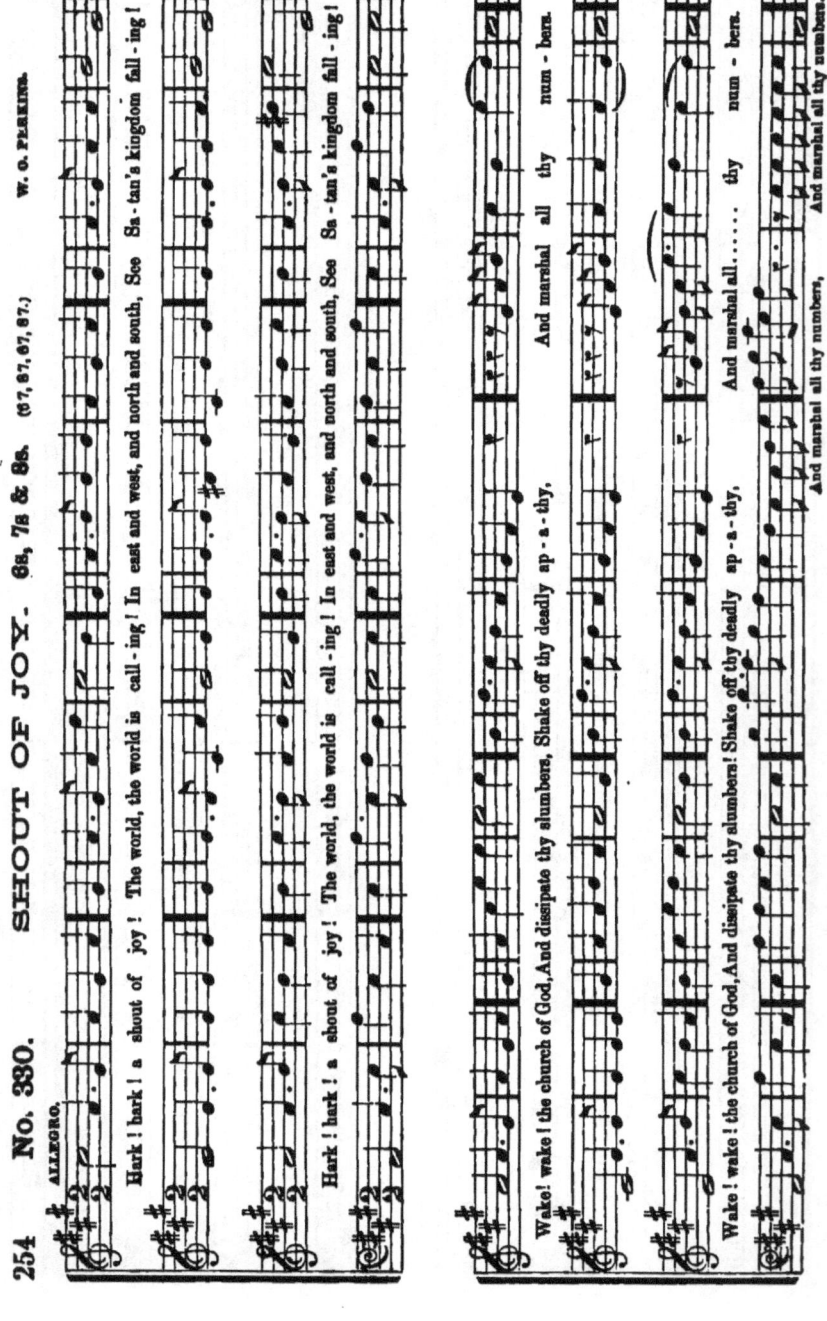

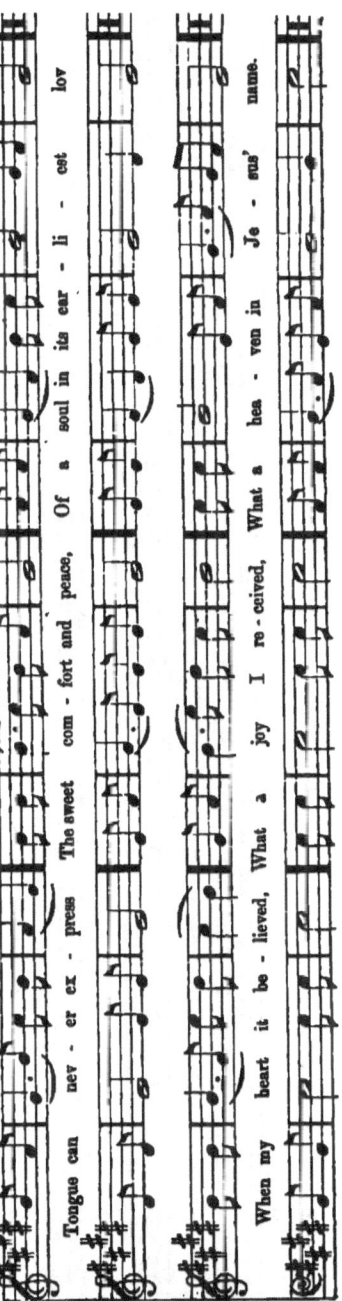

256

No. 332. POWERS. P. M. (66, 86, 88.) S. B. BALL.

LENTO.

1. Friend af-ter friend de-parts; Who hath not lost a friend? There is no union here of hearts, That finds not here an end. We've this frail world our only rest, Liv-ing or dy - ing, none were blest.

2. Be-yond the flight of time, Be-yond the vale of death, There surely is some blessed clime, Where life is not a breath, Nor life's af - fec-tions but a fire Whose sparks fly up-ward to ex - pire.

No. 388. BREWER. 6s & 10s.

LENTO.

1. Wilt thou not vis-it me? The plant be-side me feels thy gen-tle dew; Each blade of grass I see, From thy deep earth its quickening moisture drew.

2. Wilt thou not vis-it me? Thy morning calls on me with cheer-ing tone; And ev - ery hill and tree Lend but one voice, the voice of thee a - lone.

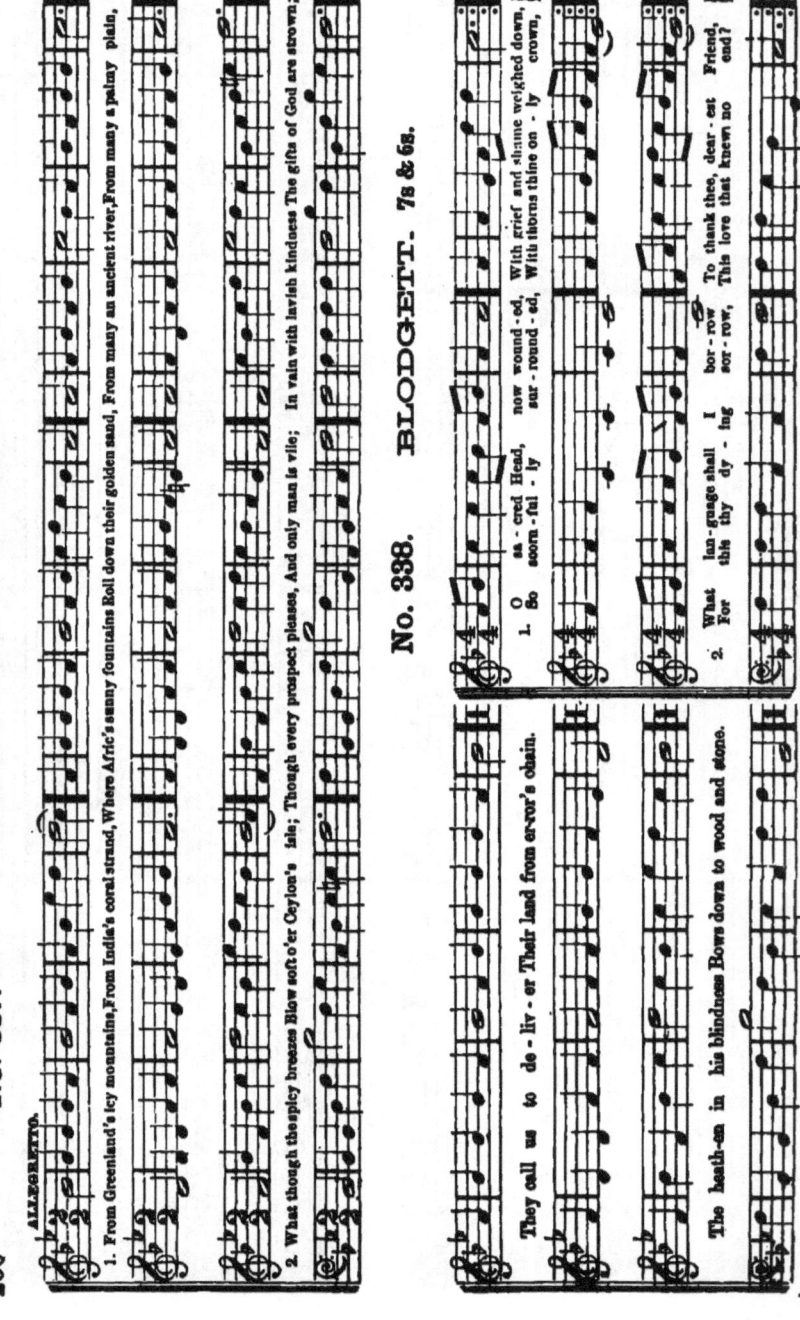

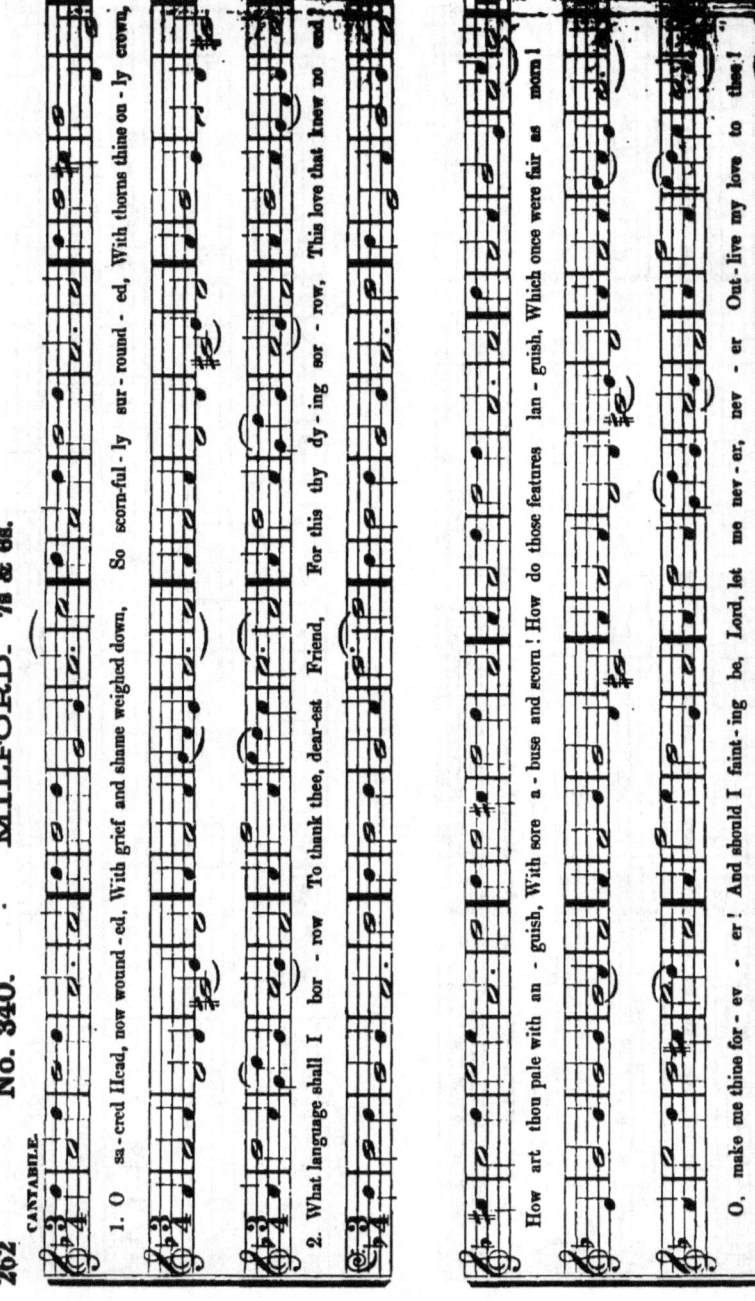

No. 341. CORONA. P. M. (7s, 8s, 7s, 7s, 8s.)

MAESTOSO.

1. Head of the Church triumph-ant, We joy-ful-ly a-dore thee; Till thou ap-pear, thy members here Shall sing like those in glo-ry:
2. Thou dost con-duct thy peo-ple Through torrents of temp-ta-tion; Nor will we fear, while thou art near, The fire of trib-u-la-tion:
   We lift our hearts and voi-ces, With blest an-ti-ci-pa-tion; And cry a-loud, and give to God The praise of our sal-va-tion.
   The world, with sin and Sa-tan, In vain our march op-pos-es; By thee we shall break thro' them all, And sing the song of Mos-es.

263

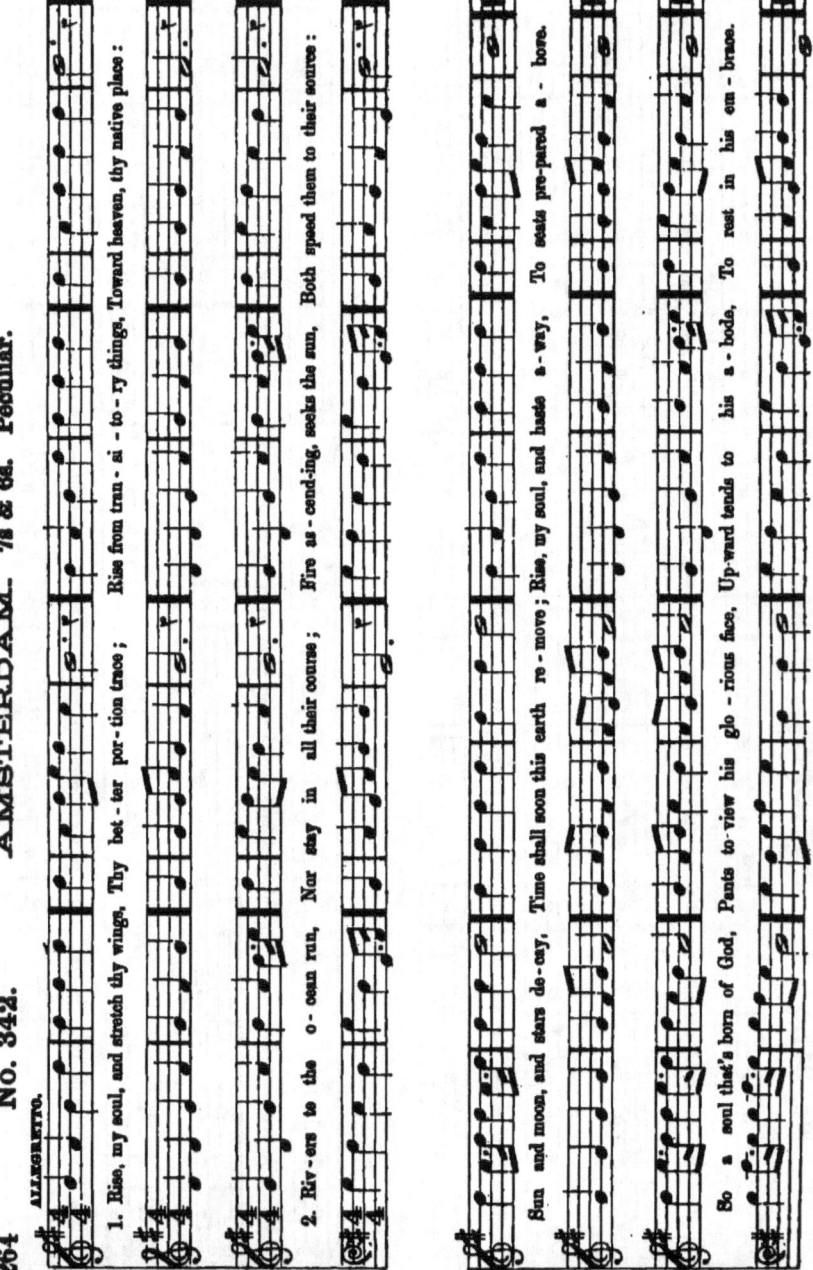

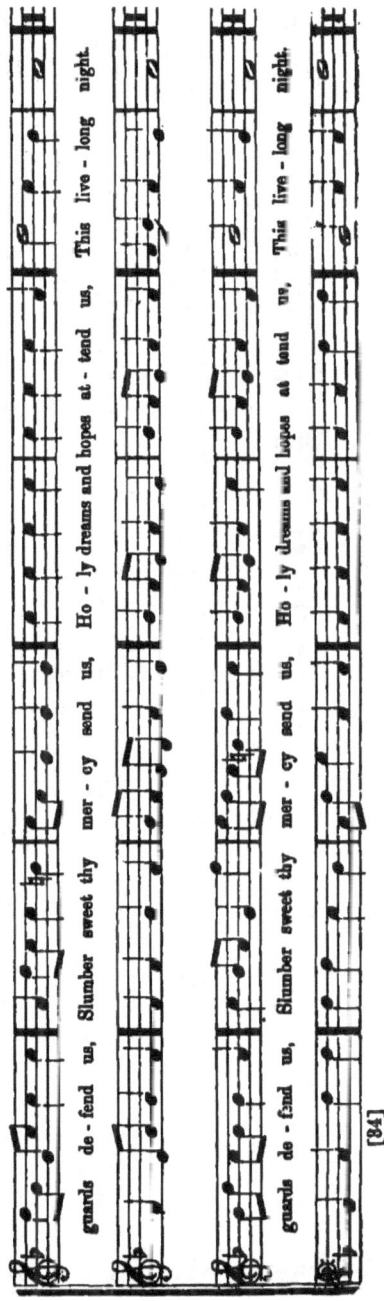

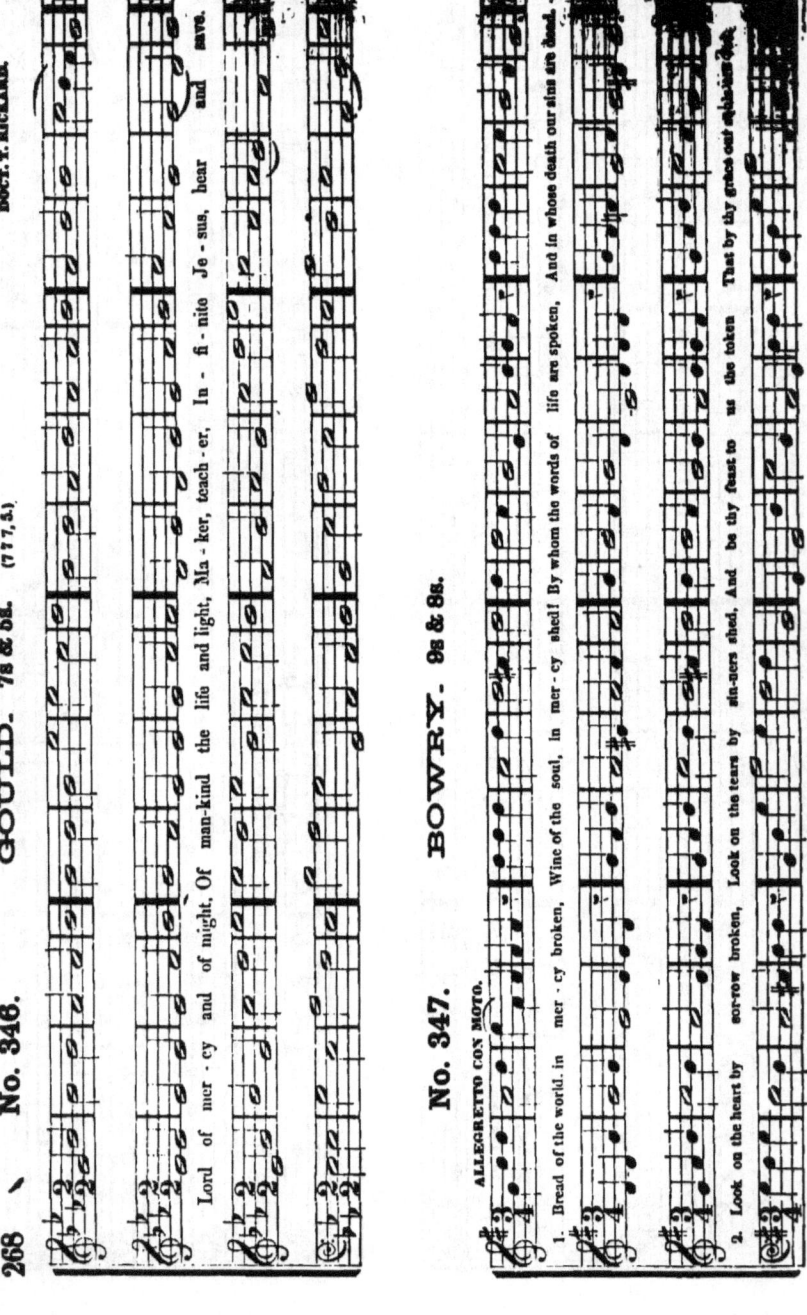

No. 348. CAMDEN. 8s & 8s 6 LINES 269

1. We come, our hearts with glad-ness glow-ing, Thee, Lord of har-vest to a - dore, For gar-ners filled to o - ver-flow - ing
2. Our praise for this a - bund-ant bless - ing With fa - vor, gracious Fa - ther, here, More deep-ly on our minds im - press - ing
3. With treasured heaps and plenteous store; To thank thee that thy Fa - ther's hand Has blest a - new our hap - py land.
4. Thy mer-cies, each suc - ces - sive year, That so our thank-ful praise may be A life de - vot - ed all to thee.

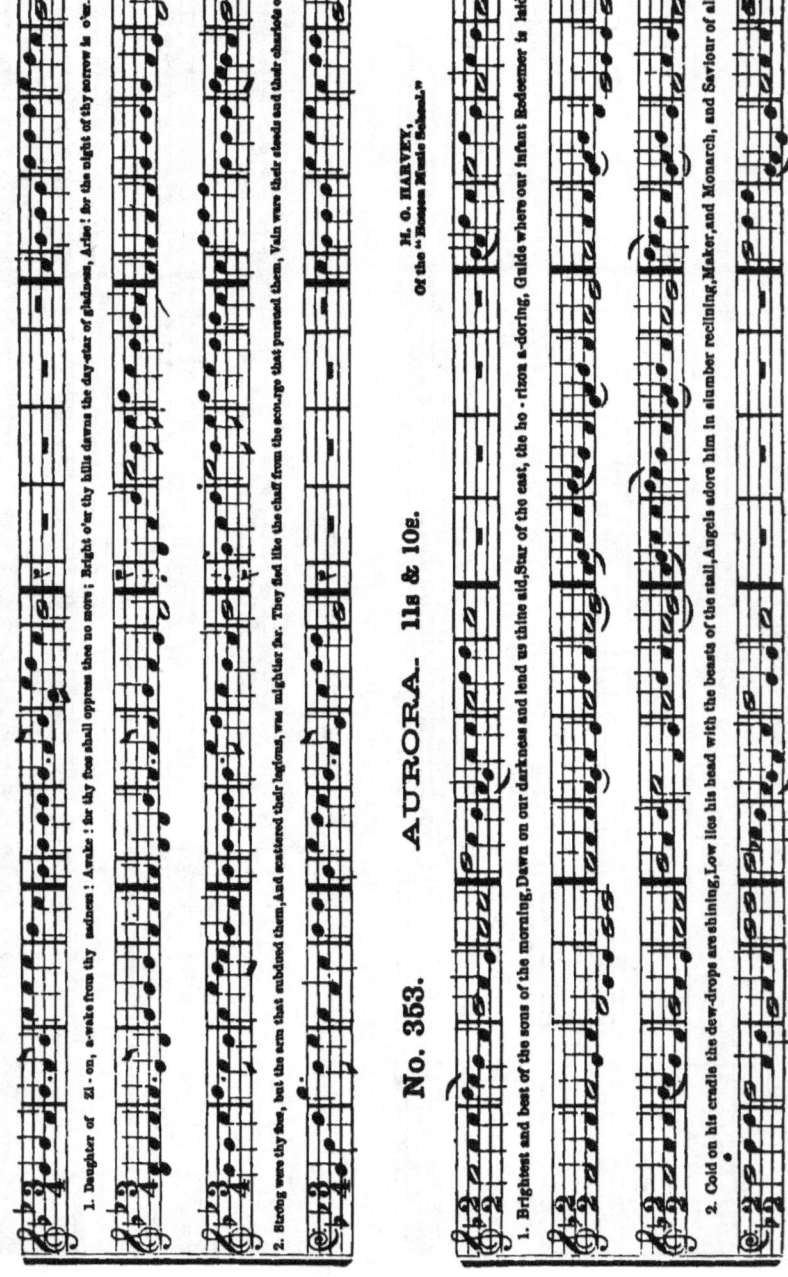

274 No. 355. LOCKPORT. 11s.

ANDANTE.

1. I would not live alway; I ask not to stay, Where storm after storm rises dark o'er the way;
2. I would not live alway; no, welcome the tomb, Since Jesus has lain there, I dread not its gloom;

I would not live alway, thus fettered by sin, Temptation without, and corruption within;
There sweet be my rest, till he bid me arise, To hail him in triumph descending the

No. 356. RESIGNATION. 11s. J. A. GOULD. 275

1. I would not live al-way; I ask not to stay, Where storm af-ter storm ris-es dark o'er the way;

2. I would not live al-way; no, wel-come the tomb, Since Je-sus has been there, I dread not its gloom;

I would not live al-way, thus fet-tered by sin, Temp-ta-tion with-out, and cor-rup-tion with-in.

There sweet be my rest till he bid me a-rise, To hail him in tri-umph de-scend-ing the skies.

278   No. 360.   MAGNIFICAT. 10s, 11s & 12s.
MAY BE USED AS A SHORT ANTHEM.

ALLEGRO CON MAESTOSO.

1. Lift your glad voi-ces in tri-umph on high, For Je-sus hath ris-en, and man shall not die; Vain were the ter-rors that gather'd a-round him, and short the do-min-ion of death and the grave; He burst from the fetters of darkness that bound him, Respiendent in

2. Glo-ry to God, in full anthems of joy; The be-ing he gave us death can-not de-stroy: Sad were the life we may part with to-mor-row, If tears were our birthright, and death were our end; But Je-sus hath cheer'd the dark valley of sorrow, And bright

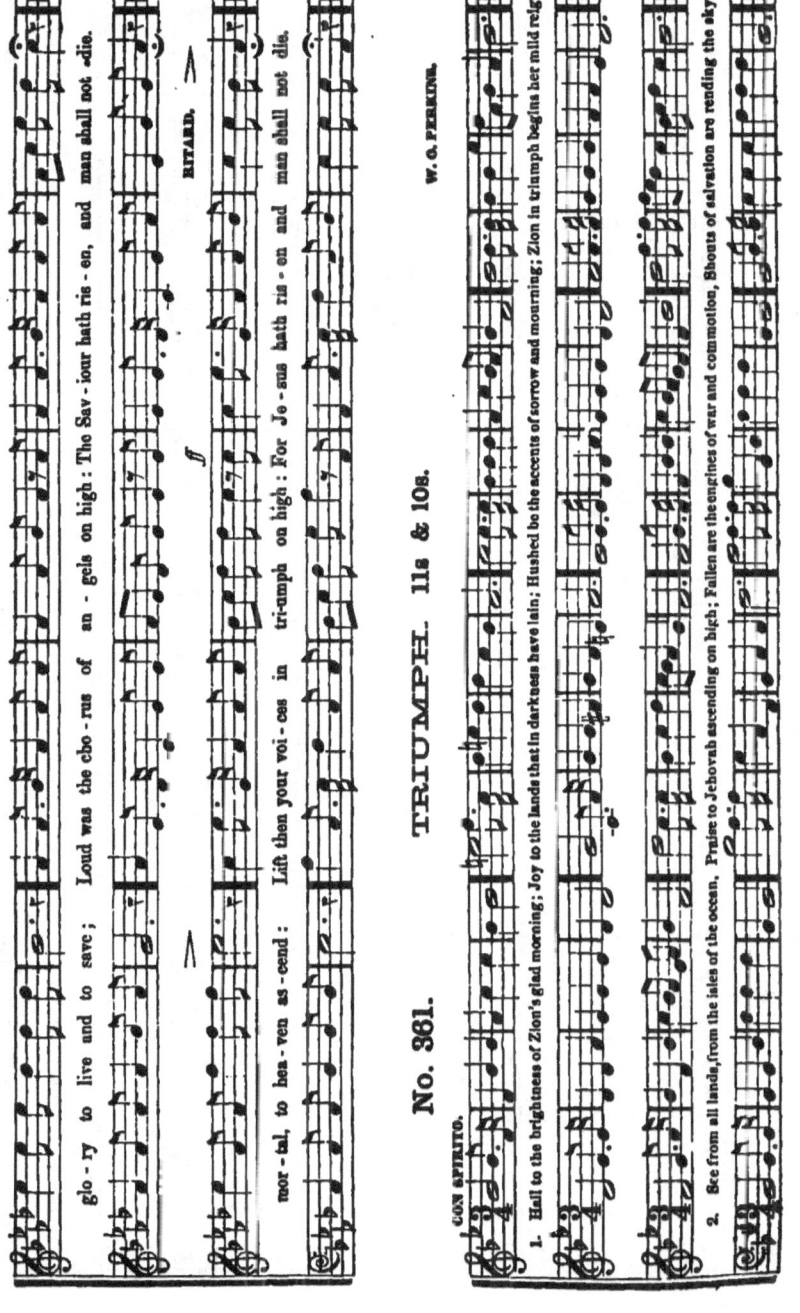

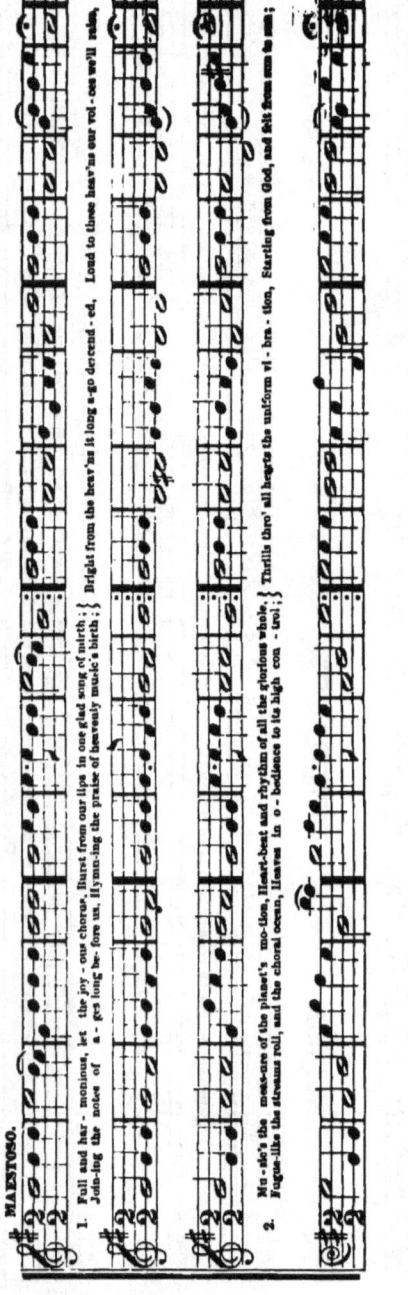
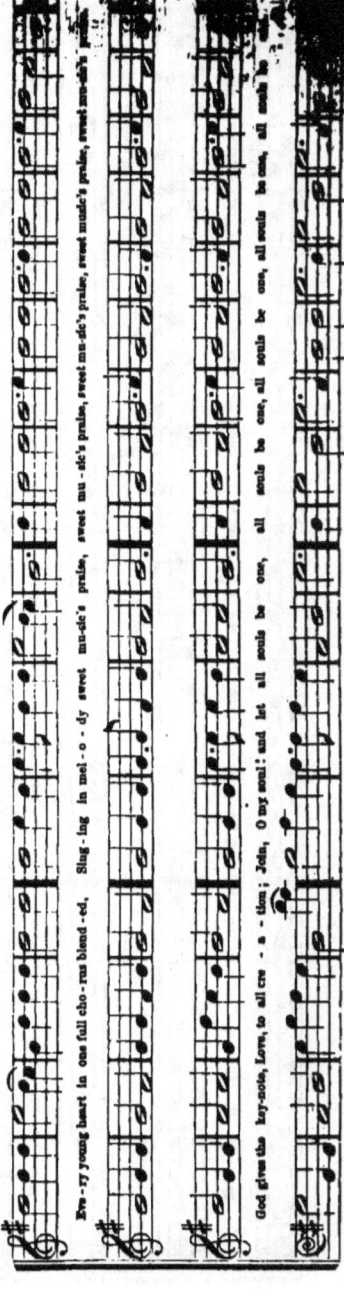

No. 364.   DEVOTION.   SENTENCE. 12s, 11s & 6s.

Cantabile.

Solo. Soprano or Tenor.

1. As down in the sun-less re-treats of the o-cean, Sweet flow-ers are spring-ing no mor-tal can see, So deep in my
2. As still to the star of its wor-ship, though cloud-ed, The nee-dle points faith-ful-ly o'er the dim sea, So, dark as I

heart, the still prayer of de-vo-tion, Unheard by the world, rises, silent, to thee, My God! si-lent to thee, Pure, warm, si-lent to thee.
roam, thro' this win-try world, shrouded, The hope of my spirit turns, trembling, to thee, My God! trembling, to thee— True, fond, trembling, to thee.

No. 365. PSALM LXXXII. "God standeth in the congregation." 283

1 God standeth in the congregation of } the mighty; he judgeth a- } mong the gods.
  Defend the poor and fatherless: do } justice to the af- } flicted and needy:
  How long will ye judge unjustly, and accept the persons of the wicked;
  Deliver the poor and needy: rid them out of the hand ...... of the wicked.

3 They know not, neither will they understand; } they walk on in darkness: all the foundations } out of course.
  of the earth are
  But ye shall die like men, and fall like one } of the princes.
  I have said, Ye are gods; and all of you are children of the Most...... High.
  Arise, O God, judge the earth for her - it- all ...... nations. A - men.
  thou shalt in-

No. 366. HYMN CHANT. "Lowly and Solemn."

1 Lowly and solemn be Thy children's cry to thee, Father di - vine!
  A hymn of suppliant breath,
  Owning that life and death A- like are thine.

2 O Father, in that hour When earth all succoring power Shall his - a - vow,
  When spear and shield and crown In faintness are cast down, Sus- tain us thou!

3 By him who bowed to take The death- cup for our sake, The thorn, the rod,
  From whom the last dismay Was not to pass away, Aid us, O God!

4 Tremblers beside the grave, We call on thee to save, Father di - vine!
  Hear, hear our suppliant breath, Keep us in life and death, Thine, only thine. A - men.

284   No. 367. HYMN CHANT. "There is an hour of peaceful rest." W. O. PERKINS.

1. There is an hour of peaceful rest, To mourning wanderers given; There is a joy for souls distressed, A balm for every wounded breast; 'Tis found a—— lone in heaven.
2. There is a home for weary souls By sin and sorrow driven, When tossed on life's tempestuous shoals, Where storms arise, and o - cean rolls, And all is—— drear but heaven.
3. There faith lifts up the tearless eye, The heart no long - er riven, And views the tempest passing by, See evening shadows quick - ly fly, And all se——rene in heaven. A - men.

No. 368.   THE LORD'S PRAYER.

1. Our Father who art in heaven, hallowed be thy name, Thy kingdom come, thy will be done in—— earth as it is in heaven.
2. Give us this day our················ dai - ly bread, And forgive us our trespasses as we forgive·· those who trespass a - gainst us.
3. And lead us not into temptation, but de - liver·· us from evil, For thine is the kingdom, and the power, and the glory, for - ever and ever. A - men.

285

No. 369. HYMN CHANT. "Jews were wrought."

1. Jews were wrought to cruel madness, Christians fled in fear and sadness, Mary stood the ...... cross be - side.
2. At its foot her foot she ...... planted, By the dreadful scene ...... undaunted, Till the gentle ...... suf - ferer died;
3. Poets oft have sung her ...... story, Painters decked her brow with glory, Priests her name ...... have dei - fied;

4. But no worship, song, or ...... glory, Touches like that simple ...... story, "Mary stood the ...... cross be - side."
5. And when under fierce ...... oppression, Goodness suffers like transgression, Christ again is ...... cru - ci - fied.
6. But if love be there; true - hearted, By no grief or terror ...... parted, Mary stands the ...... cross be - side.

No. 370. HYMN CHANT. "Thy will be done."

1. Thy will be done! In de - vious way The hurrying stream of life may run; Yet still our grateful hearts shall } say, Thy will be done!
2. Thy will be done! If o'er us shine A gladdening and a pros-perous sun, This prayer shall make it more di- } vine: Thy will be done!
3. Thy will be done! { shroud - ed o'er Our path with gloom, com - fort, one, Is ours, — to breathe, } dore, Thy will be done! A - men.
   { Though while we a- }

No. 371. HYMN CHANT. 11s & 6s. "Almighty One."

1. Almighty One! I bend in dust before thee; / Even so veiled cherubs bend; In calm and still devotion I adore thee, All-wise, all-present Friend!
2. Thou Power sublime! whose throne is firmly seated On stars and glowing suns; O, could I praise thee,—could my soul, elated, Waft thee seraphic tones,—

3. Eternity! Eternity! how solemn, How terrible the...... sound! Here, leaning on thy promises,—a column Of strength, I may be found,

Thou to the earth its emerald robes has given, Or curtained it in snow; And the bright sun, and the soft moon in heaven, Before thy presence bow.

Had I the lyres of angels,—could I bring thee An offering worthy thee,— In what bright notes of glory would I sing thee, Blest notes of ecstasy! A - men!

O, let my heart be ever thine, while beating, As when t'will cease to beat! Be thou my portion, till that awful meeting When I my God shall greet! A - men!

No. 372. HYMN CHANT. "From the recesses." 287

1. From the recesses of a lowly spirit, Our humble prayer ascends; O Father! bear it,
2. We see thy hand; it leads us, it supports us: We hear thy voice; it counsels, and it courts us:
3. O, bow long suffering, Lord! but thou dedest, To win with love the wandering; thou invitest,

4. Father and Saviour! plant with in each bosom The seeds of holiness, and bid them blossom
5. Then place them in thine ever lasting gardens, Where angels walk, and seraphs are the wardens;

Upsoaring on the wings of awe and meekness; For - give its weakness!
And then we turn away; and still thy kindness For - gives our blindness. A - men, A - men!
By smiles of mercy, not by frowns or terrors, Man from his errors.

In fragrance and in beauty bright and vernal, And spring e - ternal.
Where every flower escaped through death's dark portal, De - comes im - mortal. A - men, A - men!

288

No. 373. HYMN CHANT. 6, 10 & 4. "Saviour and dearest Friend."

1. Saviour and dearest friend, Who dying groaned for .... me; Thoughtless of self, all weakness do I bend At tho't of .... thee.
2. O, didst thou weep my tears? Then will I weep no .... more; The anguish I have felt for bitter years I've pierced thee be - fore.
3. My sorrows hast thou borne, Sinless and .... Crucified! Trembling, I thank thee, and no more will mourn, Since thou last died.

4. Bowing unto the storm That beats upon my .... head, I see thy pitying, perfect-fashioned form Suffering in - stead. A - men.
5. Thine is the heart thus bought; I cannot call it .... mine; Perish ambition! be each hope, each tho't, Henceforth di - vine!

No. 374. HYMN CHANT. "Life is onward."

1. Life is onward, use it With a forward aim; wel - fare claim. Look not to another To perform {Keep your warm hand still
   Toil is heavenly, choose it And its your will, Let not your own brother not for them.
2. Life is onward, try it, Ere the day is lost; ev - er cost. If the world should offer Every pre- Change it
   It hath virtue, buy it At what- cious gem, Look not at the scoffer,

3. Life is onward, heed it In each varied hap - pi - ness. His bright pinion o'er you Time waves {Her pro - phet - ic strain.
   dress, Your own act can speed it On to not in vain, If Hope chants before you
4. Life is onward, prize it In sunshine and hum-blest form. Hope and Joy together, Standing at Beck-on on the soul. A - men.
   in storm; O, do not despise it In its the goal, Through life's darkest weather,

290   No. 376.   SENTENCE. "Blessed is he."   L. H. SOUTHARD.

MODERATO.

Blessed is he that con-sid-er-eth the poor, Blessed is he that con-sid-er-eth the poor, The Lord will de-liv-er him in time of trouble,

Blessed is he that con-sid-er-eth the poor, Blessed is he that con-sid-er-eth the poor, The Lord will de-liv-er him in time of trouble,

The Lord will preserve him and keep him a-live; And be shall be blessed up-on earth, And he shall be blessed up-on earth.

The Lord will preserve him and keep him a-live; And he shall be blessed up-on earth, And he shall be blessed up-on earth.

No. 377. SENTENCE. "Blessed are the pure in heart."

No. 378. SENTENCE. "Nearer to Thee."

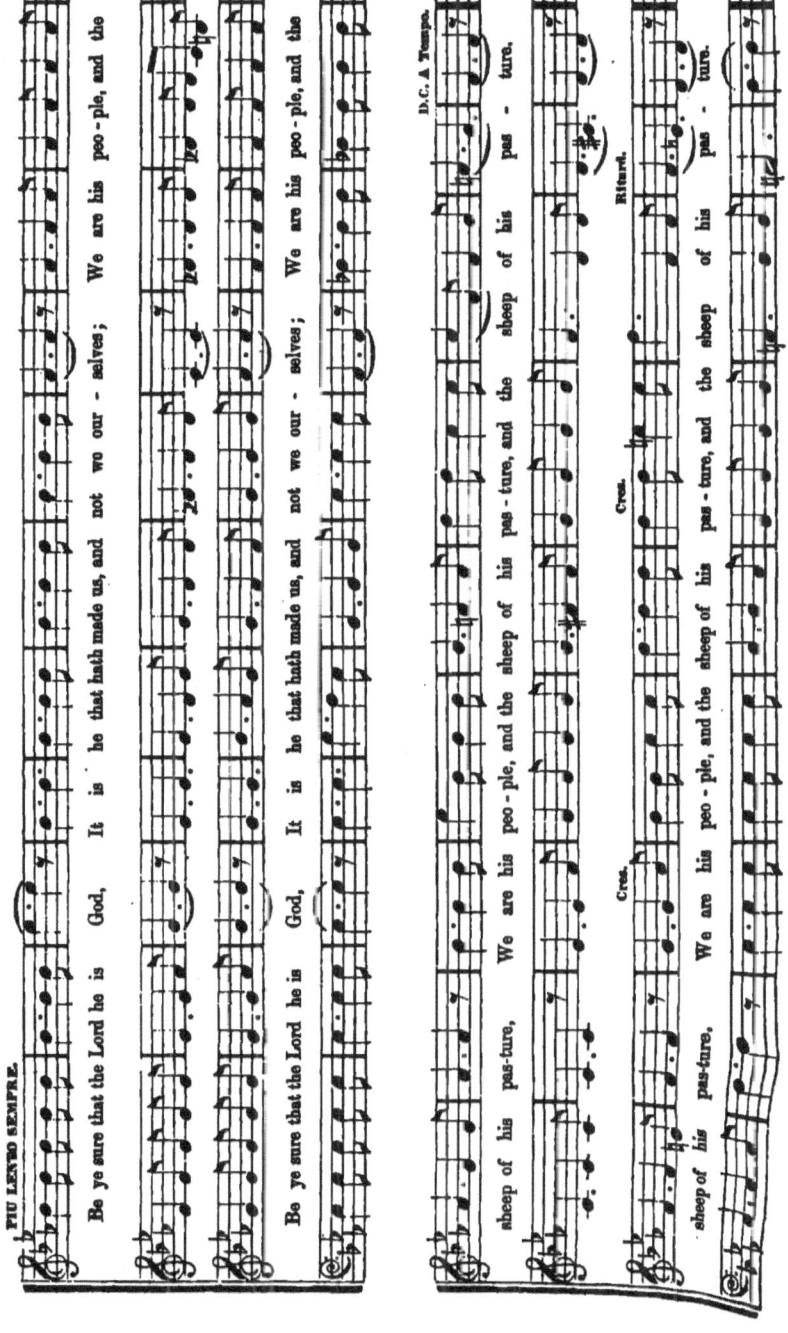

295

CONCLUDED.

NO. 381. SENTENCE. "Grant, we beseech thee."

No. 883.   SENTENCE.   "See, the Conquering Hero."   HANDEL.   297

See, the conqu'ring he - - ro come, Sound the trumpet, beat......the drum, Sports......prepare, the lau - rel bring,

See, the conqu'ring he - - ro come, Sound the trumpet, beat...... the drum, Sports.... prepare, the lau - rel bring,

Songs of tri - umph to him sing, See, the conqu'ring he - - ro come, Sound the trumpet, beat the drum.

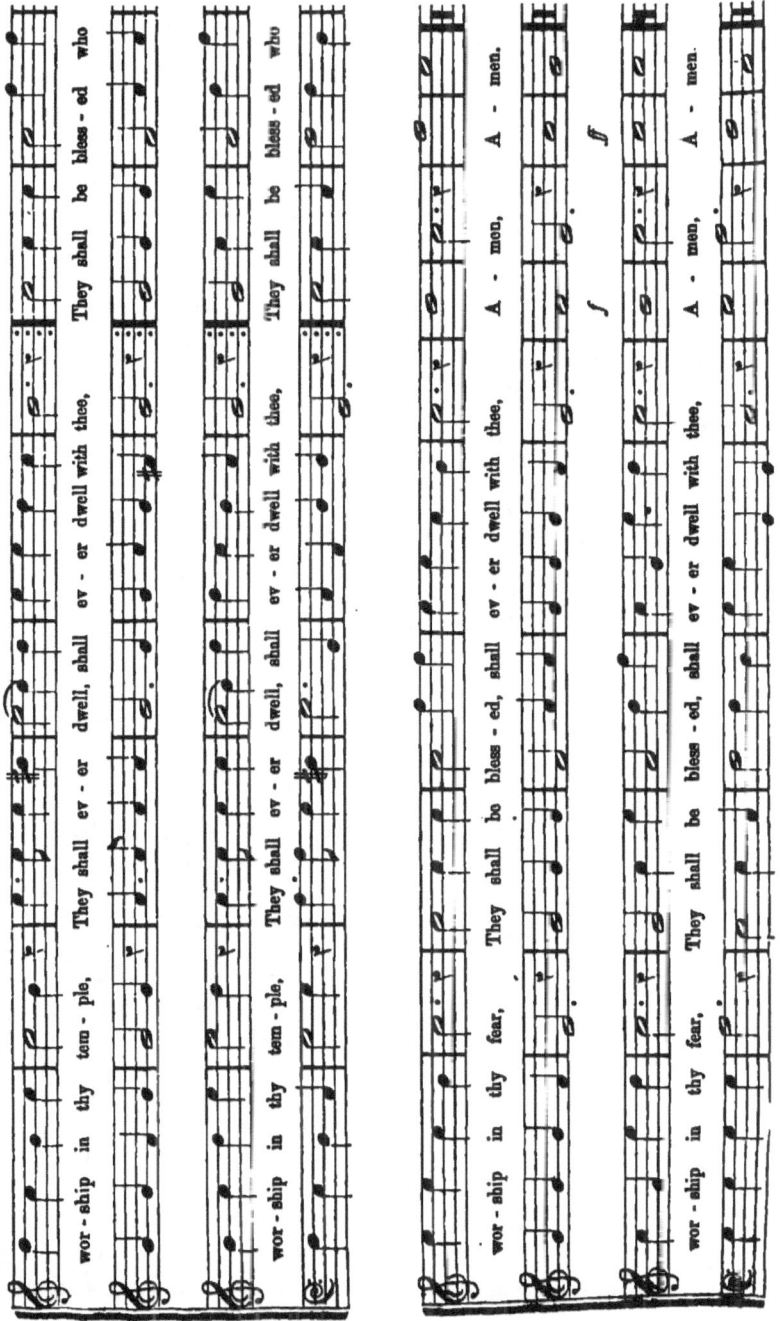

No. 386. SENTENCE. "Seek ye the Lord."

CON ESPRESSIONE.

Seek ye the Lord, Seek ye the Lord while he may be found, And call up-on him while he is near, while he is near, Call up-on him while he is near, Call up-on him while he is near.

CONCLUDED.

No. 388. SENTENCE. "Return, my soul."

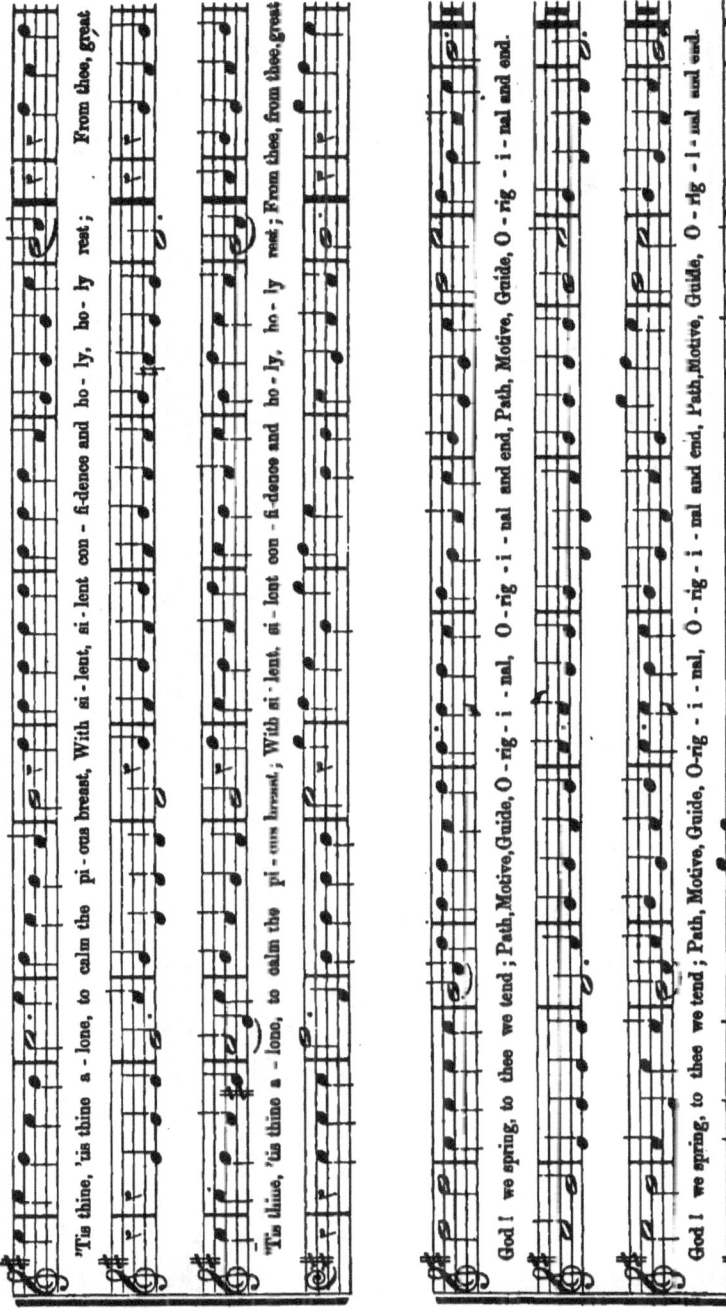

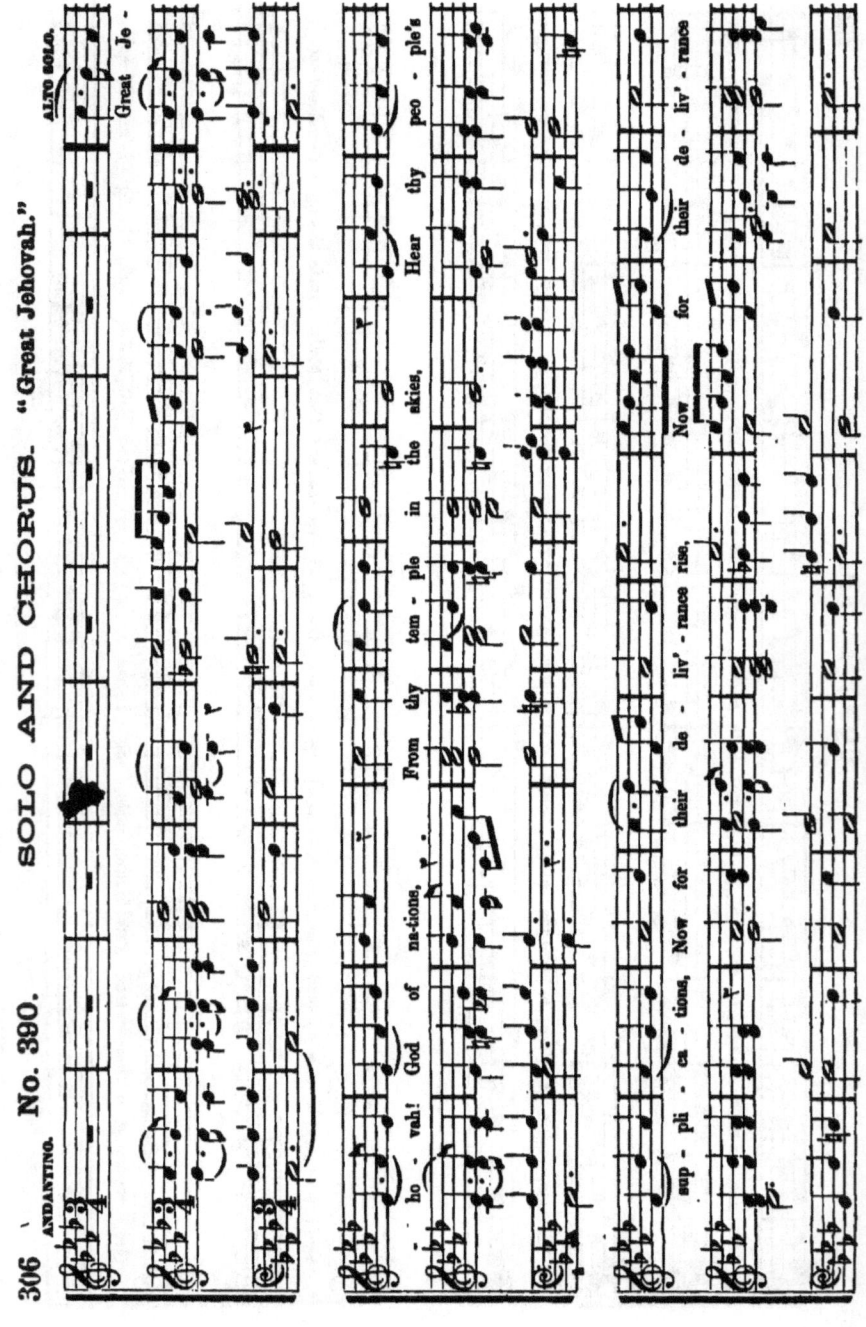

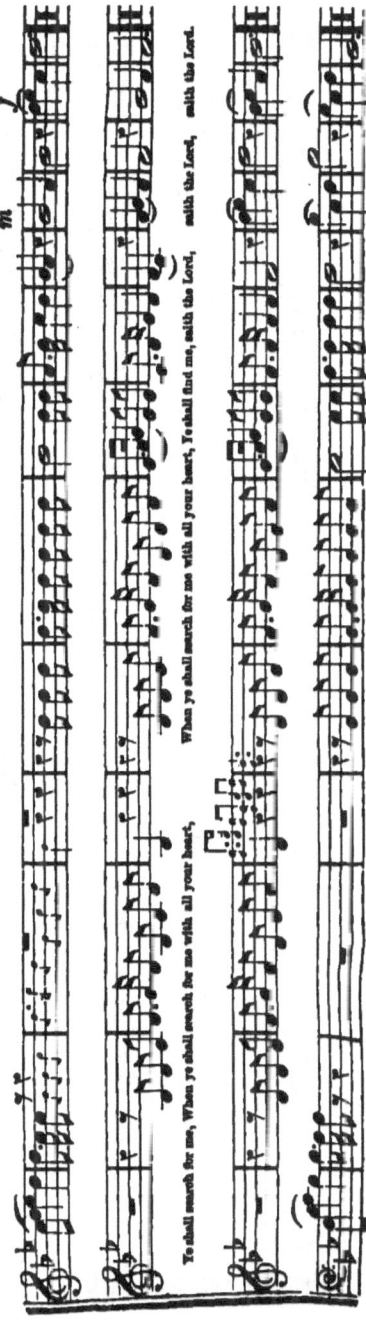

from thee stray, Keep me in the per - fect way, Fill my soul with joy di - vine, Keep me, Lord, for - ev - er thine.
Fill my soul with joy di - vine, Keep me, Lord, for - ev - er thine, Keep me, Lord, for - ev - er thine.
Fill my soul with joy di - vine, Keep me, Lord, for - ev - er thine, Keep me, Lord, for - ev - er thine.

312 No. 393. SENTENCE. "God of Israel" Arranged from A. MINK.

RELIGIOSO.

Solo. Soprano.

God of Is - rael, we a - dore thee, Keep us safe - ly through the day.

CORO.

God of Is - rael, we a - dore thee, Keep us safe - ly through the day. God of Is - rael, we a - dore thee, Keep us safe-ly

No. 396. SENTENCE. "O, how lovely is Zion." W. O. PERKINS.

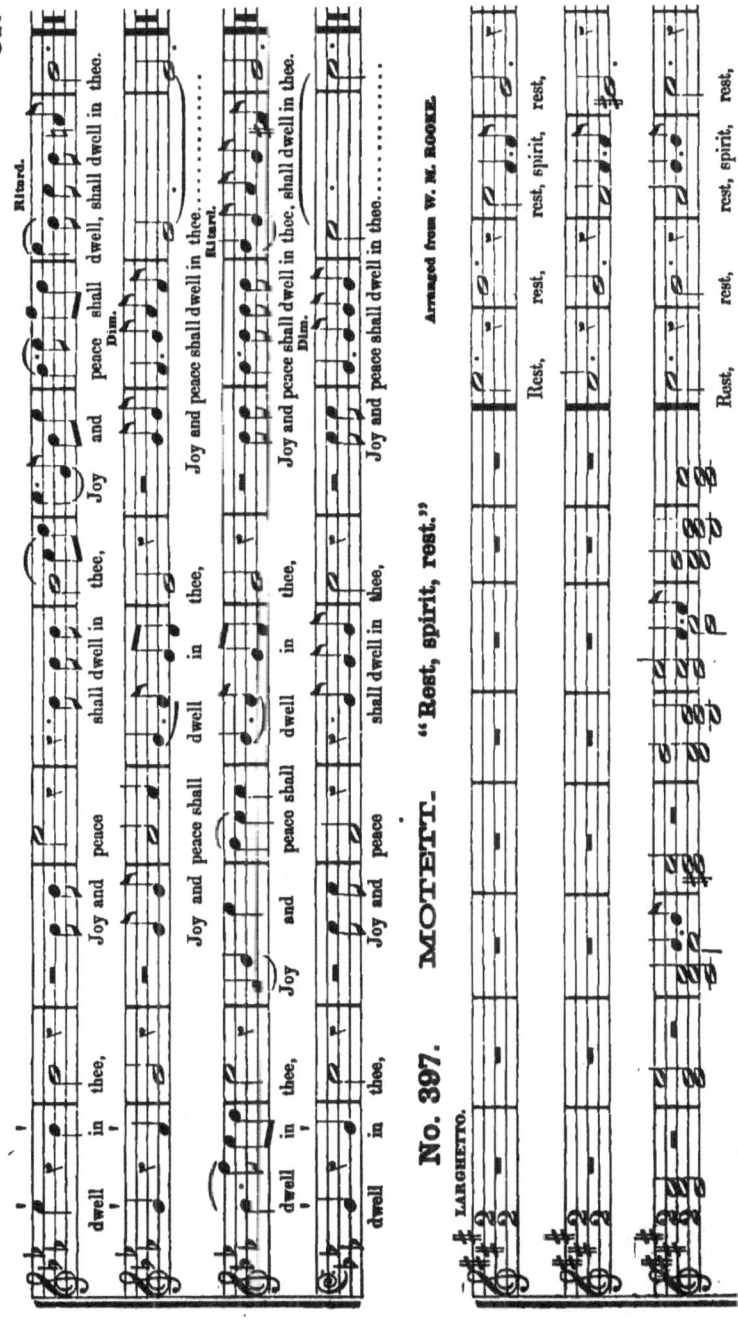

320 No. 398. DEAD MARCH. "Unveil thy bosom." From the Oratorio of "Saul," by HANDEL.

LARGHETTO.

1. Un-veil thy bo-som, faith-ful tomb; Take this new treas-ure to thy trust, And give these sa-cred rel-ics room
2. Nor pain, nor grief, nor anx-ious fear, In-vade thy bounds: no mor-tal woes, Can reach the peace-ful sleep-er here,

3. So Je-sus slept; God's dy-ing Son, Passed thro' the grave, and bless the bed; Rest here, blest saint, till from his throne

Repeat for 3d and 2d verses.

To slum-ber in the si-lent dust, To slum-ber in the si-lent dust.
While an-gels watch the soft re-pose; Nor pain, nor grief, nor mor-tal woes, While an-gels watch the soft re-pose.

The morn-ing break, and pierce the shade; Rest here, blest saint, till from his throne, The morn-ing break, and pierce the shade

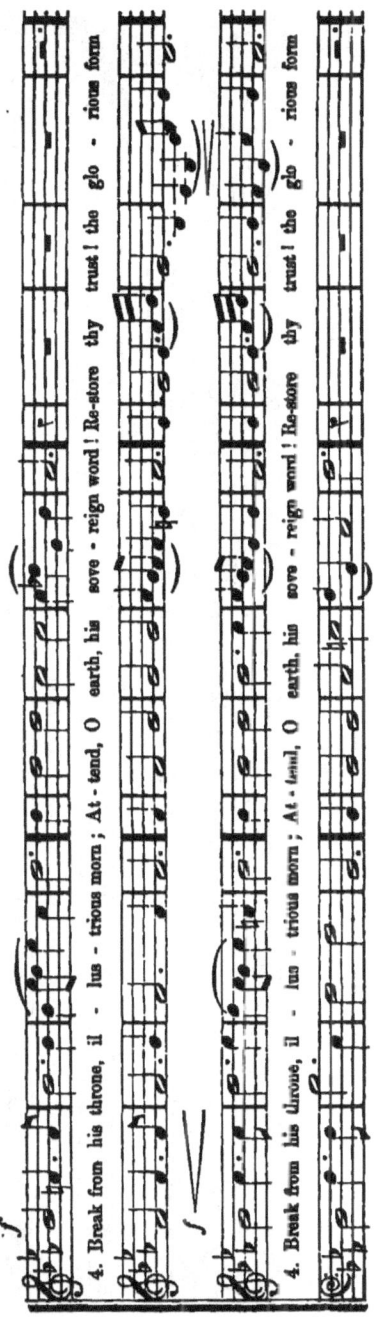

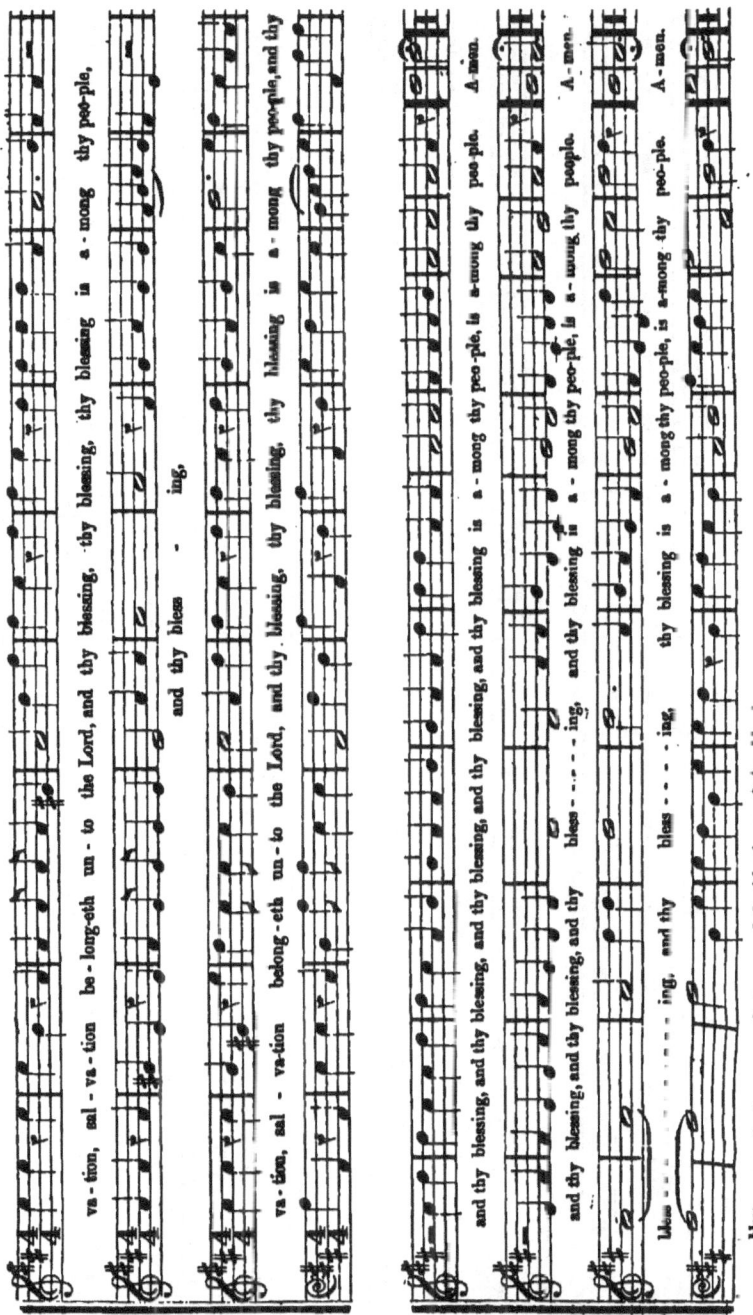

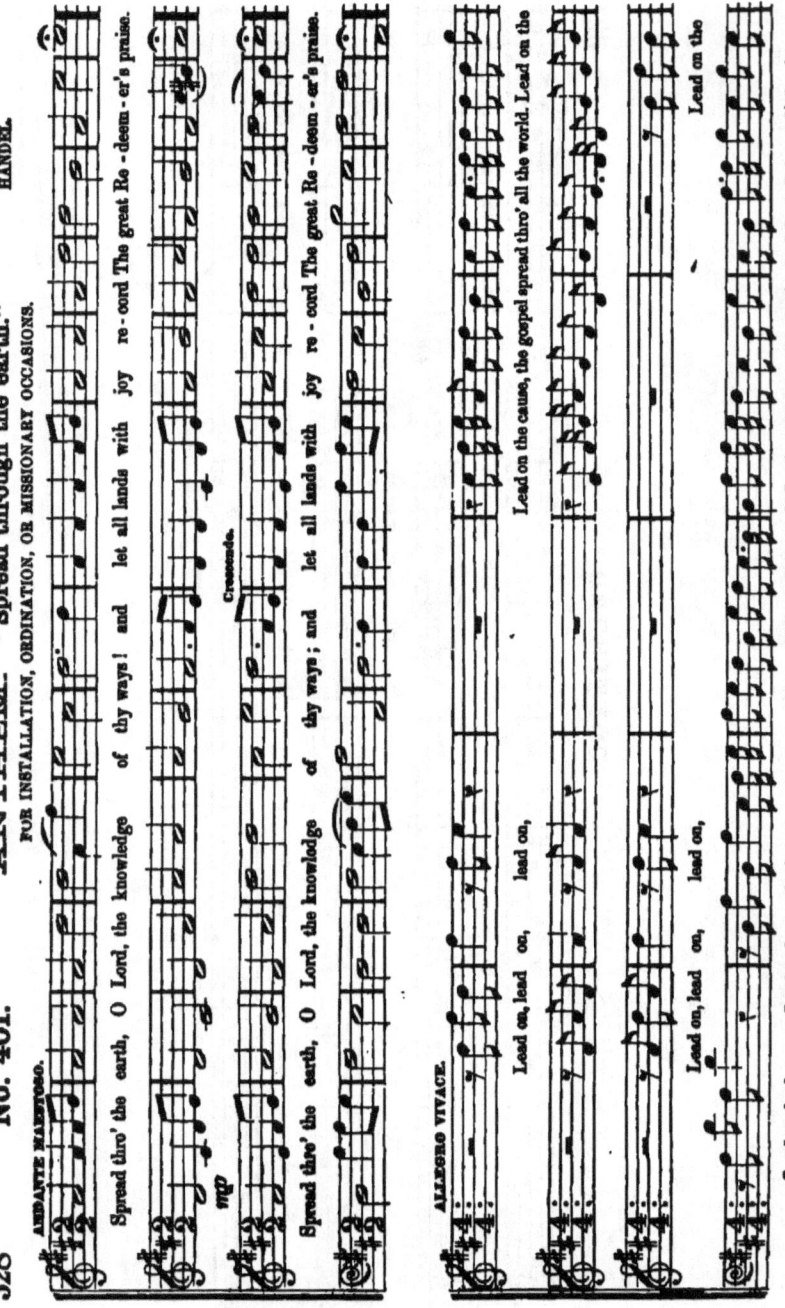

Lead on the cause, the gos - pel spread thro' all the world. Lead on, lead on, lead on the cause, Lead on, the gos - pel
spread thro' all the world, the gos - pel spread thro' all the world,
spread thro' all the world, thro' all the world. Lead on, lead on, lead on the cause. Lead on, the gos - pel
Lead on the cause, the gos - pel spread thro' all the world.
CODA, ADAGIO.
spread thro' all the world, Lead on the cause, Lead on the cause, The gos-pel spread thro' all the world.
A - men. A - men.
spread thro' all the word, Lead on the cause, Lead on the cause, The gos-pel spread thro' all the world.
A - men. A - men.

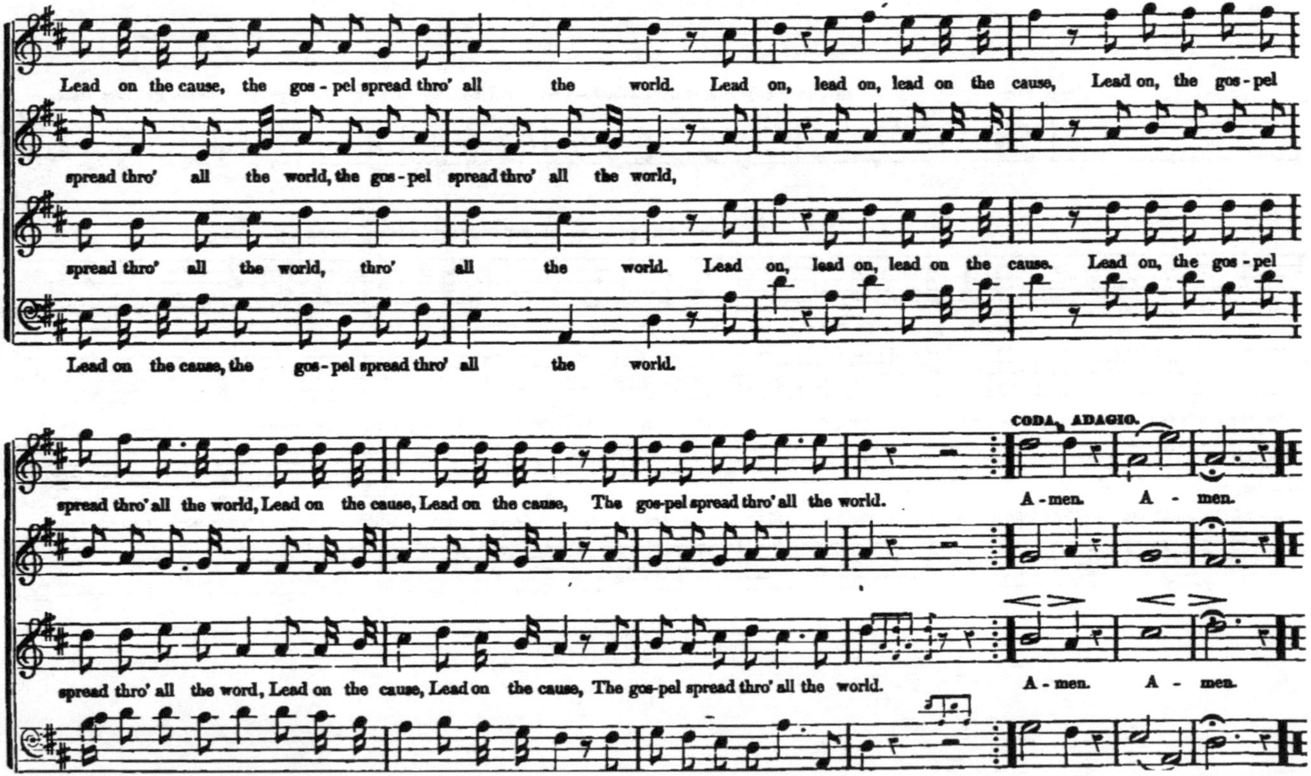

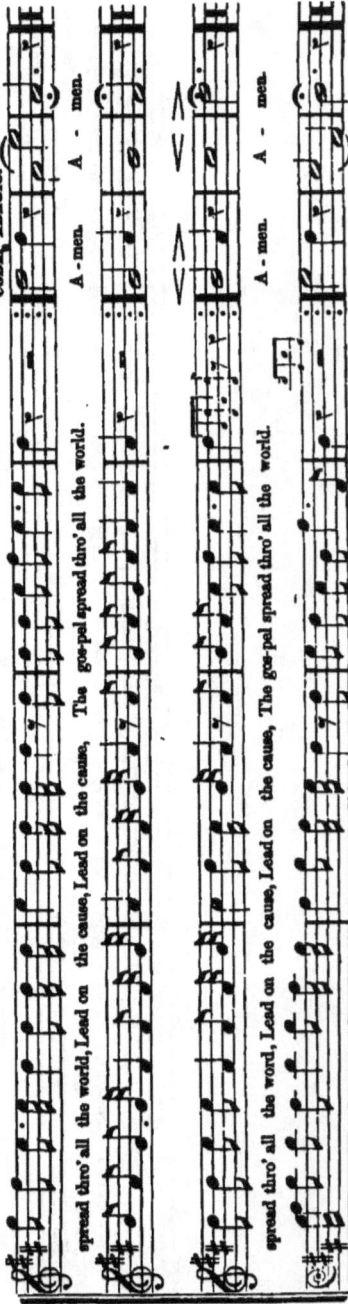

No. 402. SENTENCE. "Teach me, O Lord." NEUKOMM. 331

332. CONTINUED.

Gods! lead me, O Lord! lead me, O Lord! lead me, lead me in - - - to the

God! lead me, O Lord! lead me, O Lord! lead me in - to the paths, in-to

God! lead me, O Lord! lead me, O Lord, lead me

paths of truth: lead me in - to the paths,

paths, the paths of truth: lead me, O Lord! lead me, lead me in - to the paths,

paths of truth: lead me, O Lord! lead me in - to the paths,

in-to the paths of truth:

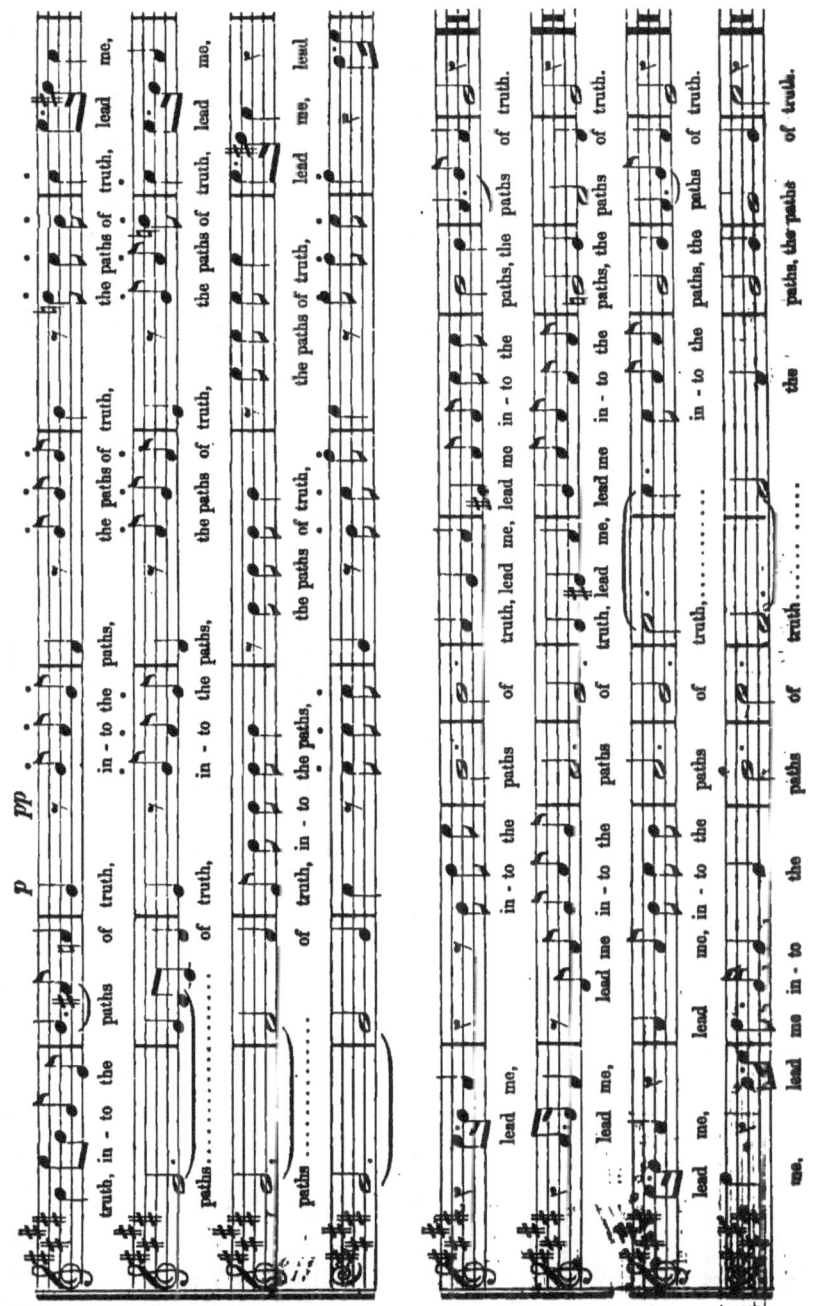

335

CONTINUED

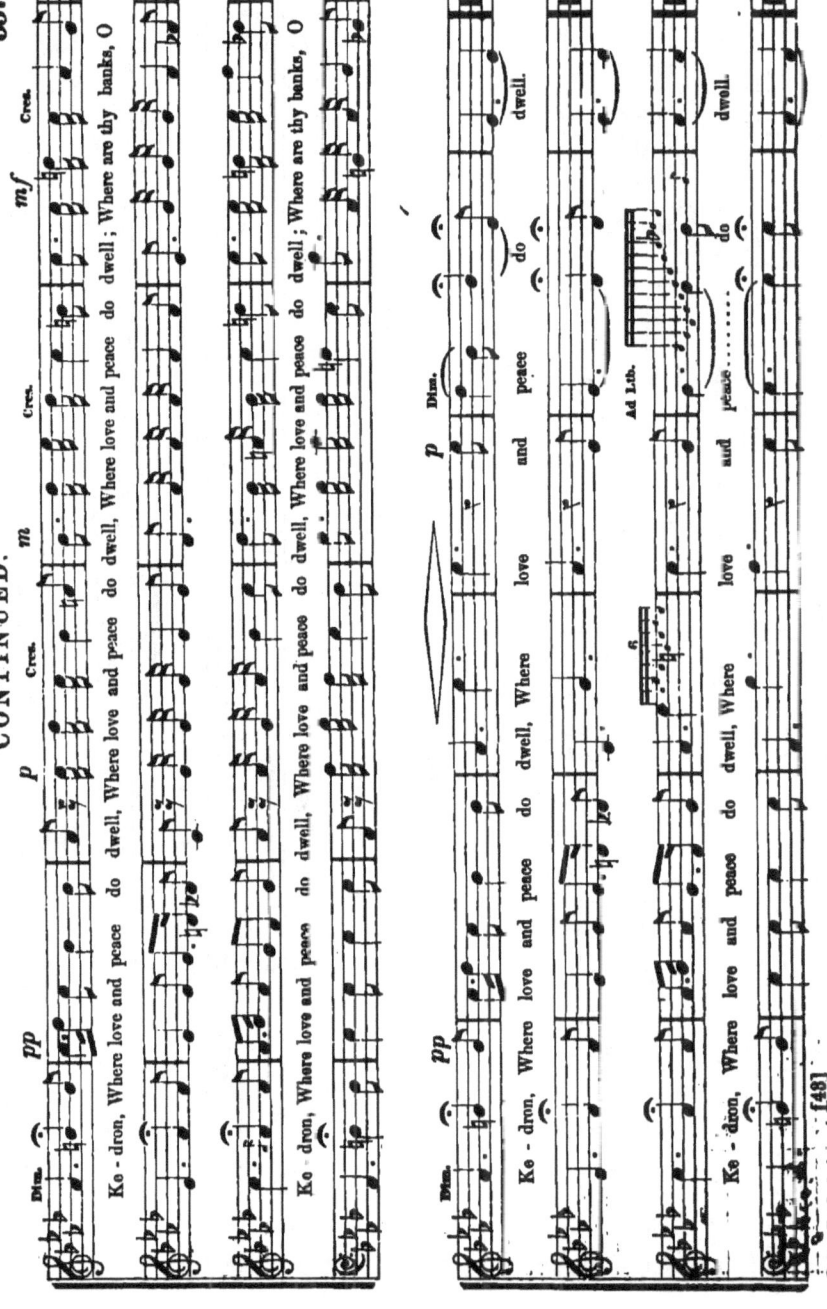

No. 406. ANTHEM. "Mighty Jehovah." 341

Arranged from BELLINI.

ALLEGRO MAESTOSO.

Migh-ty Je-ho-vah! ac-cept our prais-es; God, our Father, O hear thy children,

Migh-ty Je-ho-vah! ac-cept our prais-es; God our Fa-ther, O hear thy chil-dren,

Un-to thee we of-fer praise, Un-to thee we of-fer praise, Un-to thee we of-fer praise,

Un-to thee we of-fer praise, Un-to thee we of-fer praise, Unto thee we of-fer praise,

CONTINUED.

342

CONTINUED.

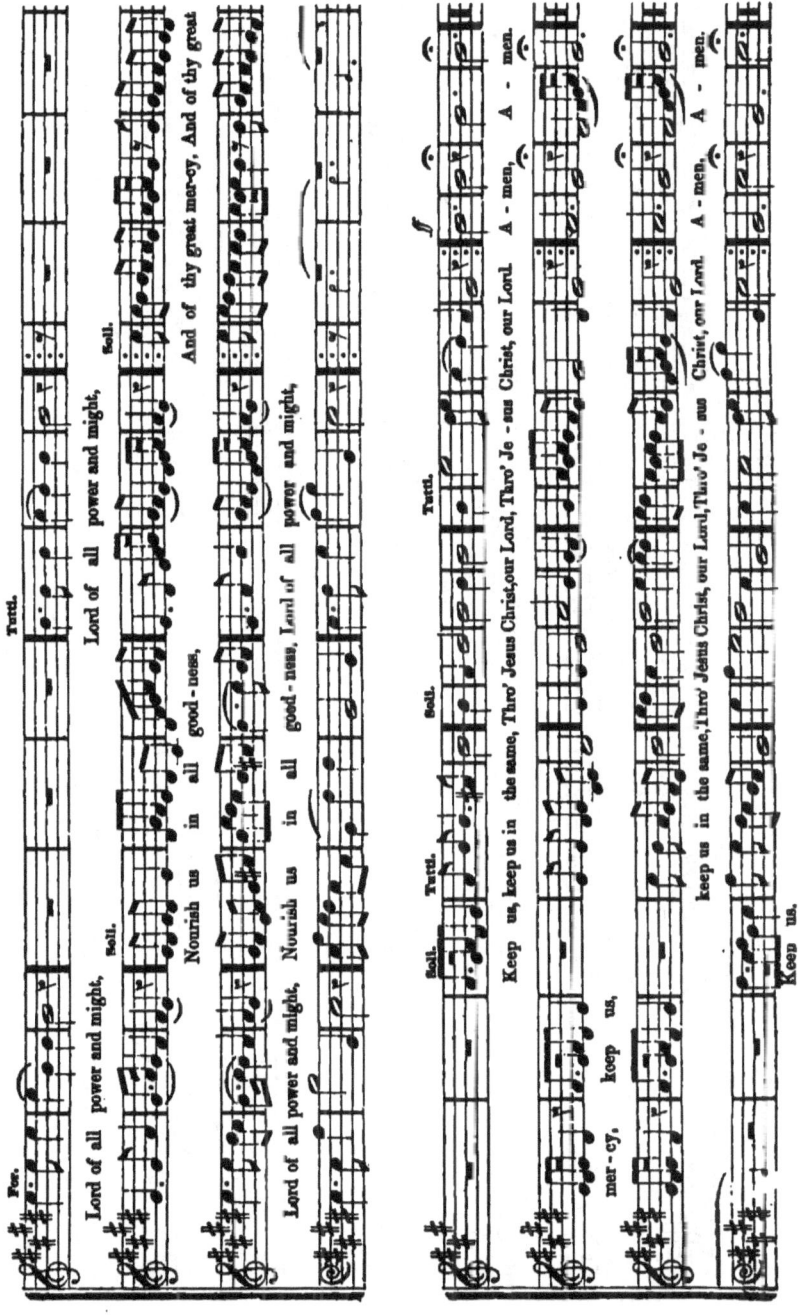

No 410. ANTHEM. "Serve ye the Mighty Lord."

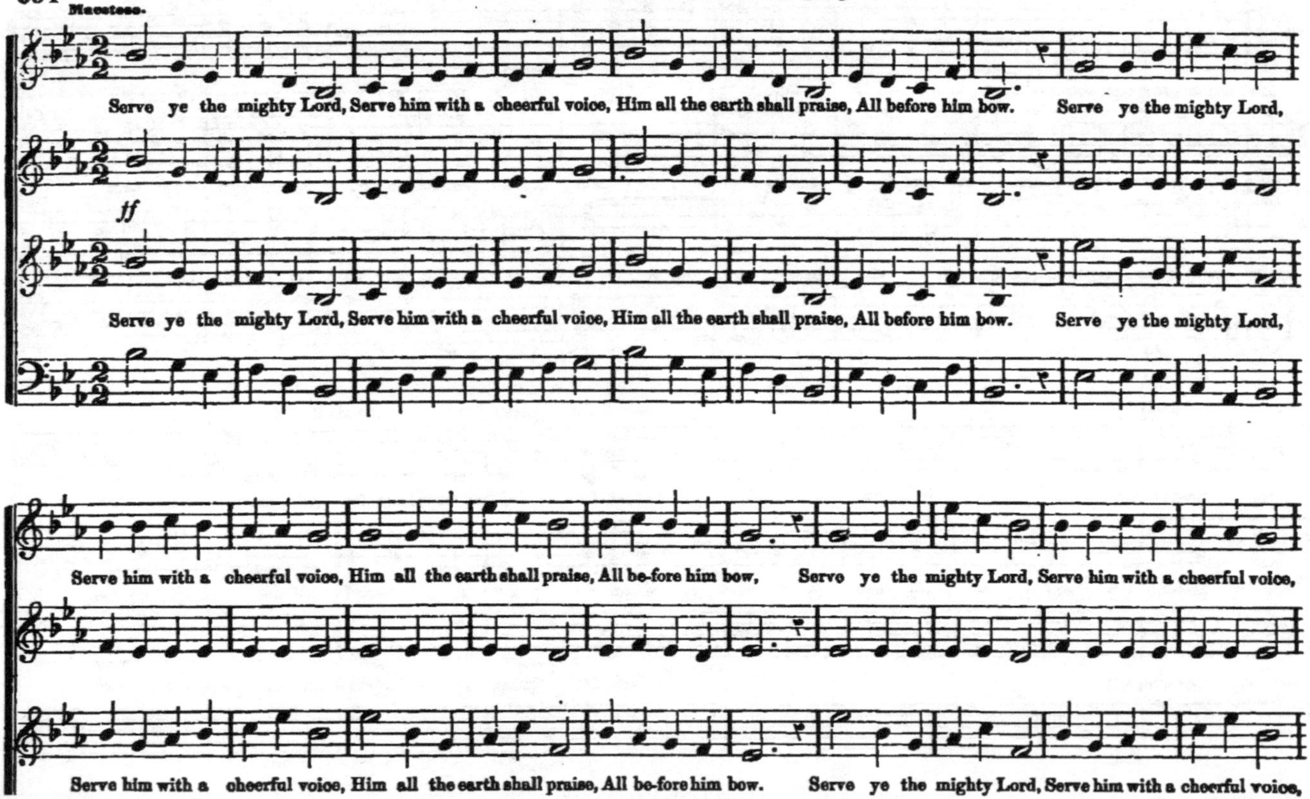

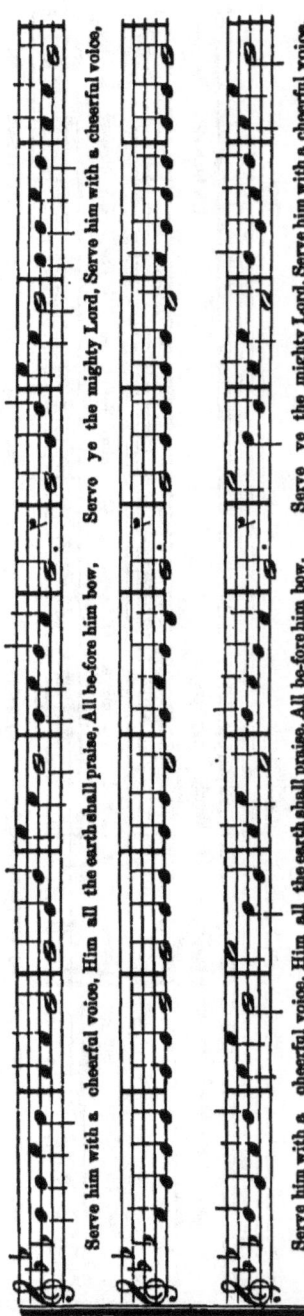

CONTINUED.

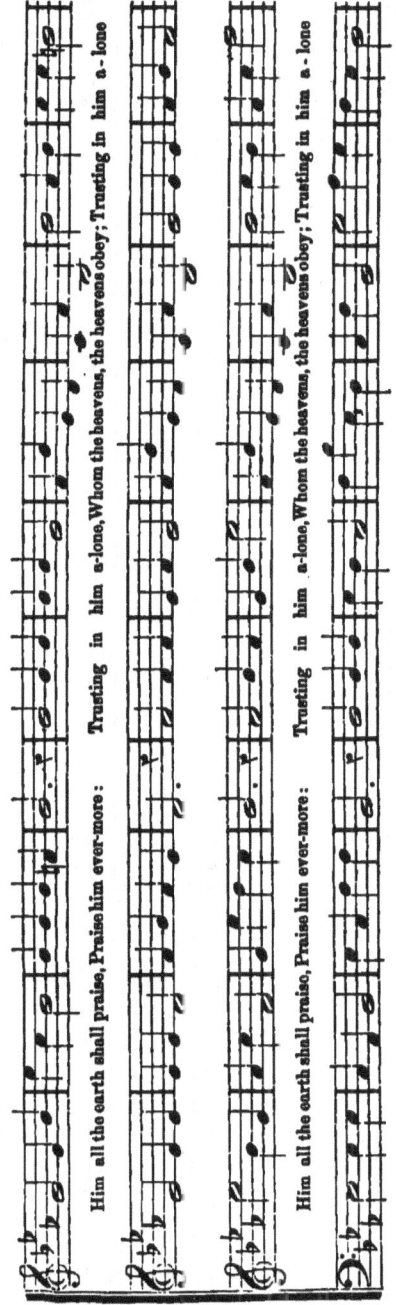

CONCLUDED.

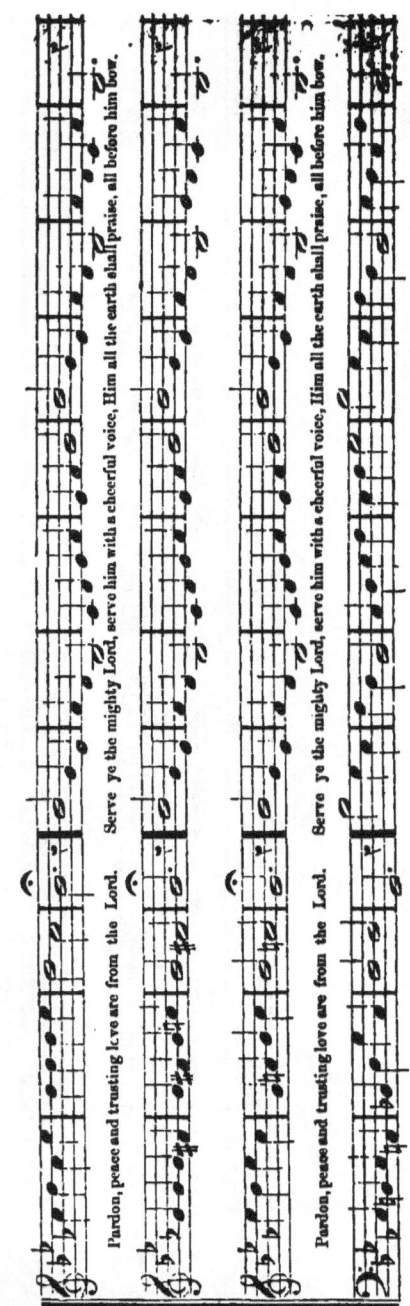

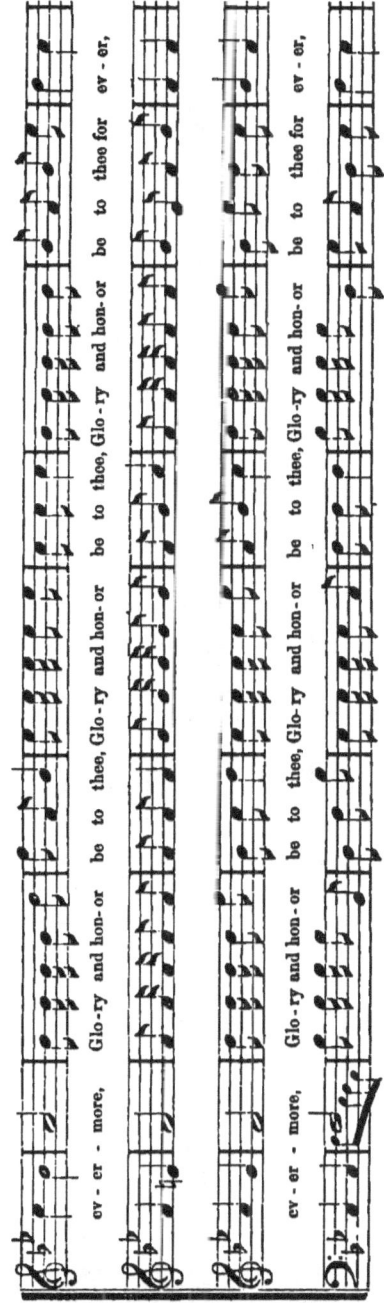
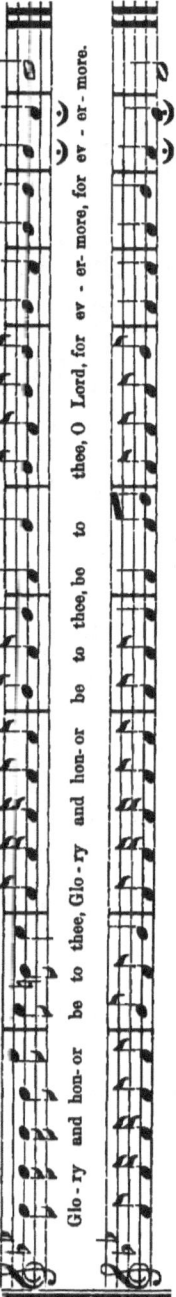

361

CONCLUDED.

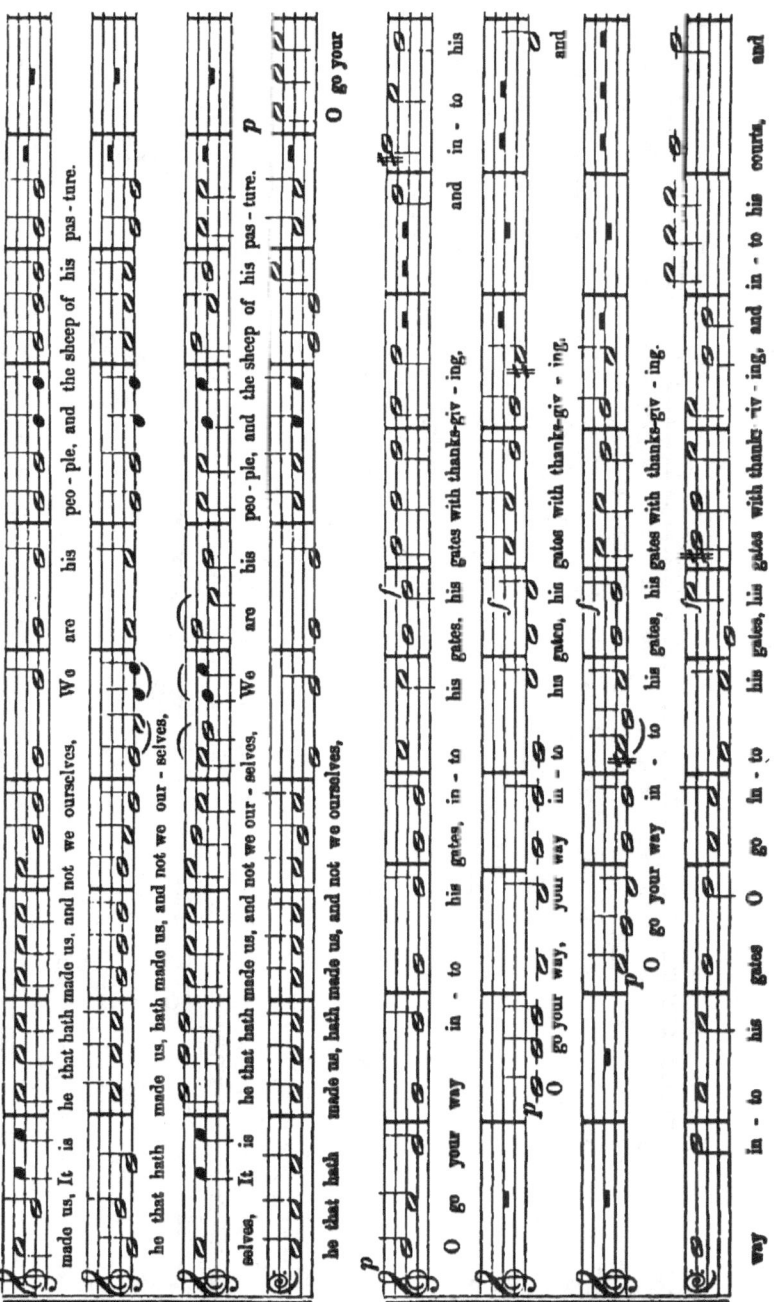

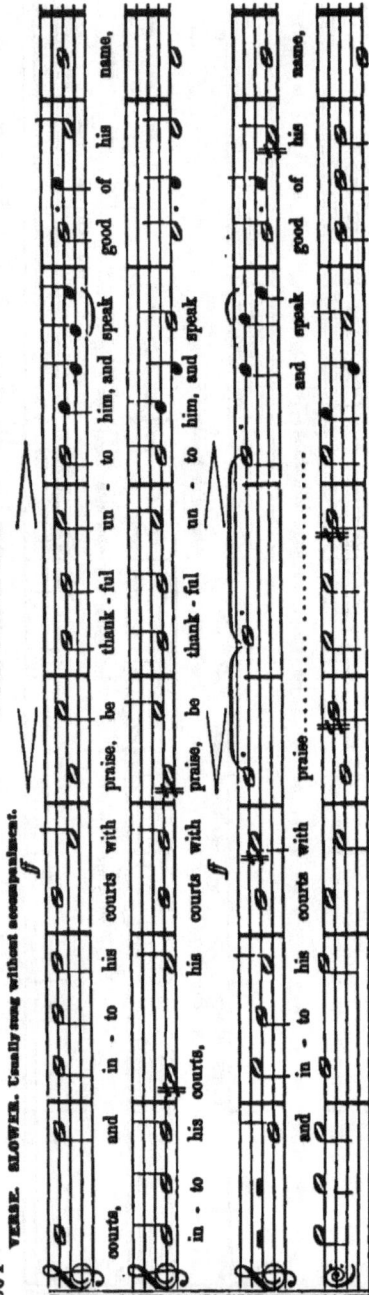

412. SOLO AND QUARTETTE. "O give ear unto me." NEUKOMM.

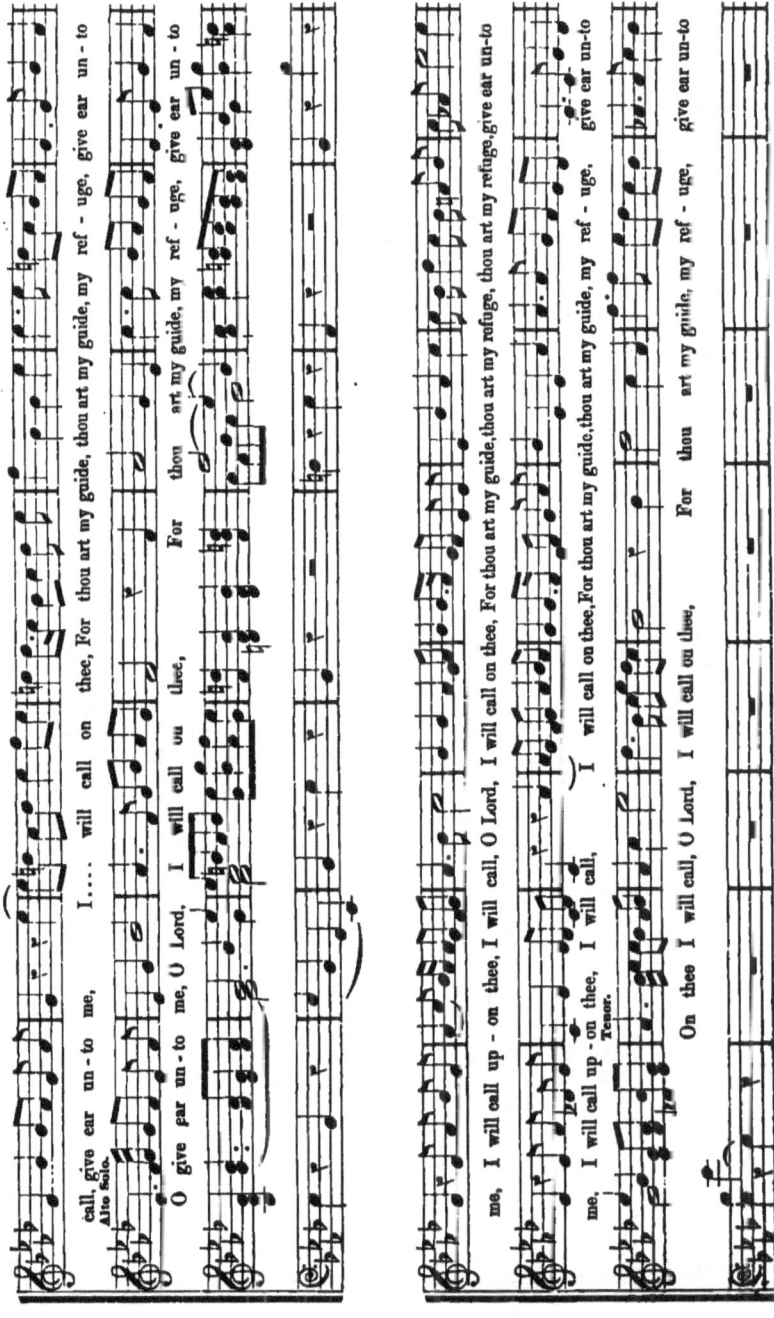

No. 413. ANTHEM. "Thanks be to God."

ALLEGRETTO.

Thanks be to God, Thanks be to God, for his un-speak-a-ble gift, Thanks be to God, Thanks be to God for his, for his un-speak-a-ble gift, Thanks be to God, for his, for his un-speak-a-ble gift.

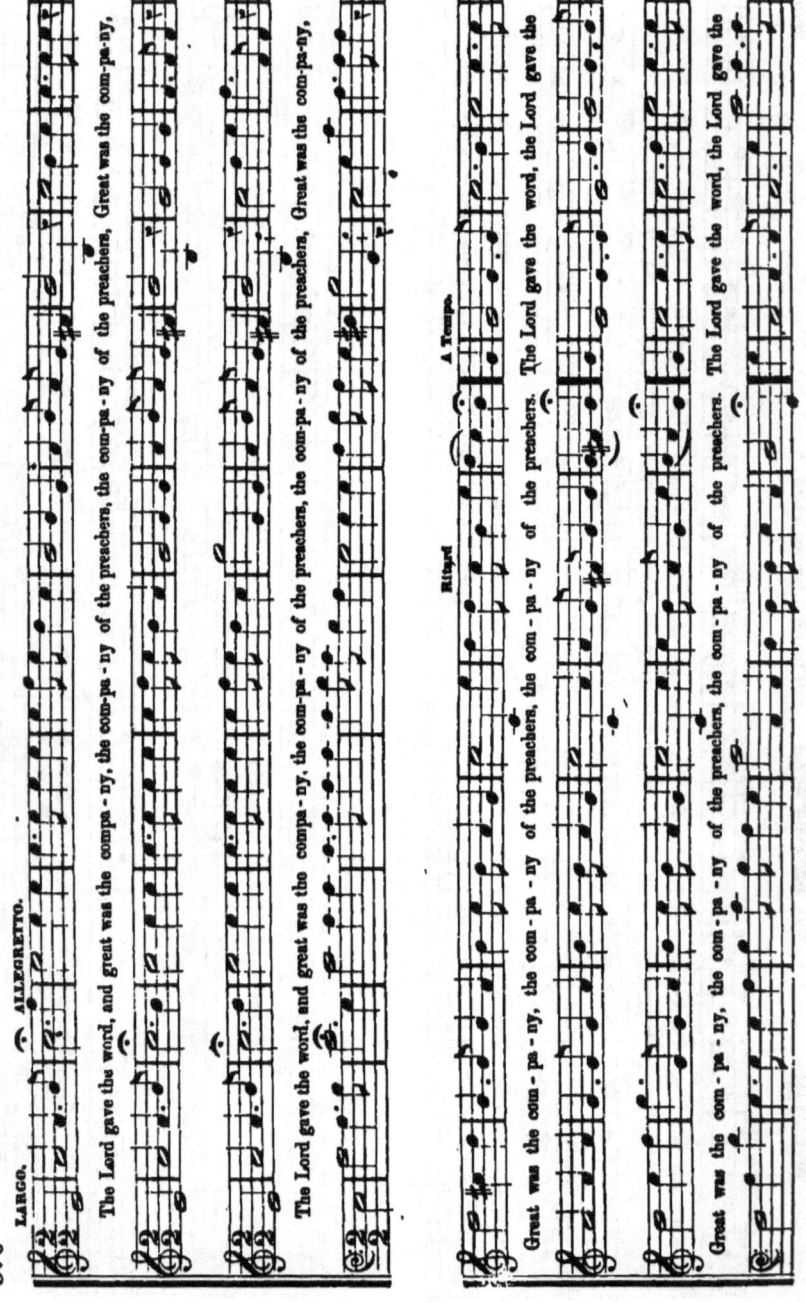

372　No. 415.　ANTHEM. "O be joyful in the Lord."　W. O. PERKINS.

CONTINUED.

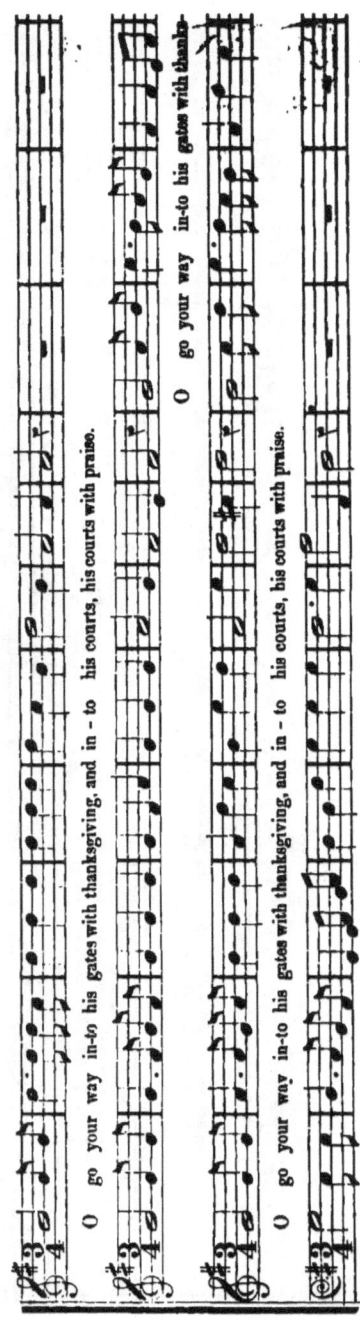

O be joy-ful in the Lord, all ye lands, O be joy-ful in the Lord, all ye lands, Be joy-ful, O be joy-ful in the Lord, be
Be joy - ful, be joy - ful, be joy-ful in the
O be joy-ful in the Lord, all ye lands, O be joy-ful in the Lord, all ye lands, Be joy - - ful, O be joy-ful in the
Be joy-ful, O be joy-ful in the Lord, be
p
Cres.
joy - ful, O be joy-ful in the Lord, all ye lands, Serve the Lord with gladness, and come before his presence with a song.
Lord, be joyful, be joy - ful in the Lord, all ye lands, Serve the Lord with glad - ness, serve the Lord, and come before his presence with a song.
p
Cres.
Lord, be joy-ful, O be joy-ful in the Lord, all ye lands, Serve the Lord with glad-ness, serve the Lord, and come before his presence with a song.
p
joy - ful, O be joy - ful in the Lord, all ye lands, Serve the Lord with gladness, serve the Lord with gladness,

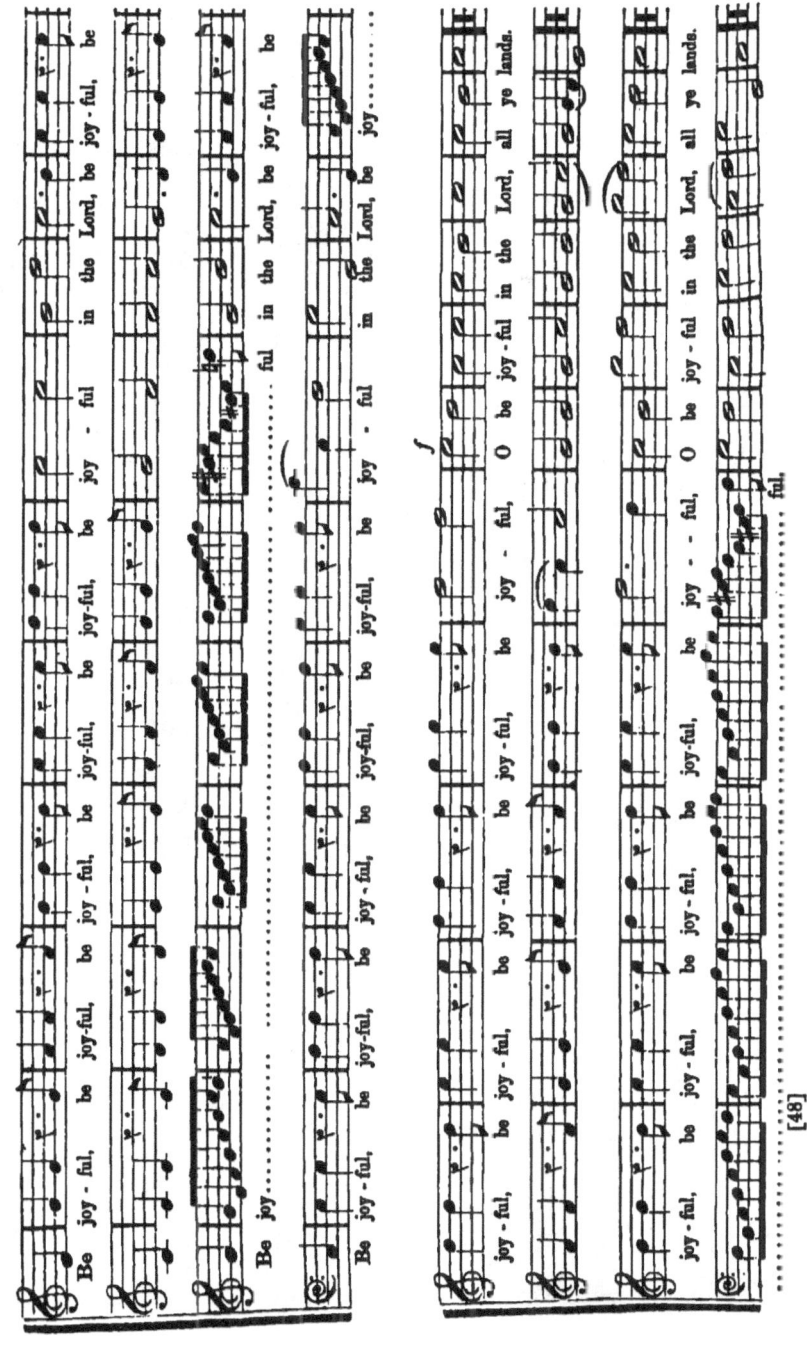

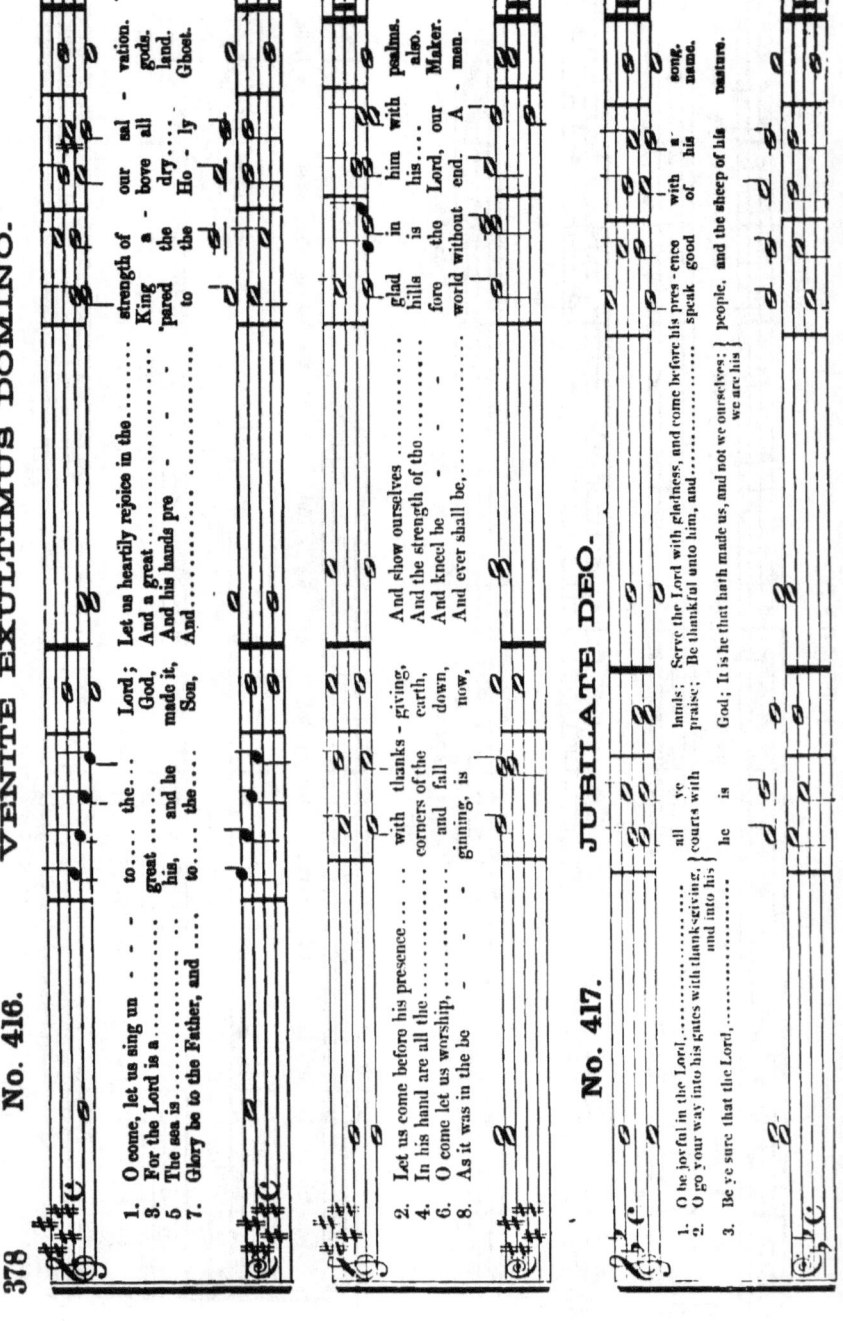

CANTATE DOMINO.

No. 418.

1. O sing unto the Lord, a new song, For he hath done marvellous things.
3. The Lord declared his salvation, His righteousness hath he openly showed, in the sight of the heathen.
5. Show yourself joyful unto the Lord, all ye lands? Sing, rejoice, O show yourselves joyful, be-fore the Lord
7. With trumpets also, and shawms; O show yourselves joyful, be-fore the Lord the King.

9. Let the floods clap their hands, and { fore the Lord; For he cometh to judge the earth.
   let the hills be joyful together, be- }

2. With his own right hand, and with his ho-ly arm; Hath he gotten him the vic-to-ry.
4. He hath remembered his mercy and { house of Israel; And all the ends of the world, have seen the sal- va-tion of our God.
   truth toward the }
6. Praise the Lord up-on the harp; Sing to the harp, with a psalm of thanks-giving.

8. Let the sea make a noise, and all that there-in is; The round world, and they that dwell there-in.
10. With righteousness shall he judge the world; And the peo-ple with equity.

379

ALPHABETICAL INDEX OF TUNES.

Tune	No.	Tune	No.	Tune	No.	Tune	No.
Ada	148	Blodgett	260	Congregational Chant	88	Franconia	143	Logan	143	Olympus	225	Seville	255
Addie	270	Borneo	78	Conover	114	Franklin	90	Lowell	90	Orford	85	Shaw	141
Addison's Hymn	60	Bowry	208	Consolation	239	Fred	219	Lyme	142	Orland	149	Shirland	138
Adieu	244	Bradbury	130	Contemplation	185	Freyburgh	142	Lyndon	200	Ormonde	124	Shout of Joy	139
Albany	179	Bradford	140	Converse	126	Galatea	209	Lyndon	200	Orpheus	91	Sicilian Hymn	213
Alben	99	Bragdon	107	Corinth	130	Gardiner	223	Lyons	223	Orson	277	Simmons	147
All is Well	292	Brattleboro'	236	Corona	263	Garland	139	Madison	112	Ortonville	112	Smyrna	308
Allston	110	Brattle street	123	Corydon	251	Glasgow	168	Magnificat	278	Ovid	89	Star of Peace	229
Alton	161	Brewer	256	Cosmos	172	Gould	242	Magnus	72	Pacific	159	Stickney	66
Amboy	78	Brookfield	246	Cranbrook	107	Grafton	197	Maine	168	Parker	72	Stockwell	140
Amelia	161	Brunswick	211	Creation	145	Grannis	215	Malden	157	Persons	243	Stonefield	76
Amherst	182	Burchmore	67	Credo	247	Greenville	68	Malone	68	Parting	131	Stoughton	75
Amphion	92	Burford	95	Crombie	228	Hamburg	141	Man	202	Peace	130	Stratton	228
Amsterdam	261	Burnham	125	Cryostom	144	Hamden	107	Manning	160	Peoria	75	Surrey	154
Anderson	65	Burnham	190	Cutler	250	Handel	178	Manoah	98	Peris	198	Tatterville	88
Andover	65	Cody	249	Dalston	118	Hanover	259	Mansa	160	Pesaro	71	Taylor	121
Another Year	62	Calmar	168	Danbury	196	Harding	119	Marcia	132	Peterboro'	122	Te Deum	152
Annenburg	290	Cambridge	125	Danvers	340	Hardwick	218	Marlboro	163	Pilppen	86	Thanksgiving	108
Apollo	81	Camden	260	Dartmouth	271	Hark, the Voice	273	Marlow (Major)	128	Pleyel's Hymn	161	Thomas	247
Appleton	83	Canaan	299	Day of Rest	220	Harlem	74	Marlow (Minor)	109	Pomfret	222	Topiady	23
Arcadia	191	Candia	174	Della	265	Harnden	69	Martin	197	Portland	273	Topsfield	308
Artus	208	Canton	118	Devotion	262	Hastings	250	Mason	151	Portuguese Hymn	259	Tremont	198
Artiegwa	108	Carl	105	Dillingham	177	Haven	202	Mazzinghi	74	Powelson	141	Trenton	77
Arnon	100	Carmen	175	Dinsmoor	252	Haydn Chant	251	Meriden	131	Powers	257	Triumph	270
Arton	256	Carroll	228	Dirge	111	Hayward	208	Michigan	97	Prague	63	Tyre	114
Ashland	103	Cassia	227	Dixon	205	Hazen	129	Middleton	206	Prayer	193	Tyro	89
Asie	233	Ceres	210	Doane	91	Herald	100	Milford	282	Putnam	98	Virgil	97
Astoria	101	Chamberlain	150	Dover	168	Hermon	109	Minerva	95	Quartette	146	Walthams toll us	103
Asylum	100	Chandler	186	Duke Street	188	Homer	207	Missionary Hymn	260	Quinsbury	93	Watchman tell us	200
Adams	101	Charity	122	Dumber	120	Howard	210	Monmouth	92	Quintette	105	Watson	157
Adland	72	Charlestown	130	Dumbarton	112	Hudson	242	Monterey	100	Rapture	100	Wayland	275
Atwood	137	Chelsea	70	Dundee	151	Hymn	217	Montpelier	277	Resignation	105	Webster	277
Auburn	164	Chester	136	Dunham	151	Italian Hymn	198	Morgan	220	Richmond	100	Wells	142
Audio	253	Chesterfield	82	Earle	126	Jasper	64	Morlington	111	Riga	217	Wenham	147
Augusta	133	Chesterville	184	Easton	199	Jordan	190	Monroe	225	Rolfo	199	Westboro'	258
Auron	272	Chicago	87	Edes	231	Joy	61	Nashville	111	Root	113	Weston	121
Bach	101	Chickering	177	Edwards	266	Julius	169	Neick to Thee	248	Roxbury	220	Whitney	88
Bailey	166	Chilton	119	Eliot	257	Kedron	104	Needham	104	Rusling	59	Wight	170
Baker	117	China	70	Ella	207	Keokuck	298	Newbury	181	Russel	105	Williams	142
Balleton	149	Choral Hymn	116	Elndorf	79	Keller	252	Newcastle	134	Runnan	240	Willingford	87
Barry	234	Christmas	226	Ensway	192	Kidder	180	Newcourt	171	Sabbath Eve	209	Wiedman	216
Barstow	134	Clare	190	Erie	184	Kingston	198	Newman	108	Rutland	70	Windsor	63
Bath	60	Claremont	67	Etta	198	Leander	212	Nile	212	Saco	236	Woodbury	129
Beavers	61,153	Cleveland	204	Evening Petition	73	Lebanon	73	Norwalk	90	Salem	155	Woodstock	67
Beethoven	241	Clifford	71	Fairfield	150	Leighton	165	Norwich	162	Sandusky	115	Woodville	166
Belgrade	219	Clinton	276	Fitchburg	157	Leonard	223	Nuremburg	214	Savannah	271	Worthing	213
Bement	267	Como ye Disconsolate	236	Floyd	150	Lewis	165	O Land of Rest	216	School Chant	117	Wyman's Chant	119
Benevento	148	Communion	223	Folsom	157	Linden	165	Old Hundred	59	Scotland	82	Young	194
Benjamin	69,156	Concord	236	Foster	207	Lindley	157	Olmuz	274	Seaver	84	Ipsilanti	160
Berlin	206	Consorella	220	Fox Row	158	Liston	77	Olivet	165	Seberth	100	Zion	229
Bethlehem				Francella	230	Lockport	158						

METRICAL INDEX.

381

L. M. Double.
Addison's Hymn... 60
Avonsburg... 62
Beethoven... 61

L. M. 6 lines.
Eaton... 64
Wenham... 63

L. M. 5 lines.
Andover... 65

L. M.
Allen... 99
Alton... 68
Amboy... 78
Amphion... 92
Anderson... 65
Applegate... 81
Appleton... 85
Atland... 72
Beavers... 80
Berlin... 69
Borneo... 78
Brunswick... 67
Burchmore... 95
Chesterville... 82
Choral Hymn... 70
Claremont... 67
Clifford... 186
Clinton... 71
Concord... 75
Congregational Chant... 88
Dover... 83
Dunham... 70
Duke Street... 91
Edwards... 87
Enway... 79
Fairfield... 73

Monmouth... 92
Newman... 79
Old Hundred... 59
Olivet... 84
Orpheus... 91
Ovid...
Parsons... 89
Peoria... 76
Pleyel's Hymn... 86
Prayer... 83
Quartette... 98
Quintette... 93
Roxbury... 68
Rutland... 87
Seaver... 82
Stickney... 66
Stonefield... 81
Stoughton... 85
Surrey... 72
Taftville... 88
Trenton... 77
Verdure... 78
Virgil... 97
Weston... 95
Wight... 82
Windham... 81
Windsor... 94
Woodstock... 73

L. M. Men's Voices.
Astoria... 101
Asylum... 101
Athens... 83
Homer... 70
Madison... 101
Montpelier... 100

C. M. Double.
Ashland... 102

Bradford... 92
Bragdon... 79
Burford... 59
Cady... 84
Cambridge... 91
Canton... 89
Charity... 76
Charlestown... 75
Chelsea... 86
Chester... 83
Chesterfield... 98
China... 93
Christmas... 68
Conover... 87
Converse... 82
Corinth... 66
Cutler... 91
Dixon... 76
Dunbarton... 98
Dundee... 88
Easton... 77
Hardwick... 89
Haydn Chant... 97
Hallston... 96
Hermon... 95
Howard... 81
Jotina... 81
Kingston... 94
Lebanon... 73
Lyme...
Lyra... 101
Malone... 101
Man... 100
Masta... 101
Marlow (Major)... 100
Marlow (Minor)... 100
Martin... 103

Watson... 140
Webster... 107
Woodbury... 125
Wyman's Chant... 118

C. M. Men's Voices.
Freyburgh... 142
Hamden... 122
Meriden... 125
Orford... 136
Rigo... 133
Rustan... 142

S. M. Double.
Creation... 114
Crysostom... 126
Franconia... 130

S. M.
Ada... 107
Amelia... 111
Armon... 120
Auburn... 112
Bailey... 126
Ballston... 119
Beethoven... 106
Benjamin... 131
Berlin... 129
Chamberlain... 111
Cranbrook... 134
Earle... 108
Fitchburg... 124
Floyd... 112
Folsom... 131
Francolla... 130
Linden... 122
Lisbon... 128
Lyman... 128
Maiden... 109

Seco... 127
Shaw... 133
Shirland... 129
Topsfield...
Wells...
Westboro'...
Whitney...

S. M. Men's Voices.
Calmar...
Dunbar...
Maine...

L. P. M.
Galatea... 145
Newcourt... 144
Russell... 143

C. P. M.
Candia... 148
Carmen... 101
Cosmos... 164
Rapture... 166
Woodville... 149

S. P. M.
Chilton... 148
Dalaton... 156
Dillingham... 159

H. M.
Albany... 151
Amherst... 190
Harding... 165
Leander... 157
Newbury... 158
Prague... 162

C. H. M.
Chicago... 157

Benevento... 155
Burnham... 158
Card... 150
Chandler... 154
Concord... 162
Danvers... 163
Dartmouth... 155
Edes... 154

S. M. Men's Voices.
Evening Petition... 168
Glasgow... 188
Granua... 168

Joy... 167
Lindley... 220
Nashville... 169
Needham... 171
Nuremburg... 170

Percla... 198
Putnam... 193
Tremont... 193
Waltham... 192
Watchman tell us... 200
Wayland... 191
Young... 194

Ss & 7s. Double.
Bethlehem... 226
Brookfield... 211
Cleveland... 204
Doane... 205
Greenville... 215
Smyrna... 203

8s & 7s.
Arius... 206
Ceres... 210
Dinsmoor... 202
Finsdorf... 207

Nile... 226

8s, 8 & 7s.
Corner... 234
Foster... 222

8, 7, 8 5.
Clare... 226

8s, 7s & 7.
Carroll... 228

6s, 7s & 6s.
Barry... 234

6s & 6s. Double.
O Land of Rest... 215

8s & 6s.
Crombie... 228
Jasper... 217
Morgan... 217
Kedron... 235

8s, 6s & 10s. 7 lines.
Chickering... 231

8 6 8, 8 6.
Communion... 230

8s, 6s & 7s.
Portland... 229

8s, 6 & 5s.
Willingford... 215

8s, 6 & 4.
Fred... 219
Thomas... 226

8s, 6s & 4. Peculiar.
Star of Peace... 229

8s & 5. 8 lines.

METRICAL INDEX, Concluded.

8s.		6s & 8s. Peculiar.		7s, 8s & 4s. Peculiar.		9s & 8s.			
Concordia	230	Belgrade	241	Canaan	253	Addie	270	Lockport	274
Gardiner	223	Lyons	277	Powers	246	Bowry	268	Portuguese Hymn	273
		Newcastle	240			Camden	269	Resignation	275
4s & 6s.		**6s.**		**6s., 7s & 8s.**		**10s.**		**11s & 10s.**	
Another Year	242	Grafton	242	Shout of Joy	254	Credo	247	Apollo	280
						Dinge	252	Aurora	272
5s & 10s.		**6s, 5s & 10s.**				Erie	252	Triumph	279
Michigan	207	Linton	245	Come ye Disconsolate	276	Italian Hymn	242		
						Missionary Hymn	200	**11s & 4s.**	
5s & 8s.		**6s & 8s.**		**6s & 4s. 7 lines. Peculiar.**		Thanksgiving	247	Richmond	277
Stockwell	241	Brewer	250	Eliot	248	**10s, 11s & 12s.**		**12s & 9s.**	
				Nearer to Thee	248	Magnificat	278	Olympus	355
6s, 7s & 4.		Corydon	239					Ellis	357
Brattleboro'	238	Simmons	245	**7s & 6s.**		**10s & 11s.**		**12s, or 12s & 11s.**	
				Amsterdam	248	Lyons	254	Scotland	281
5s, 6s & 7s.		**6s & 9s.**		**7s & 5s.**		**10s & 5s.**		**12s, 11s & 6s.**	
Kidder	238	Ellis	257	Danbury	266	Michigan	259	Devotion	282
		Olympus	255	Gould	243				
				Rollo	263	**11s.**			
						Harlem	258		

HYMN CHANTS, SENTENCES, ANTHEMS, MOTETTS, &c.

HYMN CHANTS.

Almighty One	286
From the Recesses	287
God standeth in the Congregation	283
Jews were wrought	285
Life is onward	288
Lowly and solemn	283
Saviour and dearest Friend	288
The Lord's Prayer	284
There is an hour of peaceful rest	284
Thy will be done	285

SENTENCES.

And ye shall seek me	309
Blessed are the pure in heart	291
Blessed is he	290

See, the conqu'ring Hero comes	297
God of Israel	312
Gracious Spirit	310
Grant, we beseech thee	295
Hear us, our heavenly Father	298
Heavenly Father	296
Lift up your hands	314
Nearer to Thee	291
O be joyful in the Lord	299
O, how lovely is Zion	288
Return, my soul	316
Sabbath Bell	308
Sanctus	289
Seek ye the Lord	300
Teach me, O Lord	301
The Lord is in his holy temple	331
The Lord will comfort Zion	294
Trust in the Lord	302

ANTHEMS, MOTETTS, &c.

Hark, what mean those holy voices	360
Divine Inspiration	304
God of the Fathers	350
Great Jehovah	306
I waited for the Lord	352
Lord of my Salvation	324
Lord of all power and might	348
Mighty Jehovah	341
O, be joyful in the Lord	362-372-378
O, come, let us Sing	378
O, give ear unto me	366
O God, our Father	358
O Sing unto the Lord	379
Rest, Spirit, rest	317
Salvation belongeth unto the Lord	322
Spread through the earth	328
Serve ye the mighty Lord	354
Thanks be to God	369
The Lord gave the word	370
Unveil thy bosom	320
Where are thy bowers	334
O Lord, we hear	357

INDEX OF FIRST LINES.

First Line	Page
A charge to keep I have	144
Again returns the day of holy rest	271
A glory gilds the sacred page	111, 142
Alas! I bow poor and little worth	227
A little child in bulrush ark	236
All ye who love the Lord, rejoice	120
Almighty One, I bend (Chant)	286
And is the Gospel peace and love	81
Angels, from the realms of glory	220
Another year has told its fourfold	219
Arise! arise! with joy survey	76
As down in the sunless retreats	282
Author of good, we rest on thee	184
Awake, and sing the song	156
Awake, my soul, and with the sun	86
Awake, my soul, stretch every	114, 241
Awake, my soul, to sound his praise	128
Awake, our souls! away our fears	64, 73
Behold how the Lord has girt on his	241
Behold the Man! how glorious be	101
Behold the morning Sun	150, 152
Behold the throne of grace	149
Beset with snares on every hand	66
Be thou, O God, exalted high	59
Beyond, beyond that boundless sea	104
Beyond where Kedron's waters flow	235
Blessed be thy name forever	224, 234
Blest are the pure in heart	225
Blest are the sons of peace	166
Blest are the souls that bear and	105
Blest be the everlasting God	117
Blest Instructor, from thy ways	194
Blest is the hour when cares	217, 236
Blest is the man who fears the Lord	65
Bread of heaven! on thee we feed	192
Bread of the world, in mercy broken	268
Breathe, Holy Spirit, from above	68
Brightest and best of the sons of the	272
Broad is the road that leadeth to death	84
By cool Siloam's shady rill	109
Calm on the listening ear of night	195
Child of sin and sorrow!	268
Christians! brethren! ere we part	230
Come, gracious Spirit, heavenly	100
Come hither, all ye weary souls	82
Come, Holy Spirit, calm my mind	125
Come, Holy Spirit, heavenly Dove	70
Come, kingdom of our God	157
Come, let us anew our journey	237
Come, O thou King of all thy saints	103
Come, said Jesus' sacred voice	198
Come, sound his praise abroad	148
Come, thou Almighty King	313
Come, thou desire of all thy saints	141
Come to the house of prayer	148, 161
Come, weary souls, with sin distressed	100
Come, ye disconsolate	276
Come, ye that know and fear the	133
Daughter of Zion, awake from thy	272
Dear Father, to thy mercy-seat	121
Defend me, Lord, from shame	166
Did Christ o'er sinners weep	157
Ere I sleep, for every favor	229
Eternal and immortal King	70
Eternal God, almighty cause	89
Every day hath toil and trouble	220
Far from mortal cares retreating	215
Father, adored in worlds above	83
Father of mercies, in thy word	120
Father, who in the olive shade	219
Few are thy days, and full of woe	130
Friend after friend departs	185, 256
From Greenland's icy mountains	260
From grace is not behold a branch	271
From the recesses of a lowly (Chant)	287
From whence doth this union arise	230
Full and harmonious, let the joyous	280
Gently fall the dews of eve	197, 198
Gently, Lord, O gently lead us	206, 215
Give thanks to God, he reigns above	95
Glad hearts to thee we bring	246
Glorious things of thee are	211, 213
God is our refuge and defence	160
God standeth in the congre (Chant)	268
God that makst earth and heaven	265
Go to thy rest, fair child	164
Grace, 'tis a charming sound	167
Gracious Spirit, Love divine	197
Great Framer of unnumbered	70
Great God! my Father and my	86
Great God, the followers of thy Son	83
Great is the Lord, his works of	115
Great Ruler of all nature's frame	131
Great Source of good, from thee	89
Great Spirit, by whose mighty power	107
Hail! all hail the joyful morn	196
Hail, Source of life and love	145
Hail to the brightness of Zion's glad	279
Hark! hark! a shout of joy	254
Hark! ten thousand harps and voices	228
Hark! the sounds of gladness	250
Hark! the voice of love and mercy	218
Hark! what mean those holy voices	205
Has thou midst life's empty noises	226
Head of the Church triumphant	263
Heaven is a place of rest from sin	69
High in yonder realms of light	188
How beauteous are their feet	143
How blest the righteous when he dies	76
How did my heart rejoice to hear	132
How gentle God's commands	149
How glorious is the hour	177
How pleased and blessed was I	162
How rich the blessings, O my God	81
How shall the young secure their	136
How sweet, how heavenly is the	106
How sweetly flowed the gospel's	71, 96
How sweet the melting lay	161
How sweet to leave the world awhile	101
How vain is all beneath the skies	66
I cannot always trace the way	246
I feel within a want	158
If on a quiet sea	160
I know that my Redeemer lives	97
I lift my soul to God	159
In anger, Lord, rebuke me not	124
In robes of judgment, lo, he comes	99
Israel's Shepherd, guide me, feed me	204
Jehovah, God, thy gracious power	136
Jesus, I love thy charming sound	108
Jesus shall reign where'er	73, 79, 91, 186
Jesus, the very thought of thee	142
Jesus, we thy promise claim	186
Jews were wrought to cruel (Chant)	265
Join all who love the Saviour's	100
Joy to the world, the Lord is come	110
Just as I am, without one plea	228
King of mercy, King of love	104
Leader of Israel's host, and guide	63
Let all the earth their voices raise	170
Let not despair nor fell revenge	112
Let one loud song of praise arise	80
Let others boast how strong they be	130
Let songs of endless praise	160
Let songs of praises fill the sky	140
Let us for each other care	198
Let us with a joyful mind	199
Life is onward, use it (Chant)	288
Life is the time to serve the Lord	85
Lift not thou the wailing voice	266
Lift up your heads in joyful hope	215
Lift your glad voices in triumph on	278
Long as I live I'll bless thy name	139
Lord, dismiss us with thy blessing	213
Lord, bear the voice of my complaint	109
Lord, I approach thy mercy-seat	113
Lord, I believe, thy power I own	118
Lord of boats, how lovely, fair	191, 195
Lord of mercy and of might	268
Lord of the worlds above	180
Lord, thou hast scourged our guilty	125
Lord, thou hast searched and seen	94
Lord, we adore thy vast designs	88
Lord, we bow with deep contrition	208
Lord, when thou didst ascend on	74, 91
Lord, with fervor I would praise	203
Lo, the day of rest declineth	208
Lowly and solemn be thy (Chant)	283
Magnify Jehovah's name	190
Majestic monarchs sits enthroned	100
Mark the soft falling snow	179

INDEX OF FIRST LINES.

First Line	Page
Men on earth, and saints above	191
Morning breaks upon the tomb	233
Mortals awake, with angels join	112
My dear Redeemer, and my Lord	87
My faith looks up to thee	247
My God, all nature owns thy sway	62
My God, I now appear before thee	270
My God, my Father, while I stray	217
My God, thy boundless love I praise	173
My God, whose all-pervading eye	87
My gracious God, how plain	146
My Maker and my King	152
My soul repeat his praise	154
Nearer, my God, to thee	248
No more fatigue, no more distress	98
Now let my soul, eternal King	95
Now the shades of night are gone	340
Now to the Lord a noble song 94, 99,	101
O all ye nations, praise the Lord	135
O, arm me with the mind	165
O, bless the Lord, my soul	159
O, cease my wandering soul 158,	163
O, come and dwell in me	150
O, could I speak the matchless	176
O, could our thoughts and wishes fly	118
O for a thousand tongues to sing	141
O God, mine inmost soul convert	174
O God, we praise thee, and confess	106
O God, whose presence glows in all	77
O help us, Lord, each hour of need	129
O, here if ever, God of love	119
O for a closer walk with God	133
Oh land of rest, for thee I sigh	216
O how happy are they	255
O lead me to the Rock	156
O Lord, our God, arise	163
O Lord, our heavenly King	155
O Lord, thy boundless grace impart	80
Once more, my soul, the rising day	121
One thing first and only 232,	234
Onward speed thy conquering flight	259
O praise ye the Lord, prepare a new	277
O sacred Head, now wounded 260,	...
O that the Lord would guide my	191
O Thou, from whom all good 129,	134
O Thou, that hearest the prayer of	175
O Thou, to whose all-searching	78
O Thou, who hearest prayer	250
Our blest Redeemer, ere he breathed	226
Our days are as the grass	146
Our Father God, who art in heaven	131
Our heavenly Father calls	164
Our Savior alone	151
O where are kings and empires now	240
O where shall rest be found	102
Partners of a glorious hope	155
Praise the Lord, ye heavens adore	187
Praise to God, immortal praise 193,	213
Praise to the Lord of boundless	214
Praise ye the Lord, immortal choirs	71
Quiet, Lord, my froward heart	124
Return, my soul, unto thy rest 78,	202
Return, O wanderer, now return	303
Rise, my soul, and stretch thy wings	128
Rock of Ages, cleft for me 189,	264
Save me from my foes	201
Savior and dearest friend (Chant)	141
Savior, breathe an evening blessing	288
Savior, source of every blessing 210,	106
See Israel's gentle Shepherd stand	214
Serene I lay me down	114
Sing, all ye ransomed of the Lord	119
Sing, for the blest Redeemer reigns	133
Sing to the Lord aloud	216
Sing to the Lord, ye distant lands	255
Sinners turn, why will ye die	156
Sister, thou wast mild and lovely	163
Soft be the gently breathing notes	155
Softly now the light of day	80
So let our lips and lives express	121
Source of light and life divine	234
Speak gently, it is better far	259
Spirit of charity, dispense	277
Stand up, my soul, shake off thy	107
Star of peace, to wanderers weary	134
Sweet is the memory of thy grace	175
Sweet is the prayer whose holy	78
Sweet is the work, O Lord	250
Sweet the moments, rich the 203,	212
Take my heart, O Father, take it	146
Teach me, O teach me, Lord 76,	98
The day is past and gone	164
The glories of my Maker, God	151
The God of harvest praise	240
The God who reigns alone	102
The Lord is our shepherd	155
The Lord Jehovah reigns 178,	187
The Lord my shepherd is	213
The Lord our God is clothed with	214
The Lord will come, the earth shall	71
The man who seeks thy peace	124
The mighty conqueror leaves the	202
There is a calm for those who weep	65
There is a glorious world on high	221
There is a land of pure delight	128
There is an hour of peaceful (Chant)	96
There is a stream whose gentle flow	138
The sacred morn, my God, has come	201
The saints on earth and those above	238
The spacious firmament on high	288
The Spirit in our hearts	202
The voice of free grace	214
The winter is over and gone	114
This is the first and great command	154
Thou art gone to the grave	117
Thou lovely Source of true delight	74
Thou to the childs emerald (Chant)	147
Thou who didst stoop below	122
Thro' the night air stealing	188
Thus far the Lord hath led me on	210
Thy name, Almighty God	84
Thy name be hallowed evermore	199
Thy will be done (Chant)	82
'Tis finished, the Savior cries	195
To-day the Savior calls	111
To thee, O God, we humbly pay	72
To the haven of thy breast	229
Unheard the dews around me fall,	127
Up to the gospel's sacred page	135
Wake the song of Jubilee	147
Watchmen, onward to your stations	207
Wardsman, tell us of the night	190
Weary ar with closing eye	234
What shall the dying sinner do	209
What's this that steals upon my	192
We bless thee for this sacred day	25
We come, our hearts with gladness	232
Welcome, delightful morn	269
Welcome, sweet day of rest	181
When all thy mercies, O my God	165
When I can trust my all with God	90
When Power Divine, in mortal form	127
When shall we meet again 243,	184
When verdure clothes the fertile	69
Where shall we make her grave	244
Where the mourner weeping	126
While my Redeemer's near	252
While thee I seek, protecting Power	239
While the sun's last rays are shining	133
While with ceaseless course the sun	123
Why do we mourn departing friends	209
Wilt thou not visit me 251,	267
With all our hearts, with all our	119
With grateful hearts, with joy 169,	256
With my substance I will honor	67
With sacred joy we lift our eyes	171
With silence only as their	207
Work and thou wilt bless the day	113
	277
	258
Ye boundless realms of joy	286
Ye Christian heralds, go proclaim 88,	97
Ye golden lamps of heaven, farewell	245
Ye servants of God, your Master	238
Yes, I will bless thee, O my God	92
Your harps, ye trembling saints	168
	85
	241
	141
	160

www.ingramcontent.com/pod-product-compliance
Lightning Source LLC
Chambersburg PA
CBHW030342230426
43664CB00007BA/509